Script Analysis for Actors, Directors, and Designers

SCRIPT ANALYSIS

for Actors, Directors, and Designers

THIRD EDITION

James Thomas

AMSTERDAM • BOSTON • HEIDELBERG • LONDON
NEW YORK • OXFORD • PARIS • SAN DIEGO
SAN FRANCISCO • SINGAPORE • SYDNEY • TOKYO

Focal Press is an imprint of Elsevier

ELSEVIER

Focal
Press

Focal Press is an imprint of Elsevier
30 Corporate Drive, Suite 400, Burlington, MA 01803, USA
Linacre House, Jordan Hill, Oxford OX2 8DP, UK

 Recognizing the importance of preserving what has been written, Elsevier prints its
books on acid-free paper whenever possible.

Library of Congress Cataloging-in-Publication Data
APPLICATION SUBMITTED

British Library Cataloguing-in-Publication Data
A catalogue record for this book is available from the British Library.

ISBN-13: 978-0-240-80662-4
ISBN-10: 0-240-80662-X

For information on all Focal Press publications
Visit our Web site at www.focalpress.com or www.books.elsevier.com

05 06 07 08 09   10 9 8 7 6 5 4 3 2

Printed in the United States of America

For my respected colleagues at the Moscow Art Theatre School and for the great director Anatoly Efros. Their inspiring examples make a life in the theatre significant.

In fact it is the simplest things that are most tricky to do well. To read, for example. To be able to read exactly what is written without omitting anything that is written and at the same time without adding anything of one's own. To be able to capture the exact context of the words one is reading. To be able to read!

—Jean-Louis Barrault, *Reflections on the Theatre*

Contents

CHAPTER 1

Action Analysis   1

CHAPTER 2

Foundations of the Plot: Given Circumstances   27

Foundations of the Plot: Background Story　57

Plot: External and Internal Action　81

Plot: Progressions and Structure　117

Character　145

Preface to the Third Edition

This edition retains the same support for Formalist Analysis and for its central importance in acting, directing, and design that it had when it was first published in 1992. It is still a defense of close reading of the play itself in contrast to some of its alternative methods, including modern critical theory and its fascination with matters outside the play.

What has changed is the addition of a new chapter on Action Analysis. Formalist Analysis begins with specific observations and ends up by developing conclusions about the general sense of the whole play. On the other hand, some readers have expressed the wish to see the whole picture before beginning to look at the parts. Experienced actors, directors, and designers do not move mechanically from topic to topic in their analytical work. Their reading goes back and forth, moving ahead a few steps, going backward, and thinking about undone topics lying ahead. This approach has a very different feel from that of the formalist strategy adopted in the book for teaching purposes. The chapter on Action Analysis has been added to address this question and to reinforce how each part of the analytical process influences all the others. The new material, including additional questions at the end of the first six chapters, should enhance the book's teaching and learning flexibility.

I have changed the names of a few classifications, clarified inexact or ambiguous definitions and added a few selections to the Bibliography. Most of these are minor, but two of them deserve to be explained further. One is a change of the terms "Physical and Psychological Action" to

"External and Internal Action." The reason for this should be self-explanatory. The other change takes place in the definition of Dramatic Action under the category of Character. In the previous editions, I separated the concepts of Dramatic Action and Objectives because I wanted to distinguish two different issues that are often conflated. The issues continue to be different, but in this edition I chose to defer to custom about the terminology. Hereafter, Objectives and Dramatic Action are identical concepts, and what I used to call Dramatic Action is now termed Qualities, following Michael Chekhov's usage. Readers' feedback and my own experience have cleared up my thinking about this. The revised section in Chapter 6, Character, should explain the whole thing.

Speaking of categories, this is a good place to keep something important in mind. The decision to divide plays into topics and categories is a subjective one made for teaching purposes, and dividing each category into even smaller categories is even more so. Like all categories, they are by no means rigid in actual practice. Intelligent readers will notice that many categories could be placed under more than one heading covered somewhere else in this book. One thing experienced actors, directors and designers can't help but notice is the way that many of these issues mix together, bump into each other, explain and fine-tune one another. Theatre is the art of human behavior in action. And it is the imaginative nature of theatre and the indefinite nature human behavior that cause the slippery quality of much of what is presented here. Whether a certain passage fits into one category or another is important for learning purposes, of course. But equally important is learning that a passage could belong to several categories at the same time. Such is the nature of good playwriting. Besides, script analysis is more than a labeling gun used to take possession of plays by putting labels on everything we can. Fanatical labeling can overwhelm creative imagination. By contrast, professional play analysis should stimulate creativity in acting, directing and design.

Preface to the Second Edition

This book is the outcome of teaching and directing experience acquired in theatre programs with a variety of educational objectives. In all of them, I found that at some point in the curriculum teachers require their students to analyze plays in an orderly fashion before the practical experience of acting, directing, or designing. At a growing number of prominent theatre programs, the faculty has determined that students should have at least one course devoted to this purpose. In the process of teaching these and related courses, I have examined theatre textbooks concerned with the craft of performance and literature textbooks concerned with the scholarly aspects of drama. I did not find any current text dedicated to discussing the dramatic potentials of a play in ways that are useful for actors, directors, and designers. As a consequence, in too many cases, I found otherwise talented students unable to employ their talents to their best advantage because they did not know how to study plays from an applied theatrical point of view.

This book is designed to teach the serious theatre student the skills of script analysis using a formalist approach. By this, I mean first that it uses a standard system of classifications to study the written part of a play, excluding performance, scenery, and so forth. Formalist methodology also means that the book does not cover all the topics included in the usual dramatic literature textbooks. There is no extensive attention to dramatic forms or styles; no scrutiny of historical-critical theories or sociopolitical implications; and no attention to the life, mind, or personality of the author (although the book relates to all these matters). The approach is not new. We know how scientists adopt the practice of neglecting certain data outside their own spheres of interest. Likewise professional theatre artists tend to avoid outside details and turn instead to the play itself when they are looking for the key to their work. The scientist and artist both know that the neglected information exists all the time, but they act as if it didn't for the special purposes of their work. I admit that this kind of restricted approach can claim no scholarly pretensions. The aim is practical and intended for the theatre.

Most of this book deals with play analysis, but since the acts of thinking and reading are intimately connected with this analysis, I have provided an Introduction that I hope will make those processes a little clearer. It begins with a brief sketch of the heritage of Formalist Analysis and then offers general guidelines for reading and thinking about plays.

The largest portion of the book is involved with understanding the basic dramatic potentials of a play. I have attempted to keep the design simple. Chapters two through nine treat one of the basic elements of drama described by Aristotle and later adopted by many other teachers, scholars, and theatre artists. Though all the elements depend on each other, of course, the method used is to select one element as the essence of the play for the time being and to disregard the others. This is what I believe is unique and what will prove the most useful about the book. By narrowing the point of view in this way, students can acquire the mental concentration needed to learn the individual parts of plays and their possibilities. The approach will show that each element is inseparable from the whole meaning, an understanding that is the bedrock of artistic unity. When Formalist Analysis is done well, it can feel almost like the play is acting, directing, and designing itself.

Although the basic principles and approach in this second edition are the same as in the first, there are various changes from beginning to end. Several issues have been made clearer, examples have been expanded to include four additional plays (three written since 1990), and the appendices have been expanded.

A list of questions about the topics covered is found at the end of each chapter. These questions are important learning tools. They are meant to stimulate creative thinking as actors, directors, and designers engage in the production process. By reviewing the topics one-by-one, students will be certain to cover most of the important dramatic possibilities found in a play.

Appendix A: Supplementary Topics for Script Analysis, includes introductions to other major forms of criticism: biographical and historical, textual, philosophical and moral, psychological, mythological and archetypal, feminist, structuralist and poststructuralist, Marxist, and rhetorical. Thoughtfully treated, these considerations can help to clarify, if not always justify, some fascinating components of dramatic literature. Appendix B is an Introduction to the Genres and Styles of Drama. The Bibliography at the end supplements and supports the point of view of the book and is also intended as a learning tool.

Play analysis is a practical craft that is best explained by concrete examples, but since this book is likely to be used with an anthology chosen by the teacher, I have tried to keep it self-contained. The plays used in the examples were selected to represent a wide range of playwrights, periods, genres, and styles. Those who wish to attain the most from the book should read all the plays to which I refer. Listed according to the number of their citations, they are:

Hamlet (ca. 1600) by William Shakespeare
The Wild Duck (1884) by Henrik Ibsen
A Raisin in the Sun (1959) by Lorraine Hansberry
Death of a Salesman (1949) by Arthur Miller
The Piano Lesson (1990) by August Wilson
A Lie of the Mind (1986) by Sam Shepard
Tartuffe (1669) by Molière
Mother Courage (1937) by Bertolt Brecht
Three Sisters (1901) by Anton Chekhov
The School for Scandal (1777) by Richard Brinsley Sheridan
Streamers (1976) by David Rabe
Angels in America, Parts I and II (1992) by Tony Kushner
Oedipus Rex (ca. 430 BC) by Sophocles
The Hairy Ape (1921) by Eugene O'Neill
Happy Days (1961) by Samuel Beckett

The scripts are widely available both in single editions and anthologies. In my own teaching, students select three plays for careful study: one historical, one realistic, and one modern nontraditional. For the realistic play, they choose from the list or select a title of their own. Lately, I have had success using three plays from the students' current production season and employing the classifications in the book to teach the concepts as applied to those plays. Students seem to benefit from a practical—and open-minded—connection with ongoing production work.

Besides being a system of classification and an intellectual attitude, Formalist Analysis may also be used as means of entry into a play script. When analyzing plays, it's helpful to begin with a plan, and taken all together, the classifications embody such a plan. This implies that students can go through them one-by-one, and in the beginning, they are encouraged to do just that. Formalist Analysis is an attempt to organize the study of a play, and the system of classification is the necessary instructional basis of such organization. While this may seem mechanical, it should not be troubling, because a mechanical analysis is better than none at all. At any rate, we all tend to do things mechanically while learning them. Eventually, the technique becomes hidden within the substance. Be that as it may, some people cannot even start with a plan, and they end up staring at a jumble of disconnected classifications. Play analysis takes practice, just as any kind of logical thinking does. In these cases, it may be better just to study the play randomly, letting one thought lead to another without worrying about classifications. Later on it should become clear what has been left out or misplaced. Then it may be easier to return to a plan and study the topics left out of the unorganized first attempts.

The book can accommodate different teaching plans. Although it is purposefully organized and arranged, there is no absolute need either to cover all the topics or to study them in the order they are presented. Some teachers may select fewer categories to form the organizing principles for their course; others may choose to assign the readings differently or to use the book as a foundation for other approaches to criticism. I mention only three points.

First, most of the book is within reach of serious beginning students, but the material in Chapter 8 (Dialogue), Chapter 9 (Tempo, Rhythm, and Mood), and Chapter 10 (The Style of the Play), is probably better suited to those with wider experience in play reading and production. Students need to know what kind of knowledge is expected of them if they are to become serious about their future work in the theatre. Therefore, it is appropriate to introduce subjects that are important to professional actors, directors, and designers. Apprentices may be tempted to disregard these chapters, but I hope not.

Second, it's a good idea for teachers to keep their lessons moving and not become involved in prolonged examinations of individual plays. This goal may be accomplished if, instead of getting bogged down in teaching the plays themselves, the teacher focuses on teaching the skills needed to analyze plays in general.

Third, a great deal can be gained by studying as many topics as possible in their original order. I have found that with enough practice most students sooner or later develop a mode of quick, automatic understanding. Eventually they are able to go to those topics that apply to their needs for the moment and disregard the rest.

Readers should gather from my remarks what they need to know about the scope of this book, but I wish to add a few more comments. There are many ways to understand plays, and this book is concerned with only two of them. Although in the twentieth century much of the systematic writing about plays has been in these traditions, it is not hard to find objections to Action or Formalist Analysis from those who favor other methods. Therefore, since we are concerned in this book with the closed context of the play itself, I emphasize that the attention given to this aspect does not imply that other kinds of analysis do not exist or are not important. I have simply agreed to set them aside in favor of discovering the relationships expressed within the play itself. No single method can ever be completely true, but I aim to convince readers that a large number of playable dramatic values can be discovered using these approaches.

Writing a textbook on play analysis is a challenge. This is partly because there is no standard language in theatre as there is, for example, in music. There is not even agreement in the profession about the most commonly used terms and definitions. Moreover, those who deal with plays on a daily basis usually develop their own favorite aims, methods, and terms. It follows from this lexical disorder, that there are a number of ambiguous terms and definitions involved. The definitions of climax, catastrophe, reversal, and resolution, for example, have proven to be problematic even for scholars and theorists, and sometimes it seems as if there are as many definitions of action and objectives as there are actors and directors. In other words, although the topics in this book have been carefully defined, it is not hard to find different, if not sometimes contradictory, meanings in the works of other writers and practitioners. Undoubtedly we could devote a lot more thought to determining consensus definitions of these topics if we wished to, but in a practical book it isn't a good idea to test the patience of readers with too much theory. Besides, for working artists the conditions in the play itself are more important. I hope the terms and definitions as well as the comments about the plays are at least sound and practical. They are not meant to be prescriptive or to take the place of the teacher. Readers who learned about them somewhere else may wish to use my definitions as a basis for comparison with their own instead of thinking of them as conclusive statements, of which there are very few in the arts anyway.

Acknowledgments

This book would not have been possible without the help of others, and the list of those to whom I am obligated is long. It begins with Fran Hodge, whose knowledge of play analysis and directing has set standards that in my opinion few have matched. He taught me how to think seriously about plays and play production, and his approach to the analytical process (treated in *Play Directing: Analysis, Communication, and Style*) has helped to shape the general outline of this book. None of the errors found here should be attributed to him, but most of what is good and useful can be traced to his influence.

For the invaluable opportunity to attend their rehearsals, classes, and lectures and for their patience with my endless questioning, I would like to thank the artist-teachers of the Moscow Art Theatre School-Studio, notably Anatoly Smeliansky (Rector), Oleg Gerasimov (Emeritus), Ivan Moskvin-Tarkhanov (Emeritus), Vladimir Komratov, and especially Mikhail Lobanov. Diligent readers will discover that I have additional sources, probably more than I even know myself. Among these sources are the writings of George Pierce Baker, Eric Bentley, Michael Chekhov, Harold Clurman, Francis Fergusson, John Gassner, Frank McMullan, Konstantin Stanislavski, F. Cowles Strickland, Georgi Tovstonogov, Maria Kenbel, and above all Anatoly Efros. A number of colleagues read parts or all of the manuscript and made helpful comments and criticisms. Among these are Stuart Baker, Dan Carter, John Franceschina, Richard Hornby, Gil Lazier, and Jim Wise. I also owe a debt of gratitude to

José Quintero for his support and encouragement, not to mention his inspiring example, all along the way. To everyone, my thanks.

I also wish to acknowledge the reprinted selections:

Excerpts from *The Oedipus Rex of Sophocles: An English version* translated by Dudley Fitts and Robert Fitzgerald, copyright 1949 by Harcourt Brace Jovanovich, Inc. and renewed 1977 by Cornelis Fitts and Robert Fitzgerald, reprinted by permission of the publisher.

Hamlet by William Shakespeare, *The School for Scandal* by Richard Brinsley Sheridan, and *The Wild Duck* by Henrik Ibsen are from *Plays for the Theatre: An Anthology of World Drama*, Oscar G. Brockett, ed. (New York: Holt, Rinehart, and Winston, 1984).

Tartuffe by Molière from *The Misanthrope and Other Plays*, translated by John Wood (Penguin Classics, 1959). Copyright © 1959 by John Wood. Excerpts reproduced by permission of Penguin Books Ltd.

The Hairy Ape by Eugene O'Neill (New York: Random House, 1921).

Mother Courage and Her Children from *Collected Plays*, Volume V, by Bertolt Brecht, translated by Ralph Manheim. Copyright © 1972 by Stefan S. Brecht. Reprinted by permission of Pantheon Books, a division of Random House, Inc.

Death of a Salesman by Arthur Miller. Copyright 1949, renewed © 1977 by Arthur Miller. Used by permission of Viking Penguin, a division of Viking Penguin Books USA Inc.

A Raisin in the Sun by Lorraine Hansberry (New York: Random House, 1959).

Happy Days by Samuel Beckett (New York: Grove Press, 1961).

Streamers by David Rabe. Copyright, as an unpublished work, 1970, 1975 by David William Rabe. Copyright © 1976, 1977 by David William Rabe. Reprinted by permission of Alfred A. Knopf, Inc.

Introduction

WHAT IS FORMALIST SCRIPT ANALYSIS?

Although some readers may often have heard the term formal, they may not have a firm idea of what it means. This is understandable because it has taken on many meanings over time. Formal may be associated with the practice of doing something for appearance's sake as in a formal wedding. Or it may convey a feeling of primness and stiffness. Maybe readers harbor an unconscious feeling that formal means fixed, authoritarian, and inflexible. All these meanings have in common the notion of an arrangement that gives something its essential character or what Aristotle described as "the inward shaping of an object." The etymology of the word substantiates this. Formal is based on the idea of form or shape. The Latin word *forma* means that which shapes or has been shaped, but especially the shape given to an artistic object. The English word *formula* is related to it as are conformity, inform, reform, transform, and uniform.

Studying the etymology leads to the present meaning of Formalist Analysis: the search for playable dramatic values that reveal a central unifying pattern that informs or shapes a play from the inside and coordinates all of its parts. Playable dramatic values are those features that energize actors, directors, and designers in their work. To accomplish its goal, Formalist Analysis uses a traditional system of classifications to break up a play into its parts in order to understand their nature and relationship.

Some writers may call the formalist approach *descriptive* because it is concerned with describing a play in terms of its own internal artistic context. Or it may be called *analytical* because it analyzes the elements in a play as parts of an artistic totality. Others might describe this approach as *Aristotelian* because it is based on the parts of a play originally described by Aristotle. All these are acceptable alternatives. At the risk of seeming to split hairs, however, I should point out that Formalist Analysis is different from *formal* analysis, which means the study of a play in relation to the form or literary genre to which it belongs. Different, too, from *formalistic* analysis, which is based on the terms and concepts of the Formalist Critics (for which see below). In any event, the underlying assumption of Formalist Analysis is that the plays themselves ought to be studied instead of the abstract theories or external circumstances under which they are written. For theatre students especially, plays should not be merely a means to other kinds of studies, but rather the primary objects of attention.

Formalist Analysis of drama is customarily associated with the principles and methods of Aristotle. His *Poetics* (335–322 BC) treats the six elements of drama (plot, character, dialogue, idea, "song," and production values), unity of action, probability, features of the tragic hero, plot requirements, and other subjects related to plays. Although the term *poetics* is derived from the same Greek source as is the word *poetry*, in Aristotle's sense it more correctly means creatively making, constructing, and arranging an artistic work, in this case drama. The commonsense conclusions he reached continue to influence Western literature and drama even today, and his expressions and descriptions have become part of our critical heritage.

From his survey of the writing, construction, and arrangement of the best plays of his time, Aristotle deduced principles and methods for their analysis and evaluation. His work is the basis of the formalist approach. First, he summarized the basics of drama and analyzed their inner workings and possible combinations. Second, he insisted on the importance of the artistic nature of plays. Third, he reduced concern with outside realistic or moral issues and emphasized instead strict attention to inner structural design, placing special emphasis on the importance of plot as a unifying feature. Fourth, his method was inductive rather than prescriptive. These four principles together make up the heart of the formalist tradition in criticism.

During the Roman period, and later during the Renaissance and the seventeenth century, scholars treated Aristotle's insights as rigid prescriptions. Inquiring into the historical motives behind this phenomenon is beyond the scope of this book, but we know now that the practical outcome left Aristotle with an undeserved reputation for pedantry, some of which lingers on to the present. As succeeding writers interpreted Aristotle with more insight and sensitivity, his reputation as a critic was for the most part restored.

Near the beginning of the twentieth century in Russia, scholar and critic Alexander Veselovsky extended the Aristotelian tradition by developing a system of defined aims and methods for the study of literature and drama. His system, like Aristotle's, was based on the importance of plot. Veselovsky was a member of the literary committee of Moscow's important Maly Theatre and promoted his principles among the theatre artists working there. His ideas influenced actor Mikhail Shchepkin, artistic director of the influential Maly company, and Vladimir Nemirovitch-Dantchenko, a member of the same committee and cofounder of the Moscow Art Theatre with Konstantin Stanislavski. Perhaps inspired by Veselovsky's emphasis on plot and artistic unity, Nemirovitch-Dantchenko and Stanislavski promoted similar principles and methods among their own students. No matter what, their goal was practical, not scholarly: to help actors, directors, and designers understand and perform plays as logical arrangements of actions.

Later, around the time of the Russian Revolution, formalist ideas began to be applied on an even larger scale by a group of critics known as the Russian Formalists. Headed by Viktor Shklovsky and Evgeny Zamyatin, the Formalists were characterized by their meticulous attention to the artistic aspects of literature as opposed to its social or moral connections.

After 1928, Russian Formalism was suppressed in the Soviet Union for political reasons, but its major concepts and strategies can be found in the New Criticism, which first appeared during the 1930s and flourished during the 1940s and 1950s in the West. New Criticism was an American movement led by John Crowe Ransom, Allen Tate, and Robert Penn Warren, all of whom were writers and poets as well as critics. In his book, *The New Criticism* (1941), Ransom coined the term that identified this informal group, which also included R.P. Blackmur, Kenneth Burke, Cleanth Brooks, Robert B. Heilman, William K. Wimsatt, and Ivor Winters.

Like the Russian formalists, the New Critics advocated meticulous study of the work itself. They disregarded the mind and personality of the author, literary sources, historical-critical theories, and political and social implications, which they deprecated as *historical criticism*. To emphasize their belief in the autonomy of the literary work itself, they referred to the writing as the *text* and termed their analytical approach *close reading*. Their ideas were presented in four textbooks: Wimsatt and Warren's *Understanding Poetry* (1938), Brooks and Warren's *Understanding Fiction* (1943), Brooks and Heilman's *Understanding Drama* (1948), and Brooks and Warren's guide to methodology, *Modern Rhetoric* (1958). These textbooks helped to shift the focus of literary instruction away from external concerns and back to the work itself.

The Cambridge Critics led a comparable movement in English literary criticism. Influenced by poet T. S. Eliot, this group was led by William Empson and included F.R. Leavis, I.A. Richards, Caroline Spurgeon, and G. Wilson Knight. Knight's analyses of Shakespeare's plays, notably *The Wheel of Fire* (1930), were some of the major successes of the Cambridge Critics in the field of drama.

Many of the principles of the New Criticism were adopted by succeeding generations of American writers, including Francis Fergusson (*The Idea of a Theatre*, 1949), Elder Olson, Eric Bentley, Bernard Beckerman, Richard Hornby, and Jackson G. Barry, as well as theatre educators Alexander Dean, Hardie Albright, Lawrence Carra, William Halstead, F. Cowles Strickland, Curtis Canfield, Frank McMullan, Sam Smiley, and Francis Hodge, to name only a few. Among English-speaking theatre professionals, the members of the Group Theatre beginning in the 1930s adopted the analytical methods of the Moscow Art Theatre. Formalist thinking supports the creative principles of Stella Adler, Harold Clurman, Richard Boleslavsky, Mordecai Gorelik, Elia Kazan, Robert Lewis, Sanford Meisner, Lee Strasberg, and many of their students and followers, as well as Viola Spolin, Robert Cohen, Jean Benedetti, Charles Marowitz and Uta Hagen. Among the most influential of Stanislavski's followers in America was the actor and teacher Michael Chekhov (1891–1955), whose acting principles have become so well known in film and television. After leaving Russia, Chekhov resided in Los Angeles, where he and his collaborator George Shdanoff (1905–1998) taught several generations of actors their variation of Stanislavski's principles, which was based on Imagination and also involved a type of Formalist Analysis.

Beginning in the 1960s, drama and literature were influenced by movements in politics, sociology, anthropology, and religion in ways that seemed to defy traditional methods of criticism. Accordingly, a new generation of literary critics emerged who became dissatisfied with the self-imposed limits of the formalist approach. Within a decade more wide-ranging critical approaches appeared, which were based on deconstruction, post-structuralism, hermeneutics, semiotics, and theories of reception and communication. Some of them have clarified meanings previously unknown in plays, and sometimes their fresh interpretations seem promising. So far in the rehearsal hall, however, their results have not been consistently useful. Perhaps this is because they have emphasized taking apart (hence deconstruction) while theatrical production by definition must be concerned with putting together. Moreover, some of the more recent literary theories are by definition always conditional. As the film director Andrey Tarkovsky observed, it is sort of dangerous for actors, directors, and designers never having to reach final conclusions. It is much too easy to settle for hints of intuition instead of thorough, consistent reasoning.

At any rate, even though literary criticism seems committed to sociopolitical interests outside the play, theatre practice must continue to rely on close analysis of the play itself. Some may argue that this approach is not better than any other method at its best. After all, there are selected plays and periods of history where considerations outside the script are important and should be studied. Conversely, understanding the internal nature of the play is crucial to understanding its external context. More important in the theatre, plays must eventually exist in the practical realm of live performance and not just in the intellectual realm of scholarship. On stage, at least, the play itself is obliged to remain the final controlling factor. Formalist Analysis corresponds with this point of view. It offers more than intellectual insights; it supplies practical suggestions that can energize actors, directors, and designers for their work.

To conclude, the principles of Formalist Analysis have endured in the theatre because they correspond with the nature of the thing to which they are applied. They are an outcome of how actors, directors, and designers think about plays, and they are based on the assumption that what these artists need to know about plays is what is important. Although we may not always be aware of it, the principles of Formalist Analysis help to make plays work out in production. Without them, play scripts would seem unfinished and maybe even unintelligible. Moreover, they are not just empty concepts to learn because generations of actors, directors, and designers have done so before. They are the keys that actors, directors, and designers use to check their work, to explore its possibilities, and find new directions in it. Formalist topics are not only the basis of the playwright's vision, but also a guide for actors, directors, and designers through the process of creation.

Action Analysis

This edition introduces a variant of Formalist Analysis, called Action Analysis, which concentrates heavily on plot and pays comparatively little attention to the other features of a play. This reduced type of Formalist Analysis has its own interesting history and purpose. Stanislavski developed Action Analysis during the later stages of work on his "System" of acting. He died before he could codify its principles, but his followers adopted and disseminated them. Among them was Maria Knebel (1898–1985), who was a personal student both of Stanislavski and Michael Chekhov. A director, teacher, and author of important books on acting, directing, and theatre pedagogy, Knebel started directing at the Moscow Art Theatre in 1935. She was Artistic Director of the Central Children's Theatre from 1950–1960, where the revival of the Russian theatre after Stalin began. From 1960–1985 she taught directing at the Lunacharsky State Institute for Theatre Training. There she made a conscious effort to preserve, maintain, and disseminate her teacher's final principles in their undiluted form. The principles of Action Analysis described here are adopted from her books, which are listed in the bibliography. They were translated by the author and are presented here in English for the first time.

According to Stanislavski, the concepts of the Super-Objective and Through-Action are central to the creativity of the actor (and by extension, of course, the director and designer). It is widely known that the Moscow Art Theatre originated the period of so-called table work, that is, analytical work at the table prior to scenic rehearsals on stage. During this period, the actors, under the guidance of the director, subjected to careful analysis all the motives, implications, relationships, characters, through-action, super-objective, etc. of the play. Table work made it possible to penetrate the play deeply, to define its ideological and artistic problems. It encouraged the actors to penetrate into the private world of the characters as the foundation for creation of the performance. This manner of work later became essential for all theatrical organizations, from the largest professional theatres to the smallest amateur performances.

Yet as early as 1905 Stanislavski already had misgivings about the study method he had helped to develop. Since the director as artistic leader needs to comprehend the future result of the work, the internal structure of the play—including the Super-Objective and Through-Action—must be made clear so that he or she can imagine the path that will lead the actors and designers to the final result. For that reason, the director is prepared for work much more deeply and multi-dimensionally than the actor or designer in the first period, the table period, of rehearsal. Stanislavski saw that even the most patient and sensitive directors (including him) could not avoid becoming creative despots by their need to merge the actors as soon as possible with the director's previously imagined impression of the play. Involuntarily, this practice of intensive table work had begun to deprive the actor of creative initiative. Actors and designers were becoming passive recipients of the director's plan, which, in any case, seemed to offer all the right answers. Stanislavski eventually became disenchanted with the unequal relationship that had unintentionally arisen between the director and the actors in the first stage of rehearsal. He wanted to find a way of working that would put the actors back into direct contact with the play, but still guided by the script, of course. After further study and practice, he concluded that the easiest and most accessible way to grasp a play was through its plot. He worked out a rehearsal method that combined intellectual analysis with physical action and which came to be known as "The Method of Physical Actions."

In the usual way of rehearsing, the director pushes the actor toward the characterization by trying to stir his or her imagination talking "at the table" about the contents of the play, the character, the time period, etc. Stanislavski asserted that in the early stages of work actors naturally perceive a director's ideas coolly. The actor is not prepared to digest someone else's ideas and feelings because he or she does not feel on firm ground yet and does not know what to accept or reject. For a true awareness of the essence of a play, not only intellectual and emotional, but also physical, experience are necessary. Stanislavski criticized his earlier method of extended work "at the table" where the actors sit down with scripts and pencils and, under the prodding of the director, try to penetrate the expressive life of the play. He felt that this approach separated the internal life of the play from the external and in doing so impoverished the results.

He came to believe that intellectual preparation was necessary mainly to find the core of the play, to define the chain of events and the essential actions of the characters. But as soon as the actors understand this much of the dramatic structure, after that early sensations of the theme and through-action could begin to arise almost of themselves. This manner of rapid analysis Stanislavski called *mental investigation*. As soon as this part of the work is done, Stanislavski suggested passing on to the next period of deeper analysis, which no longer exclusively occurs at the table but also in the form of real physical action. This he called the period of *physical investigation*. At this point, the actors work on the internal and external life of the play simultaneously and truly experience what he termed the *psycho-physical unity* of the creative process. The practice of integrating mental and physical processes was later labeled "Active Analysis" or "The Method of Etudes," in which an etude is an improvised sketch using the play's actions and the actors' words.

A textbook on play analysis is not the place for a discussion of rehearsal methods. Here it is enough to say that Action Analysis is in essence the intellectual part of Stanislavski's Method of Physical Actions, the part Stanislavski called mental investigation. Action Analysis offers a big picture of the whole play quickly because it concentrates on one element: plot. Formalist Analysis devotes a lot of attention to plot, too, but also to dialogue, character, idea, and tempo-rhythm-mood and style. Except for certain learning purposes, there is no particular advantage to one method over the other. Both are necessary for a thorough understanding and they are often used together in practice. Curiously, the two approaches seem to reflect the different personalities of Stanislavski and Nemirovitch-Dantchenko. As an actor and teacher, Stanislavski was always more interested in the process of rehearsal than in performance as such. Possibly for that reason, he developed an approach that minimized table work and maximized the actors' time working creatively on their feet. Nemirovitch-Dantchenko was a playwright, critic, and director whose attention was always focused on the final product, the performance and its thematic significance. He was always committed to extensive table work. The concept of the "seed" explained in Chapter 1 is his, although Stanislavski adopted it and it has been integrated into Action Analysis. Since 1989, we have been learning more about the inner world of the early Moscow Art Theatre, about the working relationship between Stanislavski and Nemirovitch-Dantchenko, and about the development of their creative principles. Sharon Carnicke's book, *Stanislavski in Focus* (1998), is recommended for those who want to know more. Also valuable is *The Russian Theatre After Stalin* (1999) by Anatoly Smeliansky.

Formalist Analysis: Plan of Work

The classifications of Formalist Analysis and their main subdivisions as used in this book, including Action Analysis, are listed below:

1. Action Analysis
   Sequence of Events: External Events
   Reviewing the Facts
   Seed
   Sequence of Events: Internal Events
   Three Major Climaxes
   Theme
   Super-Objective
   Through-Action
   Counter-Through Action
2. Foundations of the Plot: Given Circumstances
   Time
   Place
   Society
   Economics
   Politics and Law
   Intellect and Culture
   Spirituality
   The World of the Play

This sums up what most actors, directors, and designers need to know about the heritage of Formalist Analysis. The complete history, of course, is more complex than this. For example, the Freudian, Jungian, Marxian, Structuralist, and Post-Modern critics whose ideas currently influence some of the more radical methodologies are omitted from this survey. If the contributions of Freud, Jung, Marx, Sartre, Foucault and Derrida are understated, the position of the New Critics regarding the independence of the text is a little overstated. As a matter of fact, apart from their theories, there are passages in their writing that go beyond the literary work and into the areas of politics and morals. The survey is also responsible for another necessary exaggeration. By design, it leads the reader to feel a straight line of thinking, which supports the formalist tradition. This is unlikely for a diverse group of theorists dealing with such a complex subject. But having agreed about these over-simplifications, the survey is still adequate to establish the heritage of the formalist viewpoint. Those who wish to learn more can read some of the books that have been written about the history of literary criticism. Among the more informative are *Russian Formalist Criticism: Four Essays* (1965) and *A Handbook of Critical Approaches to Literature* (1992).

THE EXPRESSIVENESS OF DRAMATIC WRITING

Before we begin to study the principles of play analysis, it will be helpful to review some of the basic principles of reading in general. Initial learning about a play almost always begins with the written words of the script. But when we act, direct, or design a play, we not only read the play but the play reads us, so to speak. If we fall short in this respect, the results are there for everyone in the theatre to see. Therefore, what is done *at the table* before the rehearsals and production conferences begin is crucial. If initial perceptions are wrong, every succeeding repetition reinforces the error. If initial perceptions are confused, every succeeding repetition increases the confusion. Persistent errors and extended confusion are certain to lead down the path of artistic failure. For these reasons alone, reviewing some of the basic principles involved with reading and thinking can help theatre artists approach their work with something worthwhile to say.

When plays are treated as subdivisions of literature, they are likely to be analyzed with the same principles as those applied to fiction, poetry, and other literary genres. A number of writers have pointed out, however, that there are crucial differences between literature and drama that orthodox literary analysis may not be equipped to address by itself. To begin with, the dialogue in fiction is supplemented with generous amounts of narration to explain plot, character, idea, and feelings not otherwise apparent. Of course, some narration is always necessary in drama. We shall discuss this subject in more detail in Chapter 3, but in general, dramatic writing depends on dialogue, not narration, to convey the action. Unlike the literary author, the dramatist cannot interrupt the action to offer supplementary information or to clarify complex meanings without hampering the spirit of the play. Even when there is a narrator in the play, the words still must sound like normal speech within the context of the situation, and although stage directions are written in narrative form, they are not spoken by the actors and are not central to the dramatic action.

Another feature that contributes to the extra expressiveness of plays is their short length. Even in a very long play, the number of words is small compared to those in a standard novel. Yet although plays employ far fewer words than do novels, they must still contain at least as much dramatic potential as does a complete novel to be effective theatrically. Playwrights achieve this extra potency by infusing stage dialogue with a special expressiveness that is absent, or at least less important, in other literary forms. It is true that stage dialogue often looks very much like its literary cousin. Sometimes it even sounds so ordinary that it seems as if it was written without any conscious effort at all on the part of the playwright. But this is a crafted deception. The truth is that theatrical dialogue is a concentrated and powerful form of verbal expression. Speech is more condensed on stage and each word carries far more dramatic impact than in most other literature. Even a single utterance can pack a tremendous wallop. Because of the extra measure of expressiveness put into it by the playwright, there is more expressiveness per page in a play than in almost any other form of writing. Novelist Henry James, himself an experienced dramatist and a perceptive critic, maintained that playwriting required a more masterly sense of composition than did any other kind of writing.

Concentrated dependence on spoken dialogue plus radical compactness together creates the need and the opportunity for extra expressiveness in dramatic writing. It follows that actors, directors, and designers should learn to understand this special expressiveness to energize and illustrate every last ounce of it in production. But this does not always happen. Because the first experience of a play is a written script, the extra expressiveness is easy to overlook. There is an understandable confusion between the literary activity of reading and the theatrical activity of seeing, hearing, and feeling a play on the stage. Confusion is even more likely to occur with plays that have strong literary merit like those of Shakespeare and other authors whose works are studied in dramatic literature courses. To avoid underreading, theatre students should be aware of two important considerations about theatrical dialogue. First, the words in a script are far, far more expressive in a live performance than they are in the solitary, concentrated act of reading, and second, the words are only the tip of the iceberg, merely the visible part of what is happening deep within in a play. Energized acting, direction, and design are always required to unleash a play's potent expressiveness completely.

ANALYTICAL READING

There are no hard and fast rules for reading plays, but certain mental powers are needed to understand the special kind of expressiveness they contain. The first important power is that of analytical reading. Unfortunately in its initial stages at least, analytical reading can be hard work. Some people think that experienced professionals can sight-read a play the way some musicians sight-read a score, but this skill is as rare in the theatre as it is in music. A professional's analysis of a play is a long and painstaking process. In fact, a major characteristic of professionals is their recognition of the value of slow, methodical table work.

Another mental power consists of the ability to understand the many meanings of words and the dramatic force that may be expressed by them. Art students pay attention to shape and color; music students listen for pitch and timbre. Those who wish to make a living in the theatre should develop a sense of the expressiveness and emotion inherent in words.

Mental power also means concern for literal facts and their connections. A *fact* is a verifiable assertion about a thing, and *literal facts* are those that are frankly stated in the dialogue as true. Literal facts in drama include identification of people, places, actions, and objects, but they may also describe wishes as well as feelings and thoughts. Learning how to recognize hard facts is a basic test of artistic awareness. In the earliest readings of a play, the literal, verifiable facts should be searched out to find what is objectively being said. Furthermore, since plays are orderly arrangements by their nature, making logical connections among the facts is necessary for understanding the sequences and patterns found in them. We call these connections *implications* and *inferences*. Implications are hints or suggestions that are not directly stated, and inferences are deductions of unknown from known information, that is, deduced from literal facts and their implications.

Remember the short scene in the garden from Act 2 of Arthur Miller's play, *Death of a Salesman*. After a climactic confrontation with his son, Biff, Willy Loman decides late the same night to plant vegetables in his backyard garden. As in several earlier scenes, his absent brother Ben appears to him in his imagination, and they carry on a short dialogue. In this scene, the literal facts about planting a garden are important. We know that planting a garden requires certain external activities and special tools. Since these can be described precisely, this part of the action is easy to understand. Some of the literal facts involved with planting a garden are present: opening packages of seeds and reading the instructions, pacing off the rows for different kinds of plants, using a hoe, and planting the seeds in the ground. But most readers will see right away that planting a garden is not all that is happening here. There are things going on that are not connected with planting a garden. Planting is not done late at night with a flashlight, and a gardener does not carry on a conversation about life insurance with an imaginary figure the way Willy does. Willy is also possessed by a mysterious sense of urgency or anxiety in his task that prevents him from paying close attention to Ben. Obviously planting a garden is no longer what we normally think it is.

Implications and inferences now become important and they do not support a literal reading of the scene. A closer examination of Willy's unusual actions relates them to his innermost feelings and thoughts, particularly his profound sense of personal failure as a father. He is no longer simply planting a garden; he is performing a ritual in preparation for his imminent death. The garden scene becomes an important clue to the meaning of the whole play, which is a conflict between Willy's ideals as a salesman and his fatherly duty toward his son, Biff. Therefore, although literal facts are a helpful starting point, implications and inferences need to be considered to arrive at a complete understanding. Script analysis involves piecing the known and unknown together into a consistent and meaningful pattern just as detectives do in popular crime fiction.

LOGICAL THINKING

Evidence of all kinds is important, but so is logical thinking. Unfortunately, unawareness of the creative capacities of logical thinking is widespread, particularly among young artists. It can lead to the feeling that careful study of a play is stuffy and even inhibiting. But experienced professionals appreciate that logical thinking can uncover dramatic possibilities that make plays come alive in a new way. There is another value to consider. Audiences are becoming smarter all the time because playwrights demand far more intelligence from them today than they did in the past. Ever since Vsevelod Meyerhold and Bertolt Brecht, a good number of modern plays have been fashioned to pull in the audience by forcing them to comprehend what is happening ideologically, not just experience the play in a submissive manner. Increasing emphasis has been placed on the semantic meaning of the play and a great deal of aesthetic pleasure comes from penetrating the secret thinking of the characters. Consequently, modern acting, directing, and design need to demand the most of audience understanding. If this is to occur, the artistic team needs to be at least one step ahead of the audience in its thinking. Unless the audience is given something exciting to *think* about, unless the artistic team understands and expresses the inner *logic* of the play, the production cannot be considered truly modern in the creative sense.

Bringing some of the common fallacies of thinking encountered in play reading out of the subconscious, where they often lurk, and into the open, can help readers avoid accidental misreading. There are a few pitfalls, and they are not difficult to understand. Most of them can be classified as non-sequiturs, either as conclusions that do not follow from the facts or as reasoning that does not make sense. Sometimes readers may need to revisit the principles of logical thinking before trying to deal more thoroughly with plays. The basics can be found in any good rhetoric textbook. With the help of a good tutor, this should be enough to fill in any gaps.

Affective Fallacy (Impressionism)

According to literary critic W.K. Wimsatt, this error results from confusion between the play and its results (what it is versus what it does). It comes about when readers allow their favorite ideals or momentary enthusiasms or the momentary enthusiasms of the community to intrude on their judgment of the play. Maintaining enough emotional detachment is necessary to analyze a play correctly, but this is not always easy to do. After all, plays are meant to be emotional experiences, and many readers respond to the emotional stimuli in them. Actors, directors, and designers, for example, respond in personal ways, as indeed they should. In the scene from *Death of a Salesman* cited above, it is possible that readers could be reminded of their own families. They might be drawn in to confuse emotional memories of them with that of Willy Loman in the play. Or, alternatively, readers who sympathized with Willy's economic plight might be tempted to entangle their own point of view with the harsh economic world described in the play. Personal experiences like these can be interesting if readers are experienced artists or critics; but if not, they can lead to loose thinking or analytical lack of attention. At worst, a reader might become hopelessly, if unconsciously, bogged down in self-analysis. Nonetheless, it is possible to maintain emotional distance and still respond emotionally to a play. The solution is to try to separate intimate personal responses from what is objectively there in the play. Director Elia Kazan has stated, "The first job is to discover what the script is saying, not what it reminds you of." Absolute objectivity is impossible, of course, but impartiality and the tracing out of both routine and unusual consequences needs to be maintained as much as possible. Successful script analysis depends on it.

Fallacy of Faulty Generalization (Overexpansion)

Some readers are inclined to this reading error when they jump to a conclusion without having enough evidence. When a reader uses *all* or *never* in statements about the play with only a casual concern for the information in the play itself, further close reading will normally correct this mistake. But even more deadly in play reading is inattention to contrary examples. If, after reading *Hamlet*, for instance, a reader resorts to the worn-out generalities about "the melancholy prince" or "the man who could not make up his mind," he should test the conclusions with contradictory evidence. A little scrutiny will show that Hamlet is cheerful while welcoming the Players, and he's decisive while dealing with the Ghost. A few contrary illustrations like these should be enough to disprove the original sweeping assertions.

Fallacy of Illicit Process (Reductiveness)

This kind of error reduces complex issues to one thing, which is a frequent mistake even among experienced play readers. Reducing *Hamlet* to the Freudian Oedipus complex is an extreme instance. So is thinking that *Mother Courage* is nothing but an antiwar play, that *A Raisin in the Sun* is a plea for racial integration, that *A Lie of the Mind* is a plea against spousal abuse, that *Angels in America* is a defense of homosexuality, or that *Three Sisters* is about the degeneration of the Russian intelligentsia. The spoken or implied phrase *nothing but* is the giveaway. The motive behind attempts to reduce a play to less complex equivalents is generally disparagement.

Genetic Fallacy

Related to reductiveness is the genetic fallacy or the fallacy of origins, which is an attempt to reduce a play to its sources in the biography or social world of the artist in order to explain it. There is for any play a large body of secondary writing about its circumstances, the author's life and times, and so forth. Much of this writing is pedantic in the extreme and full of banalities. For example, the question is not what does *Death of a Salesman* tell us about Arthur Miller's personal life or about American economics during the 1940s, but rather what does it tell us about itself? There may be some connections between a play and some external features in the life and world of the author, but they are not as important as people believe them to be. No point-to-point correlation exists, and although Formalist Analysis teaches the fundamental unity of plays, it also teaches that plays are complex independent objects deserving intellectual respect. Readers should exercise caution before attempting to trace the meaning of a play to a tendency observed in the life or times of the author.

Fallacy of the Half-Truth (Debunking)

This error in logic occurs when readers use the same explanation for everything, with negative implications. In this way, the author, play, or character is discredited or debunked. Henrik Ibsen's plays often suffer from this fallacy among readers. To say that Ibsen wrote grim Victorian social dramas carries the unspoken meaning to others that his plays are (1) gloomy and humorless, (2) the result of psychological neuroses in the author's temperament, and (3) Victorian journalism masquerading as drama. Readers holding this opinion see Ibsen's plays as boring, depressing, and outdated. Another example is the statement that: "nothing really happens in Samuel Beckett's plays—there's no plot." What is the real meaning behind this half-truth? The remedy for automatic cynicism is to study the script more than once with an open mind. This is not just a question of finding any reasonable explanation and verifying it in the script but also of testing what connects to what against many points in the script.

Intentional Fallacy

This is another of Wimsatt's formulations that is central to the principles of Formalist Analysis. It means trying to determine what the author's intention was and whether it was fulfilled, instead of attending to the work itself. Examples of this are easy to find because of the modern vogue for literary criticism and the frequency with which artists insist on writing about their own works. Take the situation of Bertolt Brecht. No one can measure the amount of misunderstanding that has resulted from misapplication of his theoretical writings to productions of his plays (that is, the alienation effect, epic realism, and so forth). Wimsatt in *The Verbal Icon* argues that a work of art is detached from the author the moment it is finished. After that, the author no longer has the power to intend anything about it or to control it. Wimsatt's opinion, however, should be taken as a warning more than as a strict rule. As with the other reading errors, the antidote to use against the intentional fallacy is repeated close reading of the play itself before attempting to make a definitive statement about the author's intention.

Frigidity (Insensitivity)

The next error turns in the opposite direction. *Frigidity* is author John Gardner's term for not showing enough concern—or the right kind of concern—about the characters or situations. Frigidity here means not treating the feelings in the play with the importance and care they deserve. Frigidity also includes the inability to recognize the seriousness of things in general. The standard of comparison is the concern any decent human being would show under the circumstances. Frigidity occurs when pulling back from genuine feeling or when only looking at the surface trivialities in a conflict. Unfortunately, in the form of irony it is one of the chief characteristics of the current artistic scene. It leads to less concern for the characters, plot, and concrete meaning of a play, is one of the worst errors possible in play reading, and is often the root of other errors. The error is frigidity when actors, directors, or designers knowingly go into a production less than fully prepared.

Literal-Mindedness

Related to frigidity is the error of evaluating everything in the play on the basis of its literal resemblance to real life. When it is used as a negative judgment, a statement like "the Angel in *Angels in America* and Sutter's ghost in *The Piano Lesson* are not plausible because modern science tells us there are no such things as angels or ghosts" is a typical if crude example. This kind of thinking is a possible sign of a limited imagination as much as anything else. It may stem from misunderstanding the idea of reality in acting, sometimes called by actors *emotional honesty*. But the quality of observed reality in a play has little connection with the play's potential for expressing psychological truth. A play, after all, can be unrealistic in all its external features and still permit honest acting. A simple door can be different from one play to another, depending on the artistic plan of the production. In one play, it can be realistic while in another the actor can enter by appearing out of the darkness in a spotlight. Emotional honesty and theatrical reality are separate and distinct issues and do not contradict one another. Whatever the source of the confusion, however, the lesson is that everyday reality is irrelevant to understanding a play as an artistic experience. Plays create their own realities.

Secondhand Thinking

This error is a corollary of the intentional fallacy. Although it is not a logical fallacy, it can still be troublesome for novice play readers. It stems from relying too much on other people's opinions, especially when dealing with difficult material. The methods of the college classroom and the recent interest in radical criticism have not discouraged the habit. Unfortunately, addiction to the judgments, even of experienced critics, even when they are accurate, can inhibit self-confidence and independent thinking. Artists, especially young artists, should beware of cutting themselves off from new experiences, feelings, or words by relying on established opinion rather than on direct contact. To permit the free exercise of imagination, script analysis should initially be a solo experience. Experts can safely be consulted afterward.

Over-Reliance on Stage Directions

Secondhand thinking also extends to stage directions, which are notes incorporated in a script or added to it to convey information about its performance not already evident in the dialogue itself. Ordinarily they are concerned either with the actor's movements on stage or with scenery and stage effects. Plays written in the past tended to keep stage directions to a minimum, but over the years their use grew more widespread until, by the end of the nineteenth century, they were often long and very elaborate. The prefaces to George Bernard Shaw's plays, for instance, often run on for dozens of pages and contain explicit instructions for actors and producers. There is some evidence among modern playwrights, however, of a reversal of this trend.

But stage directions may not always belong to the author. According to the custom of most publishers, stage directions are as likely to be written by the stage manager from the original setting provided by the scene designer or written by the literary editor of the text (as in the case of Shakespeare, for example). Even when we are certain the author has written them, it is prudent to recall the advice of the late designer, Edward Gordon Craig, about the reliability of stage directions. In his treatise, *On the Art of the Theatre*, Craig contended that stage directions are an infringement on the artistic rights of actors, directors, and designers. From this he concluded that playwrights should cease using them altogether. Of course, Craig's prejudices are notorious, and his position on this subject was extreme. He did have a point, however. Stage directions are intended to supplement the dialogue, not replace it. They shouldn't be confused with the play itself. Many professional actors, directors, and designers as well as producers and agents will seldom read stage directions, any stage directions. They want to work with the play itself and allow it to tell them everything they need to know, which is the point of view of this book.

CHAPTER 1

Action Analysis

Formalist Analysis proceeds by gathering lots of detailed information from the play and then drawing general conclusions about the whole work. It uses an orderly collection of close-ups to form the big picture. This process is called *inductive reasoning*; from the verb *induce*, meaning the act of bringing forward facts or particulars. Formalist Analysis is time-consuming and thorough because it attempts to cover all the dramatic potentials of a play. This quality of thoroughness almost guarantees its functional success. Unfortunately, thoroughness is also lengthy and loaded with fine points. In the middle of a project readers can become at times so involved in the details that they lose sight of the whole play. They cannot see the forest for the trees. At some point they may need to step back and consider what result their project may lead to. The method of Action Analysis offered in this chapter provides that opportunity. Action Analysis is a reduced type of Formalist Analysis. It is not intended as a shortcut to creativity, however. It may be faster than Formalist Analysis, but by the same token it is also less complete. Action Analysis and Formalist Analysis are supposed to operate together to obtain the level of knowledge necessary for genuinely professional work.

Defining the important events and examining their internal springs will also introduce readers to some of the features of Formalist Analysis treated at more length later in the book. For example, to evaluate the events correctly, it will be necessary to consider the Given Circumstances, Background Story, Action, and Structure (Chapters 2, 3, 4, and

5), which are the lifeblood of a play. Revealing the main events from which the behavior of a character develops, readers begin to understand the motives behind the actions and start to learn about Character (Chapter 6). In addition, learning the sequence of the events and its logic, readers will come to an understanding of the ultimate goal, or Super-Objective, that governs the play and its characters, the play's Idea (Chapter 7). Action Analysis and Formalist Analysis can be learned and used in any order the reader's needs require.

SEQUENCE OF EVENTS

The easiest and most accessible grasp of a play is through an analysis of the events of its plot. Action Analysis is based on an explanation of the play's noteworthy happenings, which is called the *Sequence of Events*. Determining the important events will help to understand how the author has built the plot, from which everything else follows. Learning how to define what constitutes the important events is not as easy as it may appear to be. It takes a special range of vision to be able to distinguish the essential from the less essential. To perform Action Analysis it is nec-essary to think of plays as large pieces of action and to develop a feel for what are the important events in a play. A simple illustration will help to explain. An express train traveling, for example, from New York to Washington, D.C. stops only at major cities along the way: Hartford, New York, Philadelphia. But there is also a "local train," which stops at the smaller cities: New Haven, Baltimore, etc. To study the regions between the major cities—between Hartford and New York or between Philadel-phia and Washington, D.C.—it is useful to stop at some smaller cities, where one contains shopping districts, another suburbs, a third hills and valleys, a fourth lakes and rivers, a fifth factories, etc. It is also possible to take an intercity bus and stop at each small town, village, or rural community along the way. Stopping at them, a traveler will obtain an even better understanding of the regions between Boston and Washington, D.C. It is also possible for a "non-stop" train to travel straight from Boston to Washington, D.C. without any stops along the way. A feeling of great momentum and speed will be the result. But this "train" is for the rich—the geniuses, as Stanislavski put it. We might say that the express train is Action Analysis (Chapter 1), while the local train is Formalist

Analysis (Chapters 2–7) and the intercity bus is Advanced Analysis (Chapters 8–10). Most of us do not need to concern ourselves with the non-stop train.

Sequence of Events: External Events

The Sequence of Events begins with a list of the most important *External Events* in their original order. By "external event" we mean the simple social activity that is taking place, for example, arrivals or departures, meetings, announcements, discussions, quarrels, etc. While we're on the subject, according to Stanislavski an event consists of the intersection of two conflicting actions that cause the social activity in the first place. For example, John wants to marry Jane, but Jane does not want to marry John, which then leads to their quarrel. There is no need to be too exacting with event descriptions at this point, however, as long as they are generally accurate, whether social activities or conflicting actions. Here we'll just refer to social activities because they're simpler to describe. Shakespeare's plays make the process somewhat easier to manage because they are crowded with events and are also divided into formal scenes. As a result, it is possible to consider each scene as a single External Event. *Hamlet* will be the example used here.

What happens in 1,1 (shorthand for Act 1, Scene 1)? Several small External Events occur in the scene: the changing of the guard, the arrival of Horatio, the first appearance of the Ghost, a discussion about the previous appearance of the Ghost, the second appearance of the Ghost, a discussion about Denmark's current preparations for war and a decision to tell Hamlet about the Ghost. These are simple social events—arrivals, departures, discussions, and decisions—of a kind found in daily life under a variety of circumstances. Also, their descriptions here use as few words as possible; they are short and to the point. Brevity and an absence of literary jargon are essential goals in Action Analysis. Short, clear-cut descriptions are closest to simple human behavior, which is a merit of Action Analysis.

The next question to ask is which one of the six or seven smaller events in 1,1 form the essence of the whole scene. What single event sets the scene apart and defines its vital purpose in the play? Let's review the circumstances. All the characters in the play are important at some point, of course, but for the moment most readers would agree that the guards Francisco, Barnardo, and Marcellus, are less essential here than Horatio and the Ghost. Horatio is Hamlet's classmate and closest friend from the University of Wittenberg and the Ghost provides the reason for the scene. Earlier, Marcellus told Horatio about the first appearance of the Ghost, but the skeptical Horatio did not believe him. That is why Marcellus has asked Horatio to come and see for himself. A clever rehearsal room saying declares that anything of importance on stage happens either for the first time or the last time. First times and last times entail beginnings and ends, which are dramatic by their nature. This particular scene shows Horatio's first encounter with the Ghost. In fact, it is his first experience with anything supernatural. Moreover, as Hamlet's closest friend and confidant, Horatio will be the first one who tells him about the event. Evidently, the main point of the scene is Horatio's encounter with the Ghost. Therefore, we could describe the central external event of 1,1 as follows: Horatio encounters the Ghost.

Using a similar "express" way of thinking, the External Events in *Hamlet* can be cataloged like this:

1,1: Horatio encounters the Ghost
1,2: Claudius takes over the throne
1,3: Laertes departs for France
1,4: Hamlet meets the Ghost
1,5: Hamlet learns that Claudius murdered his father
2,1: Reynaldo departs for France
2,2: Hamlet plans to trap Claudius
3,1: Claudius eavesdrops on Hamlet and Ophelia
3,2: The "mousetrap scene"
3,3: Claudius prays
3,4: Gertrude appeals to Hamlet
4,1: Claudius takes action
4,2: Rosencrantz and Guildenstern capture Hamlet
4,3: Claudius sends Hamlet to England
4,4: Hamlet crosses paths with Fortinbras
4,5: Laertes returns to Elsinore
4,6: Horatio learns that Hamlet has returned
4,7: Claudius and Laertes conspire to kill Hamlet
5,1: Hamlet learns about Ophelia's death

5,2: Hamlet agrees to a sporting duel with Laertes
5,3: Hamlet slays Claudius

This is quite a short and snappy examination of a very complex play. Some may argue that it is too short; others may disagree with some of the descriptions. No matter. Action Analysis is not comprehensive, just rapid and functional. In any case, the descriptions here are not meant to be definitive but no more than demonstrations of the thinking process involved. Besides, sometimes a snappy attitude is useful for seeing through the avalanche of words in a play, especially a Shakespearean play. Whatever the case may be, Formalist Analysis and rehearsal lie ahead to fine-tune any over-hasty or misguided conclusions. True, many less essential events have been omitted, but at least this list gives a satisfactory outline of the External Events, which at this point is all that is needed to proceed with the next stage of Action Analysis.

REVIEWING THE FACTS

This part of Action Analysis is well explained by its title. *Reviewing the Facts* is a process that occurs at intervals throughout Action Analysis. A good time to address it occurs after defining the External Events. This stage of study asks readers to force their imaginations to deal with the characters as particular people who are living in particular circumstances. To do so, it is necessary to purge any memories of what well-known actors, directors, or designers did with the play in the past or what they or others may have written about it. Studying the play this way, readers will start to understand the conditions that generate the events together with the words and characters that express them. In the Formalist Analysis taught in the following chapters, those conditions are called the Given Circumstances, Background Story, and Character. They cover the questions, Who, What, Where, When, Why, and How, including everything that happened before the play begins and offstage between acts and scenes. Action Analysis does not require careful identification of these conditions in the same thorough way as Formalist Analysis does. Only needed at present is to ask, Who, What, Where, When, How, and Why in any convenient order. Study the questions, as a stubborn district attorney would do when cross-examining an untruthful offender, inquiring and probing and not taking anything for granted. We already performed a cursory Review of the Facts for 1,1 when attempting to define the basic External Event for that scene. A similar thinking process led to identification of the other External Events listed above for the play.

SEED

The process of Reviewing the Facts also looks for any patterns that may be latent but so far unidentified in the External Events. It may seem that scholars have covered this ground before ad nauseum. A search for *Hamlet* in the Modern Language Association database, for example, lists over three thousand articles on topics ranging from Afterlife and Allegory to Violence and Wordplay. *Hamlet* contains many patterns, but there is a difference between a pattern as a literary motif and the special kind of pattern sought in Action Analysis. The dictionary states that a motif is "a recurring prominent thematic element." Searching for interesting motifs is satisfactory in literary scholarship, where the goal is intellectual insights. The problem for actors, directors, and designers is not what motifs take account of, not what they include, but what they exclude. Motifs cover only part of a work. In the theatre, the whole play has to be produced, not just the parts that match up with a motif. Relying too much on literary motifs, sometimes actors, directors, and designers assume that the rest of the work is padding for the sake of entertainment. Or worse, lapses in taste on the part of the dramatist. Or worse still, they may apply additional motifs to fill the vacant parts, a practice that undermines the entire spirit of artistic unity.

The difficulty clears up as soon as we think about the nature of pattern in drama. While a motif may illuminate two, three, four events or more, the special pattern sought in play analysis, in Action Analysis, ought to illuminate the whole play. The creative processes of actors, directors, and designers involve a steady, consecutive embodiment of this pattern into a unified representation. Formalist Analysis reveals such a pattern using the concepts of Idea, Super-Objective, and Theme. Action Analysis accelerates the process by using an analytic concept called the Seed, which provides a concise vision of the whole play.

The concept of the Seed holds an important place in the creative insights of Vladimir Nemirovitch-Dantchenko, Stanislavski's partner and co-founder of the Moscow Art Theatre. Nemirovitch-Dantchenko was a playwright, critic, and superior director in his own right and in 1943 he also established the Moscow Art Theatre School. He never trusted that it was possible to begin rehearsal without everyone having a clear ultimate goal, the Seed, before them. In his time, he felt that the director should establish the Seed; today, actors and designers will also find it valuable to be aware of.

In simple terms, the Seed is the basic subject of the play, the central issue for the sake of which the play was written. It is a single point of origin, the simplest, most basic concept of a play. A seed is a source of development or growth and the Seed of a play is the source of its development and growth as a creative work. Traditionally, the Seed stems from one of ethical precepts found in most religions and customs in civilized societies. They include injunctions to revere God or a higher Good, to honor one's parents and children, as well as injunctions against idolatry, blasphemy, murder, adultery, theft, lying, false witness, and covetousness. Of course, precepts like "Thous shalt not kill" are very simple. If that is all the Seed is, then it could be a newspaper story that states, "Mr. Jones killed Mr. Smith. He was captured, put on trial, and sent to prison." Not interesting, probably, except for Mr. Jones, Mr. Smith, and their families.

But what about a multifaceted play such as *Hamlet*? Here a huge number of particulars are heaped on top of the Seed; variations, digressions, resulting ideas, and observations that have little obvious connection with its underlying precept, "Thou shalt not lie." That is how the Seed grows and develops into a large, impressive tree blossoming with ideas and called a play. Nemirovitch-Dantchenko explained that the Seed of his production of Leo Tolstoy's *Anna Karenina*, for example, was *passion*. Clearly, this Seed stems from the precept, "Thou shalt not commit adultery." A reader hardly perceives this when reading the novel, however, because he or she becomes involved in the particulars of life presented there. So much is happening in the novel when the characters underestimate or overestimate the role of the basic precept in their lives or when they try to offer extentuating circumstances to adjust to it. Much of this has little obvious relation to the Seed, but all the same the Seed is what holds it all together.

Understanding the Seed helps to build a production according to the harmonious unity of *all* its parts. According to Nemirovitch-Dantchenko, the Seed should *resonate in every event*. He believed it was necessary for all the participants of the production, whether they play a large role or a small role, to be connected to everyone else by means of the Seed. Earlier, we Reviewed the Facts to define the External Events. At this point, Reviewing the Facts will serve to find the Seed. Before returning to *Hamlet*, it should be acknowledged once again that the explanations presented here are intended for instruction and not as conclusive statements.

Hamlet provides a convincing example for an examination of the Seed. The ideological core, the Seed, of this play is *idealism* stemming from the precept, "Thou shalt not lie." Idealism is the practice of forming ideals from precepts and living under their influence. Hamlet is a perfect example of someone who places his ideals, in this case his ethical ideals about telling the truth, above all other considerations. Murder, false witness, coveting another's goods (i.e., the throne), and coveting another's wife are certainly present in the play, too, but in Shakespeare's treatment of the story they all emanate from "Thou shalt not lie." If this formulation of the Seed is correct, every event and every role in the play will be found within it. Here is where Reviewing the Facts comes into play again.

Hamlet has come back from the University of Wittenberg to attend his father's funeral. He is a prince, he is young, and he has led a comfortable and privileged life. Moreover, he loves to read, listen to music, and attend the theatre. He is under the influence of the academic ideas he learned in college, including philosophy, for which he has a special fascination. He is inexperienced in love. He is inexperienced in other aspects of the real world, too, in particular the rough and tumble moral code of big-time politics and statecraft. On the other hand, Hamlet is no fool. He may lack experience, but he makes up for it with his superior intelligence, sensitivity, and perception. In fact, he is almost a poet or an artist in his sensitivity to the nuances of human motives. He is also loyal and kind. In 3,2, Ophelia, who is in love with him of course, considers him noble, a courtier (gentleman), soldier (an excellent fencer), scholar, and handsome, witty, poetic, athletic, and fashionable. He attracts attention wherever he goes. Even the common people of Denmark like and admire him. Prince Hamlet.

Yet for all his obvious personal advantages, it seems as though he was born on another planet. He cannot tolerate the atmosphere of lies, murder, corruption, capricious love, disloyalty, hypocrisy, apathy, philistinism, sin, etc. that characterize much of human life on earth, or at least it may be so in Denmark. He lives in a bubble and has to breathe a special kind of pure air to survive: the air of idealism. He is a perfectionist with high standards. If he loves, it must be pure love. If he befriends, it must be totally loyal and without reservation. If he feels an emotion, it must be genuine, never forced or feigned. If he speaks, it must always be the absolute truth. Even his mastery of fencing must be letter perfect. And what a ruthless conscience he has to keep watch over his high ideals. Moreover, he expects others to have the same ideals and he can be cruel to them if they do not live up to his expectations. If the truth were told, Hamlet might even be a little proud of his idealism. After all, it makes him feel special to hold such lofty ideals. Doesn't he accept the dueling challenge as an opportunity to show off just a little? Unfortunately, Hamlet's ideal world does not exist; neither in Denmark nor anywhere else on Earth. It is a figment of his untested and over-heated *idealism*. He becomes aware of this in the end, of course, but he knows then that at least he gave the last measure of his courage striving to preserve something important: truth.

The concept of *idealism* works in a productive way for *Hamlet*, but the form of the Seed does not always have to be an abstract verbal expression ending in "ism." Actors and designers, for example, might prefer a more concrete formulation capable of stimulating the imagination as well as the intellect and will. For example, a more material form of the Seed for *Hamlet* is already apparent in the early moments of the play: the Ghost of King Hamlet. The Ghost is a concrete embodiment of Claudius's cynical defiance of idealism. Opposed to the Ghost are his enemies: Claudius, Polonius, Rosencrantz and Guildenstern, the officers of the court, and (unwittingly) Gertrude—all of whom are liars and accessories to murder. On the other side are Hamlet, Horatio, Ophelia, and the Players—all idealists in their own way. Every character's attitude toward the Ghost (that is, toward the Seed, toward the *idealism* stemming from "Thou shalt not lie"), offers actors, directors, and designers rich material for their talent and imagination. At the same time, all the events and thoughts in the play are related to a concrete subject—the Ghost of King Hamlet.

There will never be uniformity of opinion about *Hamlet* and there may be other ways to describe the Seed, in both abstract and concrete ways. Most readers would grant, however, that *idealism* and the Ghost, in one form or another, appear to resonate throughout the whole play. No matter what, these formulations may serve to explain about the Seed, how it can be identified and how it works to unify a play.

Sequence of Events: Internal Events

The Seed works to unite every moment of the play. If this is true, then idealism should be able to unite all the External Events already described above. In other words, idealism should appear in a pre-existing form inside each External Event. Here is another opportunity to undertake a Review of the Facts, this time to learn if the Seed is present throughout the play, and if so, how it expresses itself. In 1,1, Horatio encounters the Ghost. The idealism here belongs to Horatio, who, as Marcellus tells us, does not believe in ghosts. Horatio, like Hamlet, is a student at the University of Wittenberg, where he learned about the principle of scientific skepticism emerging at the time and became fascinated by it. And since there is no place for ghosts in science, Horatio does not believe in them. After all, their existence is irrational. The guards, Barnardo and Marcellus, are less educated, perhaps, but with more everyday know-how. They have seen this Ghost before and in any case they are not skeptics. They are less idealistic than Horatio, less guided by abstract book knowledge, and more in touch with the way things are presented to them in real life, whether rational or irrational. In this scene, Horatio's skepticism comes face to face for the first time with something it cannot explain. He calls it a "thing" and an "illusion" because he cannot bring himself even to say the word "ghost." Horatio becomes unnerved because the existence of the Ghost is contrary to his scientific ideals. Accordingly, we may call the Internal Event in 1,1, "The Ghost challenges Horatio's idealism," which is a way of saying that the Ghost's reality overpowers Horatio's idealism. It makes no difference here that the Ghost is not real, that it is supernatural. The point is that the appearance of the Ghost defies Horatio's academic idealism. What he learned at the University of Wittenberg does not hold true in the real world of Denmark. The thematic focus of the play is already underway.

In 1,2, Hamlet learns about the Ghost from Horatio. A short time ago Hamlet's idealism received a shock in the form of his mother's hasty marriage to his Uncle Claudius. He thought his mother was idealistically devoted to his father, whom he seems to have worshipped blindly, ideal-istically. How could she forget her husband, her ideal, so soon? Now Hamlet learns from his best friend that a ghost has appeared and that it looks like his father. Since Hamlet goes to the same philosophy classes at the University of Wittenberg as Horatio does, he does not believe in ghosts either. Horatio even feels a little ridiculous telling him about it, but after all, it looked just like Hamlet's father, the former king. Also, could it be that the Ghost has important news relating to Denmark's current political crisis? In any case, Hamlet must be told. Actually, five shocks to Hamlet's idealism occur in this scene: the throne taken away, mourning cut short for his dead father, an unfaithful mother, his return to Wittenberg forbidden, and now what seems to be the Ghost of his father. The Seed continues to be working powerfully.

Continuing to Review the Facts behind the External Events by connecting them to the Seed of idealism, we might arrive at the following Sequence of External and Internal Events in which the Seed is underlined for emphasis:

1,1: External: The Ghost appears
1,1: Internal: The Ghost challenges Horatio's idealism
1,2: External: Claudius takes over the throne
1,2: Internal: Claudius rebukes Hamlet's idealism
1,3: External: Laertes departs for France
1,3: Internal: Polonius reveals his phony ideals
1,4: External: Hamlet meets the Ghost
1,4: Internal: The Ghost tempts Hamlet's idealism
1,5: External: Hamlet learns that Claudius murdered his father
1,5: Internal: The Ghost challenges Hamlet's idealism
2,1: External: Reynaldo departs for France
2,1: Internal: Ophelia fears Hamlet has rejected her idealistic love
2,2: External: Hamlet welcomes the Players
2,2: Internal: Hamlet plans to put his idealism into action
3,1: External: Claudius eavesdrops on Hamlet
3,1: Internal: Hamlet accuses Ophelia of betraying her ideals
3,2: External: The "mousetrap scene"
3,2: Internal: Hamlet celebrates the apparent success of his idealism
3,3: External: Claudius prays
3,3: Internal: Hamlet begins to compromise his ideals

3,4: External: Gertrude appeals to Hamlet

3,4: Internal: Hamlet unconsciously betrays his ideals

4,1: External: Claudius takes action

4,1: Internal: Claudius fortifies his anti-idealism (cynical rationalism)

4,2: External: Rosencrantz and Guildenstern capture Hamlet

4,2: Internal: Hamlet torments the anti-idealism of R. & G.

4,3: External: Claudius sends Hamlet to England

4,3: Internal: Hamlet defies the anti-idealism of Claudius

4,4: External: Hamlet crosses paths with Fortinbras

4,4: Internal: Hamlet reflects on the nature of idealism

4,5: External: Laertes returns to Elsinore and sees Ophelia

4,5: Internal: Laertes's rash idealism and Ophelia's defeated idealism

4,6: External: Horatio learns that Hamlet has returned

4,6: Internal: Horatio fears that Hamlet has abandoned his ideals

4,7: External: Claudius and Laertes conspire to murder Hamlet

4,7: Internal: Claudius lures Laertes into anti-idealism

5,1: External: Hamlet learns about Ophelia's death

5,1: Internal: Hamlet recognizes that his idealism killed Ophelia

5,2: External: Hamlet agrees to a sporting duel with Laertes

5,2: Internal: Hamlet comes to terms with his impossible idealism

5,3: External: Hamlet slays Claudius

5,3: Internal: Hamlet defends himself and his newly humane ideals

All the Internal Events show a latent relationship with the Seed of idealism, which is the unifying reason for establishing the Seed in the first place. Idealism is the subject that holds everything together. To have an understanding of the Seed makes it possible to build a production according to the unity of all its parts. Notice, too, that the Seed has been obtained from the facts of the play itself and has not been laid on from any outside sources.

THREE MAJOR CLIMAXES

A vision of the whole play has come into view. The next task is to find the Three Major Climaxes that help to give the play a sense of forward motion. Regardless of its complexity, the plot of every play goes through three stages in which it emerges, develops, and concludes. We call these stages simply the beginning, middle, and end. A climax is an event of highest dramatic tension or a major turning point in the action. The beginning, middle, and end comprise the Three Major Climaxes, which by definition are the three most important events in the play. Movement from one climax to another is what drives the play and gives it a sense of momentum. Michael Chekhov taught that defining the Three Major Climaxes is vital because it exposes the basic outline of the play, which is also the goal of Action Analysis. The principle of forward motion holds even for plays showing little evidence of a traditional plot as such.

As long as Hamlet remains ignorant about how his father died, he has no material basis to take defensive action. Claudius has taken the throne away from him, of course, but Hamlet cannot do anything about that problem for the simple reason that Claudius is already in power. In addition, Hamlet has already made it clear that he is less upset about the public issues at stake than he is about the personal ones. It is not the throne that is on his mind at first, but the death of his father and the hasty remarriage of his mother. This does not stop Claudius from worrying about Hamlet's secret intentions, however.

For the First Major Climax, readers would be drawn to the scene where Hamlet's energies begin to materialize. This would be 1,5, where the Ghost reveals the true circumstances of his death and commands Hamlet to revenge his murder. This is when the Seed of idealism breaks through and begins to grow as though on steroids. Here we begin to see the evil that had been lurking around King Hamlet in the intrigues of Claudius, Gertrude and Polonius. Hamlet has comes face to face for the first time with genuine evil. He makes note of this extraordinary discovery in his journal:

HAMLET

```
O most pernicious woman! [i.e., Gertrude]
O villain, villain, smiling, damnèd villain!
  [i.e., Claudius]
My tables—meet it is I set it down [i.e., in
  his journal]
That one may smile, and smile, and be a
  villain.
At least I am sure it may be so in Denmark.
```

Learning about his father's murder provides Hamlet with grounds to take decisive action. His ideal world, so comfortable at the University of Wittenberg up to now, begins to disintegrate. Act 1,5 corresponds to our understanding of a climax because the tension of the External Events reaches a high point. It also summarizes the external plot up to that time and points forward to the middle phase of the play's development. A climax should also be an extra concentrated expression of the internal action. If the First Major Climax is 1,5 how does the Seed, the signal of a play's inner life, operate there? Hamlet's idealism suffers its first major setback. It is one thing for Claudius and Gertrude to be indifferent to King Hamlet's death; it is another thing for them to have secretly murdered him for their own hateful purposes. Another point in 1,5 is the idealism of the Ghost, that is, King Hamlet. The assassinated King expects his son, the Prince and heir apparent, to fulfill his royal responsibilities, his royal ideals. This creates a new problem of ideals, which Hamlet does not foresee the consequences of when he swears to discharge his father's command:

HAMLET

Remember thee?
Yes, from the table of my memory
I'll wipe away all trivial fond records,
All saws of books, all forms, all pressures
  past
That youth and observation copied there,
And thy commandment all alone shall live
Within the book and volume of my brain,
Unmixed with baser matter. Yes, by heaven!

Hamlet vows to give up his bookishness and devote himself to revenging his father's murder. But revenge is an ideal, too. Starting in 1,5, a clash emerges between King Hamlet's old-fashioned feudal ideals and Prince Hamlet's renaissance humanistic ideals. Idealism itself is being placed on trial.

The beginning and end of the play are polar opposites; not always, but normally. What is revealed in the beginning changes into its opposite at the end; what lies in between is the movement of action from the beginning through to the end. Opposites by definition are different, which means they should be easier to recognize than the in-between points. That is why we will look for the climax at the end, the Third Major Event, before trying to find the middle climax.

There is not much doubt that the principal scene in *Hamlet* is 5,3, when all the forces of the play clash and the future of Denmark is determined. There is little doubt either that 5,3 is the climax of the External Events, or the Third Major Climax. Four deaths, the collapse of the monarchy, a family dynasty disgraced, and a change of national leadership would be considered a major event under any circumstances.

An earlier event in 5,2, however, is worth examining for an overall understanding of the play and how the Seed works. When Hamlet recounts his adventures at sea to Horatio, the episode is not dramatic in the normal sense because it involves mainly narrative and discussion. Hamlet has returned to Denmark a changed person. He tries to explain to his friend the change that has come over him:

HAMLET

Sir, in my heart there was a kind of fighting
That would not let me sleep. Methought I lay
Worse than mutinies in the bilboes. Rashly,
And praised be rashness for it—let us know,
Our indiscretion sometimes serves us well
When our deep plots do pall, and that should
  learn us
There's a divinity that shapes our ends,
Rough-hew them how we will—

To paraphrase, "I felt all locked up inside, Horatio. I could not sleep at night. It was worse than being shackled in chains like a prisoner. I know that I rashly sent Rosencrantz and Guildenstern to their deaths and a little while ago I rashly fought with Laertes at Ophelia's grave. But sometimes rashness is a good thing. Sometimes accidental blunders work out better in the end than all the elaborate plotting and planning we could possibly do. This should teach us a lesson: there is something indescribable that shapes our destinies, no matter how much we try to interfere."

A few moments later Osric delivers Claudius' invitation for a sporting duel with Laertes, which we know is designed to lead to Hamlet's death. Hamlet knows that Osric is Claudius's lackey and that he will report everything said here to Claudius. But Hamlet merely pokes fun at Osric's manners; he does not scorn him as he did Rosencrantz and Guildenstern earlier in the play when they found themselves in a similar position. Osric is just a fool, not the embodiment of all the evil in the world. The change in Hamlet's former intolerance of any sort of hypocrisy concerns Horatio. A few moments later, Hamlet accepts Claudius's challenge, but confesses a shiver of foreboding. Horatio worries that Hamlet could still be in shock from the recent events; he should be looked after in case he does something, well, rash:

HORATIO

If your mind dislike anything, obey it. I will
forestall their repair hither and say you are
not fit.

HAMLET

Not a whit, we defy augury. There is a special
providence in the fall of a sparrow. If it be
now, 'tis not to come; if it be not to come, it
will be now; if it not be now, yet it will
come. The readiness is all. Since no man of
aught he leaves knows, what is't betimes? Let
be.

"If you have a bad feeling about this challenge," Horatio seems to say, "then please do not go through with it. I will tell the King that you do not feel well." "Never mind," replies Hamlet, "I do not believe in omens or ghosts anymore. Whatever will happen will happen. Living, being ready for life, is what matters. Anyway, since no one can know what happens after he dies, why agonize about it? Let things just happen." Hamlet's inner life has changed. He used to be scrupulously idealistic, especially about the behavior of others. He is still idealistic and honorable, but now his idealism has been tempered by personal experience and self-reflection. He is less selfish and more compassionate.

Could this event be the Third Major Climax? Despite the obvious thematic importance of this moment in the play, our choice for the Third Major Climax is still the murder scene in 5,3, described earlier. The words about Hamlet's change of heart in the episode with Horatio remain in the end only words. Hamlet's new attitude is not put to the test until later on, when Laertes exposes Claudius' plot. Hamlet does not go to the dueling challenge with a strategy for revenge, but after he uncovers the truth, he acts without hesitation. Act 5,3 is *theatrical and thematic*, while 5,2 is mainly *narrative and thematic*. The true beginning and end ought to illuminate each other by theatrical as well as thematic contrast.

The middle is the section of the play during which Hamlet's change takes place. Hamlet's obsessive pursuit of the truth behind the lies characterizes this section. It is fitting that the distinguishing event involves a company of actors. The scenes with the actors form a thematic group related to idealism, but they are too multifaceted to be treated at length here. Enough to say that Hamlet admires the actors for their professional idealism, their ability to become engaged by the ideals of characters they have never even met, the moral idealism of their plays, and the moral impact of their work on an audience's conscience. "Players are the only honest hypocrites," says Hamlet. They are fellow idealists from the same planet as he. The Second Major Climax is the "dumb show" or "play-within-a-play" or "mousetrap scene" in 3,2, when Claudius reveals his guilt while watching the players enact "The Murder of Gozago." Externally, 3,2 is a crowd scene including the whole court, fanfares, color, torches, pageantry, etc. Internally, it marks the collapse of Claudius' cynical anti-idealism (he tries to pray for forgiveness after this scene) and the apparent victory of Hamlet's idealistic search for the truth.

However, it is not until Hamlet kills Polonius, and later Rosencrantz and Guildenstern, and (indirectly) Ophelia that he begins to understand how idealism has perverted him. He always thought of himself as a good person, humane and thoughtful, yet now he has committed acts of absolute evil. During the graveyard scene, he begins to grasp how a scrupulously moral human being like himself could be forced to act like those monsters that inhabit the corrupt royal court of Elsinore. In 5,2, he apologizes to Laertes (for being responsible for the death of Polonius and Ophelia), then in 5,3 he sacrifices himself in the name of impractical idealism and for the sake of his own salvation. His death refutes Claudius's world view and for that reason it just might bring about fundamental changes in people's lives and, with any luck, the course of Denmark's history. This is why he insists that Horatio live on to tell his story:

```
As th' art a man
Give me the cup [i.e., of poison]. Let go. By
  heaven, I'll ha't!
O God, Horatio, what a wounded name,
Things standing thus unknown, shall I leave
  behind me!
If thou didst ever hold me in thy heart,
Absent thee from felicity awhile,
And in this harsh world draw thy breath in
  pain,
To tell my story.
```

It is no accident that after this discourse about idealism, Hamlet's next observation is about the arrival of "warlike" Fortinbras, who promises to honor Hamlet's death with a soldier's funeral. And so the "harsh world" resumes.

THEME

Earlier we said that a motif is "a recurring prominent thematic element." However, the dictionary states that a Theme is a specific and distinctive quality, characteristic, or concern of an artistic work. A motif and a Theme sound like the same thing, and to some readers they may be identical. But for actors, directors, and designers there is an important difference: a motif covers only part of a play while a Theme covers the whole play. Like the Seed, the Theme passes through the entire play, a condition that leads to its definition here: the Theme is the point of view that the play expresses about the Seed.

The Three Major Climaxes provide the key to the Theme of the play. Each climax forms the essence of the corresponding part of the play and illustrates the external and internal action going on at that point. Let's Review the Facts. Three climaxes mark Hamlet's line of development in the play: Hamlet commits himself to revenging his father's murder; Hamlet ruthlessly pursues the truth and in doing so he tears apart the court of Denmark; as a result, a new self-awareness emerges in Hamlet and evil is purged from Denmark. The play is a test of Hamlet's idealism.

But many plays, including *Faust* and *Waiting for Godot*, share the same Seed, the same basic subject of idealism. What distinguishes them is their *point of view* about the Seed, their attitude toward their subjects. What does the play *Hamlet* show about the character Hamlet's idealism? Like so many of Shakespeare's plays, in the end the story moves into a mystical realm where Divine Providence, in the form of humanistic idealism, eventually prevails. Hamlet's idealism is tested and adjusted, but it prevails. If the Theme is the play's point of view about idealism, then the Theme of *Hamlet* can be expressed, if only for our narrow aim here, as *impossible idealism*. Hamlet begins in a state of impossible, that is, innocent idealism. His awkward progress toward a more humanistic form of idealism constitutes the action of the play. Compare this with the Themes of *Faust* or *Waiting for Godot*. Ever since Polish critic Jan Kott's book, *Shakespeare our Contemporary* (1964), progressively-minded actors, directors, and designers have tended to interpret Shakespeare's plays skeptically, that is, as though his plays represent a world of universal corruption. In other words, Kott holds that in Shakespeare idealism as such is exposed as a cruel hoax. This is a subtle interpretive point, and perhaps outdated already. But it needs to be brought up here to remind readers that the purpose of play analysis is not to obtain the single ultimate interpretation of a play, but at all times an accurate and consistent one. Our instructional example in this chapter treats idealism as a benevolent force, which is the consensus view of Shakespeare's plays in general. In any case, we have shown how the Three Major Climaxes in *Hamlet* illustrate different stages in the development of the Theme of impossible idealism.

SUPER-OBJECTIVE

One of the advantages of defining the Three Major Climaxes is learning what gives the play a sense of forward motion. Without this feeling of forward motion, a play remains emotionally flat and uninteresting in performance. While the Theme is a satisfactory summary statement of the play's ideology, it remains just that—a fixed summary, a definitive final statement of the play's action. But in performance, the Theme is revealed through events that happen in real time. The Super-Objective is a concept that embraces the Theme, but returns a sense of forward motion to our understanding of the play. It is the Theme expressed in the form of unfolding action. The Super-Objective explains the play in terms of what it is striving to illustrate. The Super-Objective is the Theme *in progress*. For this reason, the Super-Objective is expressed as a course of action, a process, or a path, instead of the definitive statement of a result. This is a subtle distinction, but an important one for actors, directors, and designers.

The Super-Objective of *Hamlet* is "to set things right." In other words, to make things happen according to Hamlet's impossible ideals. He states this openly: "O cursed spite / That ever I was born *to set it right!*" [italics added].

A Review of the Facts shows that Hamlet attempts to set things right throughout the whole play, even after he returns to Denmark. He sets things right by agreeing to carry out the Ghost's demands, by rebuking the lies and hypocrisy of Polonius, Rosencrantz and Guildenstern, Ophelia, Gertrude, and above all Claudius in the "mousetrap scene." Hamlet's impossible idealism drives him to imagine that with enough effort he will set everything right again in Denmark. Instead, to his shock and disgust, he uncovers more deceit, lust, corruption, apathy, sycophancy, intrigue, and stupidity everywhere he turns. The characters that provide him with any real help, with any real truth, are the Ghost, Horatio, the Players, the Gravedigger, and Yorick, the deceased court jester who was his childhood friend at court. Hamlet encounters an impossible amount of wickedness to set right; however, this does not stop him from trying. Only it teaches him not to be so self-centered and self-absorbed while doing so.

THROUGH-ACTION

At this point we are seeking to understand *Hamlet* as a total story once again, that is, as *the account of a particular character performing a particular action under particular circumstances*. The second-to-last stage of Action Analysis, called the Through-Action, or sometimes the "Through-Line of Action," fulfills this purpose. The Through-Action has often been discussed in the writing of Stanislavski and his followers. The description Sharon Carnicke provides in her informative book, *Stanislavsky in Focus*, is representative. She defines the Through-Action as "A unifying, overall action that relates all moment-to-moment actions throughout the play to each other" (181). While this definition is accurate and satisfactory, it does not succeed in distinguishing the Through-Action from the Theme, Seed, and Super-Objective, which also serve to link all the actions to each other. Idealism, Hamlet's impractical nature, the corruption in Denmark, and the concepts of truth and enlightenment found in *Hamlet* are useful concepts up to a point, but helpful as they are, they still remain abstractions. Their disassociation from specific instances has been helpful for obtaining a vision of the whole. But to be effective for actors, directors, and designers, these concepts need to be translated from the abstract to the concrete, from the realm of ideas back to the realm of real human behavior shown in the play itself. The Through-Action makes it possible for these concepts to become concrete, which is one step closer to the physical expression necessary for performance.

We need to Review the Facts again and look with fresh eyes at the actions that showed us the way to the External Events, Seed, Internal Events, Three Major Climaxes, Theme, and Super-Objective in the first place. The difference is that now we have a sense of the whole play in which to frame the story. Remember that Reviewing the Facts means asking Who, What, Where, When, How, and Why. Who is Hamlet? Young, idealistic, devoted to art, philosophy, theology, and poetry. What is he doing? Eliminating corruption. Where is he doing it? In the fraudulent royal court of Denmark. When is he doing it? At a turbulent time when Denmark is threatened by war from abroad and his malevolent Uncle Claudius has taken up the throne. How does he do it? At times, sensitively and unfeelingly, elegantly and clumsily, rashly and broodingly, anguished and elated, gracefully and without grace or finesse, tenderly and violently. Why is he doing it? His father, whom he is devoted to, has ordered him to do it. It is a sacred duty.

Hamlet learned about art, literature, theology, and philosophy at the University of Wittenberg, where he lived unaffected by real life. Outside the university setting, he meets up with a reality that is as unfamiliar and unexpected as it is appalling to him. Hamlet was not equipped for this confrontation with life after being protected from it at the university, which had an unrealistic view of the outside world. After going through hell at court, he loses faith in the ideals he learned about in the classroom. They could not conform to practical reality. Then he returns to the point where he started, washed up on the shores of Denmark, "naked and alone," with only his exhausted ideals left. He has experienced for himself that ideals are important aspirations, but that the real world is a corrupt and human place after all. That is the foundation of his strength and the importance of his story to the world. Hamlet has learned how to face insanity and corruption without becoming crazy and corrupt himself.

Reviewing of the Facts leads to a description of the Through-Action as an account of what happens in the play: *An idealistic student prince who vows to purge all the corruption from the rotten state of Denmark.* This one-sentence description of the Through-Action contains all the parts of Action Analysis in dormant form. It hints that Hamlet could do a lot of damage with his idealism, not just to himself but also to others and to his country. From within the limits of this statement we can also figure out the Seed, Theme, Super-Objective, and even find clues about the Three Major Climaxes. Moreover, this account of the Through-Action also preserves the tragic tone of the play. Not everyone may agree with this description of the Through-Action, but at least its purpose and the working process behind it should be apparent.

COUNTER THROUGH-ACTION

Every action in a play meets with a counter-action, which challenges and strengthens it. Therefore, adjacent to the Through-Action and running in the opposite direction to it, passes a counter-action that is opposed to it. The Counter Through-Action is the source of the conflict in the play. Without it there is no play in the ordinary sense.

Hamlet's principal opponent is Claudius. Reviewing the Facts for the Through-Action involved asking Who, What, Where, When, How and Why. Determining the Counter Through-Action involves the same process as that of the Through-Action, except it is concerned with the story of the principal opponent of the main character (antagonist) instead of the main character (protagonist). Who, then, is Claudius? Brother of the dead king and uncle to the heir-apparent prince. He is also the new husband of his brother's widow. What is he? A cynical murderer and usurper. Where is he doing it? In medieval Denmark, which is threatened by war. When is he doing it? Following the mysterious death of the former king, who was a legendary warrior. How does he do it? By killing the king with the help of court insiders. Why does he do it? For power and the former king's wife. This analysis leads to the following description of the Counter Through-Action: *A crafty feudal lord who seizes the throne by murdering his brother the king and marrying his wife with the collusion of the court.* In this statement, notice the attention to the feudal morality of the world of the play, which provides a challenge to Hamlet's renaissance idealism and strengthens it by contrast.

SUMMARY

Action Analysis of *Hamlet* began with a list of simple events in order, then switched to the realm of abstract ideas, and then switched back again to real events in the form of a specific story. We started with the concrete facts of the External Events, advanced through several stages of mental concepts in the Seed, Theme, and Super-Objective, and then concluded by returning to the world of particular behavior in the Through-Action and Counter Through-Action. The outcome is a no-nonsense vision of the whole, a speedy way of getting to the professional guts of a play. By concentrating on the events of the plot, it becomes easier for the reader to see the progress of the dramatic action, the thematic core, the conflict, and the basic story line of the play. Moreover, Action Analysis establishes a reliable foundation with which to start rehearsals and director-designer conferences. If Action Analysis is done at the beginning of the study process, it can help actors, directors, and designers to maintain a point of reference during the more detailed method of Formalist Analysis taught in the following chapters. If it is done in company with Formalist Analysis, it can help to show how everything in a play is organically—meaning thematically—interrelated. The reduced, concentrated nature of Action Analysis leads to an appreciation of how good plays are written, how they work in practical theatre terms, and how much special ability it takes to write even a modestly successful play.

QUESTIONS

Sequence of Events: External Events   What are the most important *External Events*, the simple social activities, and how are they arranged in order? Descriptions should be short and snappy, without using literary words.

Review of the Facts   Who are the important characters involved in each event? What are they doing? Where are they doing it? When are they doing it? Why are they doing it? How are they doing it, that is, in what emotional manner? Again, thinking should be short and snappy, not too literary.

Seed   What ethical or moral precept is found at the center of the play? Murder, adultery, slander or lying, honor between parents and children, the existence of God? What is the dramatic subject stemming from this precept that provides the source of development and growth of the play as a creative work? One word will be enough to describe the Seed.

Sequence of Events: Internal Events   What are the most important *Internal Events* arranged in their order of presentation? *Internal* means the event is associated with the Seed by design. How does the Seed show up inside each External Event? Short and snappy again.

Three Major Climaxes   What are the three most important events in the play? What events form the beginning, middle, and end? What are the three events of highest dramatic tension or three major turning points in the action? Simple and direct is best.

Theme   What is the play's point of view toward the ethical precept it is built around? How do the Three Major Climaxes demonstrate the progressive development of the Theme, its beginning, middle, and end? A short phrase is often best. Too many words tend to cloud the issue.

Super-Objective   How is the Theme expressed in terms of the unfolding action of the play? What is the course of action, progress, or path of the Theme expressed in terms of the play's action? What is the chief motivating action of the play? What is the main action that emerges from the Theme? What is the fundamental action and struggle the play is intended to represent. What action does the play strive to express? The Super-Objective is best stated as a future action, something the play is attempting to achieve.

Through-Action   How can the Seed, Theme, and Super-Objective be expressed as the story of a *particular character* performing a *particular action* under *particular circumstances*? How do the Seed, Theme, and Super-Objective become concrete and specific in the story line of the main character?

Counter Through-Action   What counteraction interferes with the Through-Action, both the challenging and strengthening of it? What story line runs adjacent to the Through-Action, but runs in the opposite direction? What line of action is the main source of conflict in the play?

POSTSCRIPT _____

The method of Formalist Analysis taught in the following chapters does not require the prior experience of Action Analysis. Both methods are formalist in intent because they depend on information from the play itself instead of outside sources and they acknowledge the importance of form, or the arrangement of parts, in a play. But Formalist Analysis starts from scratch, building fact upon fact, until the overall unity of the play emerges. Additional insights may be gained from Formalist Analysis, however, by putting into play insights obtained from Action Analysis. For readers that are interested in doing this, postscripts have been added to Chapters 2 through 7 that provide questions to assist along the way.

CHAPTER 2

Foundations of the Plot: Given Circumstances

Every play consists of six components from which it derives its basic nature: plot, character, idea, dialogue, tempo-rhythm-mood (Aristotle's *music*), and production values (scenery, costumes, lighting, etc.). In this book we are concerned with the written part of a play; therefore, we will not deal with production values but only with those five parts supplied by the playwright. Aristotle arrived at this scheme in his study of the function of the parts of a play, called *Poetics*. He did not mean that all plays have these elements in the same amount or in the same way. One play may have more or fewer events in its plot than another, more complicated or simplified characters, or more or less attention devoted to idea. He meant that these six elements are present in one form or another in all those works we call plays.

The beginning of all plays is the unique combination of present and past that Stanislavski called the *Given Circumstances*. Other writers have used different terms—*social context, foundations of the plot, playwright's setting, texture, local detail*, or *literary landscape*. They all mean the same thing: the specific conditions in which the on-stage action of the play occurs.

Apprentice play readers sometimes unwittingly think of the Given Circumstances as the uninteresting parts they can pass over. The impulse may be uninformed, but it acknowledges something important. On the surface, the Given Circumstances may not seem as exciting or useful as are the other parts of a play. They are simple things—so simple that the impulse is to take them for granted, like the air we breathe. Yet assumptions that are most familiar are often hardest to recognize as important, again, like the air we breathe. The Given Circumstances are as vital to a play as plot, character, and all the other features. They put the characters and audience into the here and now of the action. Without the Given Circumstances, characters would exist in a conceptual emptiness, in some vague never-never land without any connection to real life. Given Circumstances function like silent, invisible characters. They influence all the characters, increase tensions, create complications, and move the plot forward. Given Circumstances always contain important clues to other parts of the play. They may seem to be elementary or silent or invisible, but they are the details that make it possible to know what makes the characters tick. Bringing each given circumstance into focus will help to explain how it works. This can happen only after careful analysis forces it out into the open so that it can stand up and be identified.

This chapter is concerned with the Given Circumstances that take place in the present, on stage before the audience. They spring from the time and place of the play along with the conventions, attitudes, and manners behind and around it. Under this heading, we will he concerned with eight subtopics: Time, Place, Society, Economics, Intellect and Culture, Politics and Law, Spirituality, and The World of the Play. In the next chapter, we will turn to the Given Circumstances of the past, the unseen *background story*, which includes everything that happened before the beginning of the play.

TIME

Time in the Given Circumstances has three aspects: (1) the time of the play's writing, (2) the time in which the play is set, and (3) the time that passes during the play.

Time of Composition

The time or date of the play's composition is not strategic in the early stages of script analysis because it is not part of the written play. It will become more valuable when it is studied in connection with the biography of the author, the conditions of his or her era, and the play's position within the body of the author's works. Although knowledge of the author's life and works is necessary for a complete understanding of any play, too much attention to them at this point is not necessary and can even be distracting. Sometimes confusion arises between what is learned about a play from outside sources and what is actually found in it. It is probably better to set aside external matters for later, after the process of script analysis is farther along.

Time of the Action

In many plays it is important to know the exact time, season, and year in which the action is set. This is not just for the sake of accuracy but also to help understand the whole dramatic situation better. The precision of the determination depends on the play. For instance, in *Death of a Salesman* there are references in Willy Loman's flashbacks to the boxer Gene Tunney and the football player "Red" Grange. These names establish the year of those scenes at about 1927 when Tunney was heavyweight champion and Grange played football for the Chicago Bears. Two years later the stock market crashed, ushering in the Great Depression—important time information for the play. Another incidental reference to time is the steel trust, which is the target of so much anger in *The Hairy Ape*. This reference establishes the time of that action at about 1913 when monopolies exercised their grip on the American economic scene. The war in Vietnam, which serves as the background for *Streamers*, sets that action between 1964–68, the height of the idealistic 1960s. The last days of the archconservative attorney Roy Cohn, depicted in Part One of *Angels in America*, set this play's action in 1986, when at the age of 59 Cohn died of AIDS-related illness. A virile, rapacious, crafty, and influential attorney was reduced to a miserable, frail, demented piece of human debris by the time of his death. But Roy Cohn was also known as a fighter. He survived repeated attacks from federal prosecutors, mafia bosses, and even tenured politicians. Also in 1986, the Attorney General published the first official report about AIDS. For the first time the enormous magnitude of the epidemic was beginning to be grasped by the public at large. The year 1986 can therefore be seen as both the end and the beginning of an era.

Gene Tunney, the Great Depression, the steel trust, Vietnam, Roy Cohn, and public awareness of the AIDS epidemic are important in these plays not only because they help to establish the historical context for audiences, but because they set in motion the actions and conflicts of the characters in the plays. For these reasons, the time of the action is a crucial issue. It should be determined by searching the dialogue itself for direct statements or references to historical people, places, or things. Stage directions and playwrights' notes sometimes offer information about the time of the action, but they are not as dependable or practical as the dialogue itself.

Dramatic Time

Dramatic time is the total of the time that passes during the on-stage action plus the time during intervals between acts and scenes. Some plays permit very precise determination. In *The Wild Duck*, it is possible without the help of stage directions to learn about the passage of dramatic time almost to the hour, including the hour of day and day of the week for each act. Dramatic time can also be compressed or expanded to accommodate theatrical needs. Several days pass in *The Piano Lesson*, weeks in *The Hairy Ape*, months in *Hamlet*, and years in *Three Sisters* and *Mother Courage*. Time moves forward and backward in *Death of a Salesman*, and stands still in *Happy Days*. In *A Lie of the Mind*, time moves in random lurches.

There is an interesting assortment of information about dramatic time in the opening lines of *Hamlet*:

BERNARDO

Who's there?

FRANCISCO

Nay, answer me. Stand and unfold yourself.

BERNARDO

Long live the King!

FRANCISCO

Bernardo?

BERNARDO

He.

FRANCISCO

You come most carefully upon your hour.

BERNARDO

'Tis now struck twelve; get thee to bed,
Francisco.

FRANCISCO

For this relief much thanks. 'Tis bitter cold,
And I am sick at heart.

BERNARDO

Have you had quiet guard?

FRANCISCO

Not a mouse stirring.

BERNARDO

Well; good night.

Although Francisco is on guard duty, Bernardo utters the first remark. Why? Because he is nervous to begin with and then he becomes frightened when Francisco makes a noise in the dark as he paces back and forth during his watch. Then Francisco challenges him, "Nay, answer me." Francisco, after all, is the one who is on guard duty. "Stand and unfold yourself," he says, from which we understand that it is night and Bernardo is wrapped in a cloak to protect him from the cold. The implication is that the season is winter, a fact that is confirmed a moment later when Francisco says "'Tis bitter cold." Another comment by Bernardo indicates the time of day—"'Tis now struck twelve."—and specifies the time at exactly the witching hour. The passage ends with Bernardo's expression of "good night" to further emphasize the lateness of the hour. They are afraid of something. Imaginative actors, directors, and designers should be able to grasp the mysterious tone Shakespeare has established as the cold winter night folds its cloak around the nervous characters.

Ibsen uses some of the same methods for expressing dramatic time in this selection from Act 2 of *The Wild Duck*:

(*A knocking is heard at the entrance door.*)

GINA

(*rising*) Hush, Ekdal—I think there's someone at the door.

HJALMAR

(*laying his flute on the bookcases*) There! Again!

(*Gina goes and opens the door.*)

GREGERS

(*in the passage*) Excuse me—

GINA

(*starting back slightly*) Oh!

GREGERS

Doesn't Mr. Ekdal, the photographer, live here?

GINA

Yes, he does.

HJALMAR

(*going toward the door*) Gregers! You here after all? Well, come in then.

GREGERS

(*coming in*) I told you I would come and look you up.

HJALMAR

But this evening—Have you left the party?

GREGERS

I have left the party and my father's. Good
evening, Mrs. Ekdal. I don't know whether you
recognize me?

GINA

Oh, yes, it's not difficult to know young Mr.
Werle again.

GREGERS

No, I am like my mother, and no doubt you
remember her.

HJALMAR

Left your father's house, did you say?

GREGERS

Yes, I have gone to a hotel.

HJALMAR

Indeed. Well, since you're here, take off your
coat and sit down.

GREGERS

Thanks. (*He takes off his overcoat.*)

Gregers's statement, "I told you I would come and look you up,"
refers to something he said to Hjalmar in the previous act, an act we
know occurred earlier that same evening. Its use at this point is a way
of maintaining continuity of time by connecting this scene with a prior
incident in the play. Hjalmar's reply "But this evening—Have you
left the party?" and Gregers's responses "I have left the party" and "Good
evening, Mrs. Ekdal." reinforce the continuity of time and confirm
the time of the current scene. We see also that Gregers is wearing an

overcoat because it is winter. The season is important enough for Ibsen to remind us about it again in the accompanying stage directions (which he wrote). The dramatic point is that the conditions are cold, that Gregers is a mysterious late-night visitor and, besides that, he is almost a stranger.

In the opening scene of *A Raisin in the Sun*, dramatic time is stated in the dialogue and observed in the characters' actions; it is then confirmed again in the stage directions. Ruth mentions the time three times. Travis gets out of bed and exits to the bathroom, then Ruth warns Walter Lee about being late for work.

RUTH

Come on now, boy, it's seven thirty (*He sits up at last, in a stupor of sleepiness.*) I say hurry up. Travis! You ain't the only person in the world got to use a bathroom. (*The child, a sturdy, handsome boy of ten or twelve, drags himself out of bed and almost blindly takes his towels and "today's clothes" from the drawers and a closet and goes out to the bathroom, which is in an outside hall and which is shared by another family or families on the same floor. Ruth crosses to the bedroom door at right and opens it and calls in to her husband.*) Walter Lee! . . . It's after seven thirty! Lemme see you do some waking up in there now. (*She waits.*) You better get up from there, man! It's seven thirty I tell you. (*She waits again.*) All right, you just go ahead and lay there and next thing you know Travis be finished and Mr. Johnson'll be in there and you'll be fussing and cussing around here like a mad man! And be late too! (*She waits, at the end of her patience.*) Walter Lee—it's time to get up!

Even in nonrealistic plays, conscientious detective work for the passage of time can pay dividends later on when dealing with more complicated issues. Time of day is rarely made known, for example, in *Angels in America* or *A Lie of the Mind*. Readers should try to determine the dramatic reasons for this departure from normal realistic expectations and the resulting effect sought for by its absence.

PLACE

The second subdivision of the Given Circumstances is *place*, or physical environment. Some directors and designers feel that the scenery should illustrate the environment as accurately and completely as possible, while others believe it should be mainly a starting point for exploring the play's inner spirit. Formalist Analysis does not argue for or against either of these viewpoints. A picture of the specific environment may work for some plays and an abstract scenic metaphor for others. What is important is that the physical environment influences the characters and is therefore part of the whole meaning of the play.

Geographical Locale

The first subtopic under the heading of place is *geographical locale*, meaning the country, region, or district in which the action is set. Instructions about the geography are often available in the front notes and stage directions, but readers should validate them in the dialogue wherever possible. This passage from *Hamlet* contains geographical references to the city of Wittenberg, where Hamlet has been studying, as well as to Denmark, his native country and the geographical setting for the action:

CLAUDIUS

```
For your intent
In going back to school in Wittenberg,
It is most retrograde to our desire;
And we beseech you bend you to remain
Here, in the cheer and comfort of our eye,
Our chiefest courtier, cousin and our son.
```

QUEEN
Let not thy mother lose her prayers, Hamlet.

HAMLET
I shall in all my best obey you, madam.

CLAUDIUS
Why, 'tis a loving and a fair reply.
Be as ourself in Denmark.

In addition to these locales, the play also contains geographical references to Poland, Norway, England, and France. Why Wittenburg? Why all the different countries?

The emotional associations evoked by geography can contribute to the dramatic impact of a play. Playwrights take advantage of this to add force to their works. Few can read *The Hairy Ape*, for example, without sensing the emotional associations of life at sea and life in and around New York City. *Death of a Salesman* contains several striking examples of geographical associations, as in this passage when Willy Loman complains about the deterioration of the neighborhood around his home in Brooklyn.

WILLY
The street is lined with cars. There's not a
breath of fresh air in the neighborhood. The
grass don't grow anymore, you can't raise a
carrot in the back yard. Remember those two
beautiful elm trees out there? They should've
had a law against apartment houses. Remember
when I and Biff hung the swing between them?

In this excerpt from *A Raisin in the Sun*, Mama Younger announces that she has made a down payment on a new home. Her family has been living in a crowded tenement on Chicago's South Side. They are pleased about the prospect of a place of their own. There are negative associations connected with the locale, however, which everyone knows is a white suburb.

RUTH

Oh, Walter . . . a home . . . a home. (*She comes back to Mama.*) Well—where is it? How big is it? How much it going to cost?

MAMA

Well—

RUTH

When we moving?

MAMA

(*smiling at her*) First of the month.

RUTH

(*throwing her head back with jubilance*) Praise God!

MAMA

(*tentatively, still looking at her son's back turned against her and Ruth*) It's—it's a nice house too . . . (*She cannot help speaking directly to him. An imploring quality in her voice, her manner, makes her almost like a girl now.*) Three bedrooms—nice big one for you and Ruth . . . Me . . . and Beneatha still have to share our room, but Travis have one of his own—and (*with difficulty*) I figure if the—new baby—is a boy, we could get one of them double-decker outfits . . . And there's a yard with a little patch of dirt where I could maybe get to grow me a few flowers . . . And a nice big basement . . .

RUTH

Walter, honey, be glad—

MAMA

(*still to his back, fingering things on the table*) 'Course I don't want to make it sound fancier than it is . . . It's just a plain little old house—but it's made good and solid—and it will be ours. Walter Lee—it makes a difference in a man when he can walk on floors that belong to him . . .

RUTH

Where is it?

MAMA

(*frightened at this telling*) Well—well—it's out there in Clybourne Park—(*Ruth's radiance fades abruptly, and Walter finally turns slowly to face his mother with incredulity and hostility.*)

MAMA

(*matter-of-factly*) Four o six Clybourne Street, Clybourne Park.

RUTH

Clybourne Park? Mama, there ain't no colored people living in Clybourne Park.

MAMA

Well, I guess there's going to be some now.

Playwrights choose geographical locales to evoke emotional associations as well as for realism. In *A Lie of the Mind*, the geographical locales are remote towns in Oklahoma and Montana, depicted in the play as inhospitable regions attractive to society's loners. What is the dramatic rationale for selecting these geographical locales?

Specific Locale

The specific locale is the place in which the scenic action occurs. A reader's first impulse is to rely on stage directions for information about the specific locale. Published scripts often include notes and diagrams of the scenery, such as the 200-word description of the military cadre room in *Streamers* or the transparent multilevel Loman house in *Death of a Salesman*. Scenery notes and diagrams can be interesting and useful, but they are only the editor or the stage manager's description of the original production, not usually the author's own writing. This may not be a problem for those who are reading a play for study purposes, but it is a serious issue for designers or directors who are preparing a performance of their own. Since modern theatre conventions require distinctive scenery for every production, editorial notes about an earlier production should not always be used as a guide.

Dialogue is a more productive source of information. Statements similar to, "So this is your quarters, Hjalmar—this is your home" in *The Wild Duck* and "Lord, ain't nothing so dreary as the view from this window on a dreary day, is there?" in *A Raisin in the Sun* are helpful references to the specific locale in those plays. Some plays may include details about the architectural layout. Mrs. Sorby instructs the servants in Act 1 of *The Wild Duck*, "Tell them to serve the coffee in the music room, Pettersen." Anfisa opens Act 3 of *Three Sisters* by saying:

ANFISA

They're sitting down there under the stairs
now. "Please come upstairs," I tell them. "We
can't have this, can we?" They're crying. "We
don't know where father is," they say. "He
might have been burnt to death." What an idea!
Then there are those other people out in the
yard as well, they're in their nightclothes,
too.

The Prozorov family is being displaced from one specific locale in their house to another, until they are pushed out altogether. This sense of displacement is experienced by the characters on both sides of the outcome and is central to the meaning of the play.

Specific locale can also be understood through inference. In this passage from *The School for Scandal*, Charles Surface is about to auction his family portraits to pay his debts. He points to the paintings in the portrait gallery of his eighteenth-century house where the sale takes place.

(*Enter* CHARLES SURFACE, SIR OLIVER SURFACE, MOSES, and CARELESS.)

CHARLES SURFACE
Walk in, gentlemen, pray walk in—here they are, the family of the Surfaces up to the [Norman] Conquest.

SIR OLIVER (*disguised as* MASTER PREMIUM).
And, in my opinion, a goodly collection.

CHARLES SURFACE
Ay, ay, these are done in the true spirit of portrait painting; no *volontère grace* or expression. Not like the works of your modern Raphaels, who give you the strongest resemblance, yet contrive to make your portrait independent of you; so that you may sink the original and not hurt the picture. No, no; the merit of these is the inveterate likeness—all stiff and awkward as the originals, and like nothing in human nature besides.

SIR OLIVER
Ah! We shall never see such figures of men again.

CHARLES SURFACE
I hope not. Well, you see, Master Premium, what a domestic character I am; here I sit of an evening surrounded by my family.

When Charles says, "Walk in, gentlemen, pray walk in," we imagine him entering a picture gallery and inviting the others to follow. When he says, ". . . here they are, the family of the Surfaces up to the Conquest." he is pointing to the paintings. His sarcastic description of the paintings ("the merit of these is the inveterate likeness—all stiff and awkward as the originals, and like nothing in human nature besides.") is a clue to what the paintings look like. Geographical and specific locale are productive objects for study by actors and directors as well as designers.

SOCIETY

Plays show social groups living together under the same closed environment. In this section we will ask, "What are the social groups in the play and what characterizes their interactions with one another?" The term *society* covers not only the specific identity of these groups, but also the behavioral standards shared by their members. A dominant group enforces these standards, but the possibility of secondary groups should not be overlooked as an aid to understanding the identity and values of the dominant group.

Arthur Miller contends that the author's choice of social groups determines the dramatic form of the play. Communication among family members is different from that with strangers, and private behavior is different from public. Interest in the family leads to writing realistic plays dealing with personal issues, while interest in social groups outside the family leads to nonrealistic forms. Miller's observation is interesting, but it should not be applied too rigidly. The implications that result from the choice of social groups are numerous and complex, and there are some obvious contrary examples. His ideas help us to understand how the choice of social groups and the meaning of a play may be interconnected.

Families

The most common social group, and the most important in the majority of modern plays, is the family. This is logical because we are all sons, daughters, sisters, and brothers before we are anything else. And since the family is the most basic social unit, playwrights cannot stray too far from it without losing touch with their audiences. The dramatic importance of families lays in the emotional tone that attends specific social relationships, such as love between husband and wife, pressures between parent and child, and competition among siblings.

Seven family members are identified in the garden scene from *Death of a Salesman* that we looked at in the Introduction. They are Willy's father, Willy as a father, Willy's wife, Willy's sons Biff and Happy, Willy's brother Ben, and Ben as the uncle of Biff and Happy. Almost every member of the Loman family and their family relationship to each other is specified or alluded to in this scene. This establishes expectations that may be confirmed or perhaps repudiated in the play.

Claudius's opening lines in Hamlet explain his family relationship to his deceased brother and his new relationship to his brother's wife, which many would interpret as dishonorable if not incestuous. Once more, the normal expectations associated with the family provide the grounds for dramatic conflict.

CLAUDIUS
Though yet of Hamlet our dear brother's death
The memory be green, and that it us befitted
To bear our hearts in grief, and our whole
  kingdom
To be contracted in one brow of woe,
Yet so far has discretion fought with nature
That we with wisest sorrow think on him
Together with remembrance of ourselves.
Therefore, our sometime sister, now our queen,
The imperial jointress to this warlike state,
Have we, as with a defeated joy,
With an auspicious and a drooping eye,
With mirth in funeral and dirge in marriage,
In equal scale, weighing delight with dole,
Taken to wife.

The dramatic point behind the complex family relationships in *The Piano Lesson* may seem hard to comprehend at first, but upon closer examination they form an unbroken bond going all the way back to slavery times. This bond exerts a powerful influence on the characters, and opens a window into the basic subject, or "lesson," of the play. The characters that ignore it risk losing their identities as free human beings.

Families form the core of such dissimilar plays as *Three Sisters, A Lie of the Mind, Mother Courage*, and *Angels in America*. A study of these examples indicates how universal the attraction of family groups is, above all in modern drama. Family love or its absence can be found at the heart of many, many plays.

Love and Friendship

Friendships are sympathetic social groups outside the family. We find important examples of friendship in David Rabe's play *Streamers*, where the social groups are defined by the friendships that exist among the military trainees. An important friendship exists between Hamlet and Horatio in *Hamlet*; Gregers Werle and Hjalmar Ekdal in *The Wild Duck*; Walter, Willy, and Bobo in *A Raisin in the Sun*; Willy and Charley in *Death of a Salesman*; and Roy Cohn and Louis Ironson in *Angels in America*. As with family relationships, friendships have emotional and behavioral expectations that may be confirmed, or just as often violated, in the play.

Love forms another kind of social group outside the family. Love entails not only the dominant heterosexual form but all forms, including homosexual love, the love of a parent for a child, love between siblings, and obsessive and destructive love. There are many examples in the study plays: Oedipus and Jocasta, Hamlet and Ophelia, Tartuffe and Elmire, Mrs. Sorby and Mr. Werle, Mother Courage and the Chaplain, Richie and Carlyle, Winnie and Willie, Louis Ironson and Prior Walter, Berniece and Avery, and Jake and Beth, to name only a few. Apart from the family unit, friendship and love are among the most interesting and dramatic social groups found in plays. Readers should have little difficulty finding more examples and determining how they confirm or contradict normal expectations. Make a note that in modern plays love can simultaneously confirm and deny expectations, a paradox that for some readers may obscure the real issues at stake. Jake's love for Beth in *A Lie of the Mind* is a case in point. Some readers may deny that real love can exist in such an abusive relationship. Jake is an example of a lover-abuser, and Beth could be considered an "enabler" whose behavior abets that of her tormentor. The fact that in spite of everything, real, mature love somehow manages to emerge from their abusive relationship is the point of the play.

Occupation

Another social group outside of the family is the occupational group. This group is defined by what characters do to earn a living and their interactions with others having the same or different professions. Merchant seamen form the central occupational group in *The Hairy Ape*, for instance, as do professional soldiers in *Mother Courage*, *Streamers*, and *Three Sisters*. Occupational groups occur in historical plays where we might not expect to encounter such issues. Professional actors, soldiers, and gravediggers are represented in *Hamlet*, process servers in *Tartuffe*, and moneylenders in *The School for Scandal*. Information about occupational groups provides clues to the characters' motives and suggests emotional values that could be underscored in production. Why does *Angels in America* deal with attorneys, doctors, religious and other educated power figures and those who serve or support them?

Social Status

Social status designates a character's position or rank in society. Status distinctions often stem from wealth or power. They are based on a privileged group whose members are accustomed to giving orders and having them carried out by those on lower rungs of the status ladder. Characters on the lower end show deference to those above them by using formal titles and various kinds of submissive behavior, such as bows, curtsies, and salutes. We observe this at work in *Hamlet*, where only Claudius and Gertrude address Hamlet by his given name. All the others, including Ophelia and Horatio, say "Prince Hamlet" or "my lord."

Although class distinctions can also be found in many other older plays like *Oedipus Rex*, *Tartuffe*, and *The School for Scandal*, they are seldom the subject of explicit attention there. Social class was a normal part of everyday life in the past and it is still customary in many regions of the world today. When class distinctions are taken for granted in the action, no special need exists to provide explanations in the dialogue. Information should be deduced from characters' behavior. There may not be much information about the inner workings of the class system in *Hamlet* or *Tartuffe*, but class distinctions are nevertheless of paramount importance. In other words, reflexively assuming democratic social customs in historical plays can be a mistake. Sometimes it may be necessary to supplement script analysis with outside research to understand the significance of their class distinctions.

In twentieth-century civilization social status may not be as obvious as its historical counterpart was, but it can be just as forceful and repressive. While aristocratic birth was the main source of high status in the past, in the present day it often appears as an outcome of education, financial or political power, ethnicity, or sexual orientation, and in these forms it may be easier for modern readers to recognize. For example, social status based on money turns up in *The Wild Duck*, *Mother Courage*, *Death of a Salesman*, *The Piano Lesson*, and *Three Sisters*; status based on education is found in *The Hairy Ape* and *Three Sisters*; ethnic discrimination influences the social status of the characters in *A Raisin in the Sun*, *Streamers*, and *The Piano Lesson*; and social status associated with sexual orientation is a feature of *Streamers* and *Angels in America*. Understanding overt and hidden social status is essential in these and other modern plays.

Social Standards

Social standards are the shared beliefs and behaviors regarded as necessary by the characters and to which they are expected to conform. An example is, "Thou shalt not kill," but there are many others equally powerful though less obvious. Social standards don't need to be proven or even stated in the dialogue because characters accept them as true without question. Characters believe in them, and conversely their behavior and beliefs are conditioned by the social standards. Social standards are often so important that violation produces shock, horror, moral revulsion, indignation, and segregation, and even justifies the use of extreme penalties to enforce conformity. Characters offended most by violations of the social standards are those who endorse them strongest.

In former times, social standards were determined by established religion, class, politics, inherited family position, and national culture. In historical plays, for example, the characters tend to be controlled by religious, aristocratic, or nationalistic forces—royal power, for example, in *Oedipus Rex* and *Hamlet.* In twentieth-century society, the overt influence of older forms of social control has lessened. At the present time it is science, belief in equality, and the values of the dominant middle class that determine the standards of belief and behavior for most people. The powerful influences of social standards may be repulsive to those who are independent-minded, but understanding and dealing with these influences is necessary nonetheless. Today the unwritten laws of social standards are often the only laws that dramatic characters can be counted on to obey.

One way social standards operate is through the use of euphemisms in the dialogue. A euphemism is an inoffensive term that is substituted for an offensive one. Thus euphemisms are evidence of social standards at work through avoidance of unacceptable words. Examples may be found in *The Wild Duck.* In the first scene the servant Jensen, referring to Mr. Ekdal, says to Pettersen, "I've heard tell as he's been a lively customer in his day." They both understand that "lively customer" is a euphemism for someone who is sexually reckless, a womanizer. In the climactic scene at the end of Act 1, Gregers accuses his father of having been "interested in" their former household servant Gina Hansen. In this context, "interested in" is a euphemism for sexual relations. Both Gregers and Mr. Werle use euphemisms when referring to the deceased Mrs. Werle. Gregers refers to her "break down" and her "unfortunate weakness." Mr. Werle says that she was "morbid" and "overstrained." He also says, "her eyes were—clouded now and then." These are euphemisms for alcoholism and drug addiction, which were almost as common in the late nineteenth century as they are today, even though social standards prohibited talking about them.

Social standards are disclosed in other ways, too. When Jensen says earlier, "I've heard tell . . ." it is a hint that there is gossip in town about Werle's family. This is confirmed later when Mr. Werle explains to Gregers why he didn't provide more help to Old Ekdal. He says, "I've had a slur cast on my reputation . . . I have done all I could without positively laying myself open to all sorts of suspicion and gossip."

Then, referring to the fact that Mrs. Sorby is currently living with him, he says, "A woman so situated may easily find herself in a false position in the eyes of the world. For that matter, it does a man no good either." Clearly Mr. Werle is controlled by his fear of scandal or even rumors of scandal. It could ruin his position in society. More evidence of this veiled type of social control occurs when Hjalmar confesses that he "kept the blinds down" over the windows when his father was in prison. Euphemisms and other kinds of evidence in *The Wild Duck* show the existence of powerful social standards about marriage, sex, alcohol, drugs, mental health, politics, government contracts, and even relations between labor and management. The reward for conforming to these standards is economic success and social approval; the penalty for violation is malicious gossip, public scandal, social ostracism, and prison.

Social standards often create a harsh and unforgiving world. The old saying that sticks and stones can break our bones but words can never hurt us is not true in plays. Words, especially epithets and slurs, are used to criticize violation of prevailing social standards, and they certainly have the power to hurt. They are meant to cause shame, embarrassment, and guilt and they work very well. Notice this harsh exchange of epithets between the Jew Roy Cohn and the black homosexual Belize from *Angels in America.* The topic is Belize's demand for access to Roy's unauthorized supply of the scarce AIDS drug AZT.

> BELIZE
>
> You expect pity?
>
> ROY
>
> (*a beat, then*) I expect you to hand over those keys and move your nigger ass out of my room.
>
> BELIZE
>
> What did you say?
>
> ROY
>
> Move your nigger cunt spade faggot lackey ass out of my room.

                              BELIZE

        (*Overlapping starting on "spade"*) Shit-for-
        brains filthy-mouthed selfish motherfucking
        cowardly cocksucking cloven-hoofed pig.

                               ROY

        (*Overlapping*) Mongrel. Dingo. Slave. Ape.

                              BELIZE

        Kike.

                               ROY

        Now you're talking!

                              BELIZE

        Greedy kike.

                               ROY

        Now you can have a bottle. But only one.

These offensive epithets call attention to the outsider social status of Roy
as a Jew and Belize as a black and a homosexual. They are meant to hurt
and hurt badly. In this incident the words hurt so much that they almost
transcend offensiveness by calling attention to the fact that both characters share a hidden bond, the unfortunate bond of exclusion from mainstream society. On a similar note, why is Baron Tuzenbach an outsider in
Three Sisters?

ECONOMICS

Economics is concerned with both large-scale monetary systems the characters live under and the smaller-scale financial transactions they engage
in within those systems. It may seem that the study of economics is far
from our stated principle of fixing on the play itself, but economics is
more important in script analysis than it first appears. Among the study
plays, *Tartuffe*, *The School for Scandal*, *The Wild Duck*, *The Hairy Ape*,
Mother Courage, *Death of a Salesman*, *A Raisin in the Sun*, *Three Sisters*,

The Piano Lesson, and *Angels in America* share a deep concern with money. Sometimes money concerns appear where we least expect them, for example in the plays of Anton Chekhov. In *The Cherry Orchard*, it is important to identify information about real estate development, mortgages, banking, borrowing and lending, agricultural marketing, and the daily financial affairs of a large country estate, not to mention the economic impact of the law passed in 1861 freeing the serfs. Andrey's unauthorized mortgage of the Prozorov estate forms a major part of *Three Sisters*. Gaining or losing money (for the most part losing it) has been and continues to be one of the favorite plot resources of dramatists.

According to economists, there are four principal financial systems. *Mercantilism* is colonialism with state control of manufacturing and exports. In a *laissez-faire* economic system, business is permitted to follow the unwritten "natural laws" of economics. Private property, profit, and credit form the basis of *capitalism*. *Socialism* necessitates public ownership of manufacturing, services, and natural resources. These four economic systems seldom exist in isolation, but present themselves in various combinations. On a smaller scale, economics in drama relates to any private financial dealings in which the characters are involved.

Capitalism is the system which most of us are familiar with and the one we most encounter in the plays we usually read. Since capitalism is based on individual freedom and free enterprise, it can be enormously rewarding for successful entrepreneurs, but it can be very hard on characters with limited financial talent, influence, or resources. In *Death of a Salesman*, Willy Loman struggles to live within a ruthless capitalist system dominated by the self-interested values of high-powered business interests. His personal economic concerns consist of meeting the regular payments for his refrigerator, automobile, life insurance, and home. Willy's personal economics are so important to him that they are elevated almost to symbolic status in the play. In the kitchen of Joe Meilziner's famous setting for the play, the Hastings refrigerator is the only appliance.

Mercantilism is the economic system in *The School for Scandal*. The important economic circumstances are the loans made to Charles Surface based on his credit from the family's colonial exports, the auction of his family home and its furnishings, and the sizable financial resources controlled by Sir Oliver Surface. International trading, which plays a major role in mercantilism, influences the timing of Charles's loans and the timely arrival of Sir Oliver. The character of Long, the Cockney seaman in *The Hairy Ape*, stirs up his companions with Marxist arguments about "the damned Capitalist clarss" [sic]. He also introduces Yank to New York's expensive Fifth Avenue shopping district to awaken his "clarss consciousness" [sic].

Economics can be an important issue in script analysis, but a word of caution. Because economics is so close to each of us, special care should be taken against projecting personal convictions or experiences into a play. As with the other analytical concepts, readers should search for conditions that are actually present in the play.

POLITICS AND LAW

The term *politics and law* refers to all governmental institutions and activities, including the rules of conduct or legislation set up by political authorities. Political and legal conditions normally rely on the mutual consent of the governed (i.e., the characters). Their importance in plays is identified through the respect or disregard that the governed characters show for political and legal matters. In *Oedipus Rex*, the public oath Oedipus undertakes to track down the murderer of Laius is an example of a political condition. For him and the population of Thebes, this oath has the force of law. Moreover, the absolute political authority of Oedipus is understood and accepted by everyone without question. There is no need for him to explain or justify himself.

Politics is at work in the pact made between King Hamlet and King Fortinbras that Horatio discloses in 1,1 of *Hamlet*. Horatio informs his companions that this pact has serious political consequences for Denmark and Norway. First, Denmark has gained political control of Norway; second, young Fortinbras of Norway has raised a military challenge against Claudius to regain his country's independence; and third, Claudius has responded by placing Denmark on military alert. Danish weapons makers are working around the clock to prepare for an impending war. The feeling of war is in the air, and everyone is frightened and tense.

Politics plays a role in *Angels in America*, too. Roy Cohn is a successful lawyer and political power broker. His wish to influence political decisions made at the highest level in Washington, D.C., forms the basis of his relationship with Joe Pitt. Louis Ironson, Prior's faithless companion, is a political liberal who exhibits an intense interest in debating the fine ethical points of topical political issues. Joe Pitt and his family are political conservatives who admire and respect the political values that were in the ascendant in this country in 1986. *Angels in America* consists in large part of dramatic illustrations of the complex dynamics formed by the mixture of these opposing political ideologies.

INTELLECT AND CULTURE

According to philosophers, intellect and culture are among humanity's highest social activities. Culture denoting the customary beliefs, social forms, and material traits of a racial, religious, or social group has already been discussed under Given Circumstances. In this chapter, the expression *intellect and culture* refers to enlightenment and excellence of taste acquired by intellectual and aesthetic training. Every society has its intellectuals and artists, or at least it has people who spend a large part of their time dealing with ideas and culture. The life of the mind is protected in most societies because in an important way it helps to shape the course of life in general. Although there may be no specialized professional roles for intellect or art, intellectual and creative life plays a substantial role in creating culture in its broader sense, too. Sometimes intellectuals and artists attempt to influence political action and social change.

Intellectual life is not reserved for scholars and artists. It may appear in non-professional ways, besides. At this position of the intellectual and artistic scale are found those characters with formal schooling and refined artistic taste. Hamlet, for example, is most at home in Wittenberg, which is an isolated intellectual and artistic environment. He is the product of a refined university education that trained him to appreciate poetry, philosophy, and theatre. He prefers the life of the mind to the life of action exemplified by Claudius, Fortinbras, and Laertes. He is out of place in a pragmatic and warlike society such as Denmark. At another place on the scale are found characters who are uneducated or may even scorn the life of the mind. In *The Hairy Ape*, Yank rejects the world of learning, though paradoxically he is the most clever and self-aware character in the play. In fact, it is the quality of Yank's native intellect that leads to his downfall. In *A Raisin in the Sun*, Walter Lee Younger has been denied ordinary learning opportunities. As a result, he is scornful of the educational dreams of his sister, Beneatha, as well as those of her college friend, George Murchison. In *Death of a Salesman*, Willy Loman preaches against the ideals of formal schooling. He encourages the cultivation of a winning personality because he believes this is what has made him a successful salesman.

Formal education does not always go hand-in-hand with wisdom. Gregers Werle is the most educated person in *The Wild Duck*, yet he is helpless in carrying out the simplest of chores such as lighting a stove. He also lacks the kind of sensitivity and humane wisdom possessed by Gina, the uneducated former housemaid who is one target of his machinations. Humane wisdom, minus the advantages of a formal education, also characterizes Mama Younger in *A Raisin in the Sun* as well as Boy Willie in *The Piano Lesson*. Anfisa, the former serf and now household servant in *Three Sisters*, is perhaps the wisest and most well adjusted character in the play. It is the educated characters in that play that cannot understand what is happening to them. Likewise with Hamlet.

SPIRITUALITY

In its narrowest sense, *spirituality* entails the formal religious features in a play. Evidence of spirituality includes any beliefs in divine, spiritual, or supernatural powers that must be obeyed or worshiped. It can be seen in the presence of religious organizations, ceremonies, and traditions and in religious values openly espoused by the characters.

Spirituality as such does not figure in *The Hairy Ape*, *Death of a Salesman*, or *Streamers*. Spirituality plays a small but strategic role in *The Wild Duck* through the character of Reverend Molvik, in *Mother Courage* through the Chaplain, and in *Happy Days* through Winnie's repeated prayers. Religious values are important in *A Raisin in the Sun*, *The Piano Lesson*, and *Angels in America*. *Oedipus Rex* contains many religious references, including prayers by the Chorus. *Hamlet* also includes important spiritual conditions, notably the references to religious ceremonies, traditions, and beliefs. *Tartuffe* is about the hypocrisy of religious societies that were influential in Moliére's time. Sometimes, too, characters may be guided by spiritual considerations that remain hidden or unspoken. Readers should be on the alert for any evidence of noticeably spiritual morality in character actions as well as in their words.

The cumulative effect of all the Given Circumstances plus the social standards they embody creates *the world of the play*. The characters usually reveal that world through their behavior more than their words. They show whether the world they inhabit is a place that is good or bad, friendly or unfriendly, amusing or frightening, benign or dangerous, lovable or hateful.

At the beginning of this chapter, there was a statement that without living through the Given Circumstances, the characters would exist in an abstract emptiness without any connection to real life. How many times has an audience experienced the feeling of looking into such a environmental void while watching a play? This occurs when productions give insufficient attention to understanding and illustrating the world of the play. To create that world it is necessary to know which Given Circumstances exert the most influence over the characters and which social standards dominate their beliefs and behavior.

In *Oedipus Rex*, spiritual forces control the characters. Their world is a fearful place dominated by fickle and unforgiving gods who do not hesitate to send plagues and famines to punish those who disagree with them. The world of *Hamlet* also is inhospitable. As punishment for his sins, King Hamlet has been condemned to wander among the living and to suffer the fires of purgatory among the dead. For his part, young Hamlet is compelled to undertake a violent and bloody revenge that he is mentally and morally unsuited to perform. Since strong political counter forces are at work in the play too, the reader will have to determine whether the world of *Hamlet* is mainly a spiritual or political one. The world of *Tartuffe*, on the other hand, is controlled by religion and politics working in harmony. Orgon suffers at the hands of Tartuffe throughout most of the play, but in the end, the King's political power sets everything right. The characters in *The Piano Lesson* live in a harsh economic, social, and political world, but one that can be improved by a compassionate spirituality. The world of the play is dissimilar in each of the two parts of *Angels in America*. A rough and unfeeling form of justice governs the world of Part I, while a modern and humane form of forgiveness guides Part II.

The dramatic worlds created in many modern plays are dominated by social considerations that can be as cruel and unforgiving as could be the gods of old. In *The Wild Duck*, a petty financial crime leads to the complete and permanent social ruin of the Ekdal family. In *Death of a Salesman*, Willy Loman is the victim of a world dominated by coldblooded, profit-hungry money interests. Mindless violence is the controlling circumstance in the world of *Streamers*. A mysterious force that seems to toy with the characters as they attempt to make sense out of their lives controls the world of *Happy Days*.

Studying the world of the play also offers an opportunity to get an early feel for the characters. As already observed, the world of the play is formed by the Given Circumstances that control the characters. Accordingly, a character's point of view to the world of the play, called his or her *position* or *attitude*, reveals his or her identity. Different characters in a play will exhibit different attitudes. For example, every character in *Tartuffe* has a different attitude toward religion and their individual attitudes toward this subject in turn determine their behavior in the play. To Orgon religion means extravagant public devoutness. He admires Tartuffe for this characteristic, which he interprets as saintliness. He hopes that Tartuffe will teach him how to achieve peace of mind and how to stop worrying about what he views as his family's immoral behavior. According to Orgon, Tartuffe must take the family under control and teach them how to behave morally. The other characters express their own points of view toward religion. For Madame Pernelle, it means social status and respectability; Elmire views religion as a private affair of conscience; Dorine considers it a refuge for gossips; for Cleante religion is "pious flummery" or flattery; Marianne sees religion as a tiresome family duty; and for Tartuffe religion is a con game and a means to easy wealth. The King alone seems to believe that religion equates with virtuous conduct. Thus each character expresses a different point of view about the spiritual-moral forces that control the world of the play.

SUMMARY

This chapter contained a review of the Given Circumstances that readers should try to identify in the study of plays. We also attempted to discover the dramatic possibilities or playable values within each given circumstance. It is not too much of an exaggeration to say that once the Given Circumstances are identified, the rest of the play will fall into place more or less by itself. Of course, not all the Given Circumstances will be useful on every occasion. And when a play does not make use of a particular given circumstance, it would not be practical to dwell on it in analysis. As in most situations, over time readers will develop their own instincts for what is most useful. Because these instincts are among the unteachable skills of play analysis, this text cannot equip students with them. It can only point the way.

QUESTIONS

Time   In what year and season does the action occur? Can the passage of time during the play be determined? The time between the scenes and acts? The hour of day for each scene? Each act?

Place   In what country, region, or city does the action occur? Are any geographical features described? In what specific locale does the action occur? What is the specific location for each scene, including the ground plan and other architectural features if possible?

Society   What are the family relationships? What are the friendships and love relationships? What occupational groups are depicted? What social classes are represented? What are the social standards, the behavior expectations? Are they spoken about or implied? Are they enforced openly or indirectly? What social group controls the social standards? What are the rewards for conformity? What are the penalties for violating social standards?

Economics   What is the general economic system in the play? Any specific examples of business activities or transactions? Does money exercise any control over the characters? Who controls the economic circumstances? How do they exert control? What are the rewards for economic success? The penalties for violating the economic standards?

Politics and Law   What is the system of government that serves as the background for the play? Any specific examples of political or legal activities, actions, or ceremonies? Do politics or law exercise any control over the characters? Who controls the political and legal circumstances in the play? How do they exert control? What are the rewards for political and legal compliance? The penalties for violating the political and legal standards?

Intellect and Culture   What is the general level of culture and artistic taste of the characters? Any examples of intellectual or creative activities? Any characters more or less educated or creative than others? Does intellect or culture exercise any control over the characters? Who controls the intellectual and artistic circumstances in the play? How do they exert their control? What are the rewards for intellectual and creative conformity? What are the penalties for violating intellectual and artistic standards?

Spirituality   What is the accepted code of religious or spiritual belief? Any examples of religious or spiritual activities or ceremonies? Does spirituality exercise any control over the characters? Who controls the spiritual circumstances in the play? How do they exert control? What are the rewards for spiritual conformity? What are the penalties for violating the spiritual standards?

The World of the Play   Describe the world of the play, the distinctive social universe created by the Given Circumstances and social standards. How does the world of the play influence the conduct and attitude of characters in the play? What are the different points of view expressed by the characters toward their world?

POSTSCRIPT FOR ACTION ANALYSIS

After Action Analysis, search for the play's Seed, or Subject, hidden within the Given Circumstances. How does the Seed influence the Given Circumstances? Why did the playwright choose these specific Given Circumstances from the whole range of other possibilities? How would the play be different with other Given Circumstances? In what way does connecting the Seed with the Given Circumstances help the play grow and develop?

CHAPTER 3

Foundations of the Plot: Background Story

Now that we have studied the present, we can turn our attention to the past. The lives of the characters begin long before they appear on stage, and their pasts are indispensable for understanding their present lives on stage. Every dramatic story has a past, but the conventional time and space features of the theatre require special writing skill to illustrate all of it on stage. Playwrights employ a unique kind of narration to reveal the past at the same time the stage action is still going on. *Exposition* is the standard term for this dramatic convention, but sometimes it is also referred to as *previous action* or *antecedent action*. The word exposition comes from the Latin root *exposito*, meaning to put forward or to expose. This term has proven useful because exposition is a way of exposing the hidden parts of a play.

Unfortunately, the abstract term *exposition* often calls up an uncritical response. According to some, exposition tells the audience everything they need to know about the past to understand what they are going to see; it is considered a playwriting annoyance. It involves a certain amount of dullness, but skillful dramatists are able to handle it without holding up the action of the play. This explanation carries unpleasant overtones. It gives the impression that exposition is an awkward technical requirement that obstructs the flow of the plot. The unpleasantness increases when scholars talk about *protactic characters* such as the

Chorus in classical Greek tragedies or certain servants in modern plays, introduced, it is said, for disclosing exposition.

Actors, directors, and designers cannot let the matter rest here. What exposition means to theatre artists is a vital element in the full-scale understanding of a play. We should attempt to understand the past in a way that makes it compelling, not a clumsy obstacle to overcome. This involves several important adjustments in ways of thinking about a play. First, the notion that what has already happened is somehow dull and undramatic must be set aside. After all, for the characters themselves, it is just the opposite. To them the past is not just an abstract literary concept, but rather their own lives—everything good and bad that has happened to them. Second, the past should be understood as an integral part of the play, not a clumsy literary burden. It helps in understanding the characters that are themselves talking about the past, it creates moods, and it generates conflicts. Third, to be reminded of the dramatic possibilities of the past, replace the static term *exposition* with the more energetic term *background story*, or the film term *back story*. The basic lesson here for actors, directors, and designers is that background story does not interfere with the flow of the action. On the contrary, it propels the play forward in explosive surges and with an increasing sense of urgency.

Background story involves everything that happened before the beginning of the play. Time and again it is crucial to know what went on prior to the stage action. In *Oedipus Rex* the fate of Jocasta's infant son is an example. Did Jocasta bind the infant's feet and turn him over to a household servant with orders to abandon him? Where did the Corinthian Messenger obtain the infant he gave to King Polybus and Queen Merope? He claims that he obtained the infant from one of Laius' herdsmen. But why did the herdsman give the baby to him in the first place? Did the infant belong to the herdsman? If not, who gave it to him and why? Is the shepherd the herdsman who gave the infant to the Corinthian Messenger? If the answer is yes, why is he unwilling to acknowledge it? All these questions and many more about the background story are decisive in the plot of *Oedipus Rex*.

The past becomes even more intricate when it is employed as Ibsen did in, for example, *The Wild Duck*. In the excerpt from Act 1 that follows, Gregers Werle has returned home after a long absence. He has a sharp disagreement with his father about the fate of the Ekdal family, who used to be their close friends. But we should guard against unjustifiable assumptions about the past. Reliability should not depend on Gregers' recollections nor on those of any single character. By the way, it is a good idea to get into the habit of underlining the background story as we do here to distinguish it from the on-stage action.

GREGERS

How has that family been allowed to go so miserably to the wall?

WERLE

You mean the Ekdals, I suppose?

GREGERS

Yes, I mean the Ekdals. Lieutenant Ekdal who was once so closely associated with you?

WERLE

Much too closely; I have felt that to my cost for many a year. It is thanks to him that I—yes I—have had a kind of slur cast upon my reputation.

GREGERS

(*softly*) Are you sure that he alone was to blame?

WERLE

Who else do you suppose?

GREGERS

You and he acted together in that affair of the forests—

WERLE

But was it not Ekdal that drew the map of the tracts we had bought—that fraudulent map! It was he who felled all the timber illegally on government ground. In fact, the whole

> management was in his hands. I was quite in the
> dark as to what Lieutenant Ekdal was doing.

>   GREGERS
> Lieutenant Ekdal himself seems to have been
> very much in the dark about what he was doing.

>   WERLE
> That may be. But the fact is that he was found
> guilty and I was acquitted.

>   GREGERS
> Yes, I know that nothing was proved against
> you.

Since the interpretations of the past presented by these characters are incompatible or at least incomplete, readers are obliged to formulate their own accounts. This involves understanding what happened and why in a very detailed way. It also means knowing whose version of the past is correct and how much of it is reliable. In the excerpt here, the characters disagree about the reasons for the decline of the Ekdals. Gregers indicts his father for it, while Mr. Werle seems to lay the blame on Lieutenant Ekdal, the head of the family and Werle's former business partner. Later in the play, Lieutenant Ekdal offers his own interpretation to his son, Hjalmar and to his daughter-in-law, Gina. Who is right? Who benefits from each version? In such cases, readers should examine each version of the story skeptically, as trial lawyers do.

TECHNIQUE

Let's first study the basic techniques playwrights employ to disclose background story and then consider some ways of identifying it. By approaching the topic in this way, it should be easier to understand the workings of the background story in the play as a whole.

Background story emerges in two ways. It appears in extended passages near the beginning of a play or in fragments distributed throughout the action. There is no advantage in craftsmanship or plausibility either way. The choice depends on the author's goals and the practical requirements of the play. Playwriting fashions also play a part. Both methods have been used in a wide assortment of plays, can be used simultaneously, and are capable of revealing the past without interrupting the flow of the action or harming the play's plausibility.

Historical Technique

In plays written before the nineteenth century, the background story tends to emerge early in extended speeches. Note how this operates in *Hamlet*. We studied 1,1 for its political conditions in the last chapter. Horatio's lengthy speech consists of 29 lines explaining the reasons behind Denmark's preparations for war. In the next scene, Claudius has a speech of 34 lines expressing his gratitude to the court for their support during the recent transfer of power. He also explains his strategy for dealing with the political threat posed by Fortinbras. At the end of this scene, more background story is disclosed. In a famous soliloquy of about 50 lines, Hamlet reveals his feelings about his father's recent death and his mother's hasty remarriage. In 1,3 Laertes censures Ophelia in a speech of 34 lines, warning her not to be misled by Hamlet's fondness for her. Besides being a warning to Ophelia, this is also background story. In 1,4 the Ghost materializes, then in a discourse of 50 lines in 1,5 he discloses the circumstances of his death. At this point in the play, the characters have revealed most of the background story in five speeches totaling about 200 lines. Most of the background stories in *Tartuffe* and *The School for Scandal* unfolds in a few long speeches early in those plays, too.

The technique of early extended narration has advantages and disadvantages. On one hand, it focuses attention because it collects all the essential facts of the background story together at the beginning of the play. This permits the dramatist to devote the remainder of the play to the development of on-stage action, which is a considerable writing and performance benefit. On the other hand, extended narration can be a burden on actors and audiences. For actors, it is essential to express all the important background information in densely packed speeches, while at the same time maintaining emotional honesty and logical consistency. Audiences must digest most of the background story at one time and note who the important characters are and what they did. And they must remember it throughout the action that follows.

Early Modern Technique

For artistic reasons, another method of disclosing the background story was added to that of extended speeches. Most of the background story still appeared at the beginning of the play, but now it was broken into smaller pieces and shared among several characters. Although the absence of long speeches in this method seemed to provide plays with a more plausible appearance of everyday reality, its initial use was somewhat simple by current standards. A typical instance involved an opening scene in which two servants perform routine household duties while gossiping about their employer. This type of opening was so widespread in nineteenth-century realistic drama that it came to be called the *below-stairs scene* because it almost always involved servants, whose working quarters were located downstairs.

Ibsen used a refined variation of this method in the opening scene of *The Wild Duck*, where Pettersen, the old family servant, and Jensen, a hired helper, observe, explain, and otherwise account for a dinner party that's happening off stage at the same time. The parallel off-stage scene lends plausibility to the on-stage discussion of background story, but there is another refinement as well. Unlike other early realistic playwrights, Ibsen seldom treated his secondary characters as simple dramatic functionaries. He provided them with a distinct character and with an intense personal interest in the plot. Both Pettersen and Jensen are distinctive personalities, and they have personal reasons for gossiping about the people in the other room.

In his later work, Ibsen refined his method. Instead of revealing so much of the background story in the early scenes, he began to distribute it in fragments throughout the entire play. Scholars call this the *retrospective method* because the on-stage action moves forward while the past unfolds backward, retrospectively. The key to its effective use was to keep from revealing the most significant background information until as late as possible in the action when it was most effective. As time went on,

Ibsen and other early modern dramatists—Anton Chekhov, August Strindberg, and George Bernard Shaw—became adept at this method. They learned how to distribute the background story in bits and pieces throughout their plays, and they knew where and how to place the information so that its disclosure would be as dramatic as possible. In their best works, no single piece of background story is revealed until it is of maximum service to the action—in other words, until it has maximum impact on the characters. The past unfolds one small fact at a time with a skillful sense of theatrical timing.

The retrospective method was actually the rediscovery of a historical model that had remained for the most part unused for almost 2,400 years. Few dramatists ever handled it better than Sophocles did in *Oedipus Rex*. The plot of this play is a murder mystery told retrospectively. A detective (Oedipus) searching for a murderer inquires into his past and step-by-step discovers to his horror that the criminal turns out to be himself. In spite of its early date of composition, *Oedipus Rex* remains an excellent example of retrospective technique. Both *Oedipus Rex* and *The Wild Duck* are models of background story craftsmanship that reward patient analysis.

Modern Technique

Beginning in the 1940s, certain forward-thinking authors began to push the limits of the retrospective method. They did this by concealing the background story so that audiences had a difficult time even detecting its presence. This new approach might be called *deep background story*. Audiences were perplexed by these unorthodox plays. Without knowing the past it was next to impossible for anyone to know what was going on except the actors, and they were often as perplexed as the audience was. The early playwrights of Theatre of the Absurd—Edward Albee, Samuel Beckett, Jean Genêt, and Harold Pinter—were skilled at crafting plays with deep background stories. In their plays and in those of many like-minded dramatists, the background story is concealed so that it is almost impossible to uncover without a great deal of detective work.

Appearances to the contrary, plays must have a past of some kind. Even the absurdists and their followers could not abandon need for it altogether. Critics were fond of attributing the unusual moods in these plays to intellectual factors like the "illogical and purposeless nature of existence." What the absurdists did was to rediscover the entertainment value of being cryptic. Curiosity and attention can he heightened if the audience is not allowed in on the secret. Mysterious undertones are created when the background story is withheld, a technique used by August Strindberg in *The Ghost Sonata* in 1907 and by Edgar Allen Poe as early as 1841 in his short stories.

Absurdist plays and their stylistic relatives needed a new approach to acting and production to meet the challenge of expressing the hidden undertones that were their hallmark. Talented young directors, actors, and designers developed innovative performance techniques suitable for these unusual works. Now that we have observed the background story technique of the absurdists in use for over a generation, we understand that there was no magic involved in what they were doing. Deep background story is a radical extension of the retrospective method employed by early realistic playwrights and even before. The main difference lies in limiting the quantity of background story and then disclosing what is left of it by means of intricate, complicated hints instead of by frank narration. To perform such plays, actors and directors need to pay close attention to two important factors. They must first employ patient and imaginative detective work during the analytical stages of rehearsal to expose every last ounce of background information. Second, they should use meticulous application of tempo, rhythm, and mood in production to illuminate every veiled hint and casual allusion that these plays depend on for their effects. What cannot be spoken must be acted out through the subtle interplay of facial and bodily adjustments.

The plays of Albee, Beckett, Genêt, and Pinter may have been perplexing at first, but it is instructive to remember that for similar reasons the plays of Ibsen, Chekhov, and Strindberg were also difficult for their contemporaries to understand. Ibsen felt compelled to provide detailed stage directions, and Strindberg wrote explanatory prefaces to help actors understand their then-unconventional plays. We know that Chekhov's plays were also misunderstood when they were produced. They required the talent of Stanislavski with considerable assistance from Nemirovitch-Dantchenko to uncover and communicate the background stories in his plays.

Agreeing that plays require background story, of what does it consist? Background story takes on several forms: events, character descriptions, and feelings. Which is most important is determined by the nature of the play, the characters, and the situations in the play.

Events

A background story event is something noteworthy that happened to a character in the past, something vital. Past events are always important because they provide the source material for the on-stage conflicts. Here are some background passages that contain important past events. In *Streamers*, Sergeant Cokes boasts, "I told 'em when they wanted to send me back [to Vietnam] I ain't got no leukemia; they wanna check it. They think I got it. I don't think I got it." The fateful event here is Cokes's lying about his illness so that he could be allowed to return to the war. Really, they knew about his illness but sent him back to Vietnam anyway. Two crucial past events are disclosed in Mama Younger's announcement to her son Walter in *A Raisin in the Sun*, "Son—do you know your wife is expecting another baby?" The surprises for Walter are that Ruth is pregnant and that his wife didn't tell him about it. Another example is Hjalmar Ekdal's confession in *The Wild Duck* that his father "considered" suicide when he was sent to jail. Hjalmar says to Gregers melodramatically, "When the sentence of imprisonment was passed—he had the pistol in his hand." In *Oedipus Rex* when Oedipus asks who found him as an infant, the Corinthian Messenger discloses a momentous past event, "It was another shepherd gave you to me." At this moment Oedipus finds out that he is not the son of Polybus and Merope as he thought. In *Mother Courage*, the Recruiter reveals an important past event when he says to the Sergeant, "The general wants me to recruit four platoons by the twelfth." The fact that the General will have him shot if he doesn't enlist ninety men by the end of the week explains why the Recruiter doesn't show much sympathy dealing with recruits later in the play. Sally says to her mother, Lorraine, in *A Lie of the Mind*, "Right then I knew what Jake had in mind." "What?" asks Lorraine. "Jake had decided to kill him." Background stories are composed of pivotal events like these.

Again, the caution is that readers should not always take characters' descriptions of past events at face value. It's not that characters lie; they just tell their own versions of the truth as they see it. Even a lie told as a truth, however, can be revealing if it is studied with care. In Hjalmar Ekdal's scene discussed in the first paragraph of this section, his accidental use of the word "considered" instead of "attempted" when he speaks about his father's experience is revealing. For one thing, an attempted suicide is far different from a considered suicide, which implies a kind of cowardice. Moreover, even though the event was real enough, it is not as important as the selfish use Hjalmar makes of it at this moment in the play. His purpose in confessing the event to Gregers is not to gain sympathy for his father but to express how he suffered from his father's social disgrace. This is also a useful example of how background story can provide important information about other dimensions of the play.

Character Descriptions

Recalling the events of the past leads to a concern with the characters involved in those events. In *Tartuffe*, Orgon offers this description of his daughter's suitor: "I had promised you to Valere, but apart from the fact that he's said to be a bit of a gambler, I suspect him of being a free thinker." Orgon is disclosing his evaluation of a character in the past. Horatio reveals to Hamlet his recollection of King Hamlet's character: "I saw him once; he was a goodly king." Joseph Surface receives this admiring description from Sir Peter Teazle in *The School for Scandal*: "Joseph is indeed what a youth should be—everyone in the world speaks well of him." Speaking to Gregers Werle, Dr. Relling says of Lieutenant Ekdal in *The Wild Duck*: "The old lieutenant has been an ass all his days." Willy Loman recalls his brother Ben in *Death of a Salesman*: "There was the only man I ever met who knew all the answers." Mama Younger in *A Raisin in the Sun* recalls her deceased husband, "God knows there was plenty wrong with Walter Younger—hard-headed, mean, kind of wild with women—plenty wrong with him. But he sure loved his children." In *Angels in America*, Roy Cohn listens to

Joe Pitt explaining why he cannot move to Washington, D.C. with his wife:

JOE

```
The pills were something she started when she
miscarried or . . . no, she took some before
that. She had a really bad time at home, when
she was a kid, her home was really bad. I think
a lot of drinking and physical stuff. She
doesn't talk about it, instead she talks about
. . . the sky falling down, people with knives
hiding under sofas. Monsters. Mormons. Everyone
thinks Mormons aren't supposed to behave that
way, but we do. It's not lying, or being two-
faced. Everyone tries very hard to live, up to
God's strictures, which are very . . . um . . .
```

Character descriptions in the background story often reveal as much about the speaker as they do about the person being remembered.

Feelings

Characters reveal their past feelings in a variety of ways. When, in *The Wild Duck*, Hjalmar Ekdal's father went to prison for fraud, it was also an unpleasant time for Hjalmar: "I kept the blinds drawn down over both my windows. When I peeped out I saw the sun shining as if nothing had happened. I could not understand it. I saw people going along the street, laughing and talking about indifferent things. I could not understand it. It seemed to me that the whole of existence must be at a standstill—as if under an eclipse." To which Gregers Werle adds, "I felt that too, when my mother died." In *Happy Days* Winnie expresses her gladness about three memorable events in her past: "My first ball! (*long pause*) My second ball! (*long pause, close eyes*) My first kiss!" In *Death of a Salesman*, Willy Loman tells Linda how he has felt when traveling alone on the road: "I get so lonely—especially when business is bad and there's nobody to talk to. I get the feeling that I'll never sell anything again." Paddy, the sentimental Irish stoker in *The Hairy Ape*, remembers how happy he felt being at sea when he was young: "A warm sun on the clean decks. Sun warming the blood of you, and wind over the miles of shiny green ocean like strong drink to your lungs." The frustration of Walter Younger's past expresses itself through sense impressions in *A Raisin in the Sun*: "Sometimes it's like I can see the future stretched out in front of me—just plain as day. The future, Mama. Hanging over there at the edge of my days. Just waiting for me—a big, looming blank space—full of nothing." Doaker speaks about his niece, Berniece, to Boy Willie in *The Piano Lesson*: "She still got [her husband] Crawley on her mind. He been dead three years but she still holding on to him. She need to go out here and let one of those fellows grab a whole handful of whatever she got. She act like it done got precious." Lorraine's past feelings of despair about her husband's departure are the subject of these remarks to her daughter, Beth, in *A Lie of the Mind*:

LORRAINE

Wonder? Did I ever wonder? You know a man your whole life. You grow up with him. You're almost raised together. You go to school on the same bus together. You go through tornadoes together in the same basement. You go through a war together. You have babies together. And then one day he just up and disappears into thin air. Did I ever wonder? Yeah. You bet your sweet life I wondered. But you know where all that wondering got me? Nowhere. Absolutely nowhere. Because here I am. Alone. Just the same as though he'd never even existed.

Past feelings expressed through the background story are also valuable for beginning to understand character.

Combining Events, Character Descriptions, and Feelings

To learn how past events, character descriptions, and feelings work together in longer passages of dialogue, we will consider three examples.

The first and third passages use traditional straightforward narration, the second uses the retrospective method. As we said earlier, *Hamlet* falls into the class of play in which background story appears in long passages early in the action. The murder of King Hamlet is the single most important fact of the background story. In 1,5 the Ghost reveals to Hamlet the circumstances surrounding this event in several prolonged speeches. Background story in this scene is a seamless merging of past events, feelings, and character descriptions. The Ghost begins by disclosing his suffering in purgatory ever since his death. Again, background story is underlined.

GHOST

I am thy father's spirit,
Doom'd for a certain term to walk the night,
And for the day confin'd to fast in fires,
Till the foul crimes done in my days of nature
Are burnt and purg'd away.

In the next 11 lines he describes in sensory terms how Hamlet would feel if he knew what his father has suffered.

GHOST

But that I am forbid
To tell the secrets my prison-house,
I could a tale unfold whose lightest word
Would harrow up thy soul, freeze thy young
   blood,
Make thy two eyes, like stars, start from their
   spheres,
Thy knotted and combined locks to part,
And each particular hair to stand on end,
Like quills upon the fretful porpentine.
But this eternal blazon must not be
To ears of flesh and blood.

Now the Ghost discloses that he was murdered, which is the pivotal event of the background story. He adds his personal feeling that blood ties and incest made the crime even worse.

                        GHOST

List, List, O, List!

If thou didst ever thy dear father love—

                        HAMLET

O God!

                        GHOST

Revenge his foul and most unnatural <u>murder</u>.

                        HAMLET

<u>Murder</u>!

                        GHOST

<u>Murder most foul</u>, as in the best it is;

<u>But this most foul, strange, and unnatural.</u>

A few lines later, the Ghost picks up the thread of the events once again.

                        GHOST

Now, Hamlet, hear;

<u>'Tis given out that, sleeping in my orchard</u>

<u>A serpent stung me; so the whole ear of Denmark</u>

<u>Is by a forged process of my death</u>

<u>Rankly abused; but know, thou noble youth,</u>

<u>The serpent that did sting thy father's life</u>

<u>Now wears his crown.</u>

                        HAMLET

O my prophetic soul!

<u>My uncle</u>!

The Ghost adds a character description of Claudius, condemning the incestuous relationship with Gertrude and the murder of his own brother.

                        GHOST

<u>Ay, that incestuous, that adulterate beast,</u>

<u>With wicked witchcraft of his wits, with</u>

   <u>traitorous gifts</u>—

```
O wicked wit and gifts that have the power
So to seduce—won to his shameful lust
The will of my most seeming virtuous queen.
```

Now follows 11 lines contrasting King Hamlet's idealistic love of Gertrude with Claudius's cynical lust.

```
O Hamlet, what a falling off was there,
From me, whose love was of that dignity
That it went hand in hand even with the vow
I made to her in marriage; and to decline
Upon a wretch whose natural gifts were poor
To those of mine!
```

The next 16 lines are a vivid account of the murder itself.

```
But soft! methinks I scent the morning air.
Brief let me be. Sleeping within my orchard,
My custom always of the afternoon,
Upon my secure hour thy uncle stole,
With juice of cursed hebona in a vial,
And in the porches of mine ears did pour
The leprous distillment; whose effect
Holds such an enmity with blood of man
That swift as quicksilver it courses through
The natural gates and alleys of the body;
And with a sudden vigour it doth posset
And curd, like eager droppings into milk,
The thin and wholesome blood. So did it mine;
And a most instant tetter bark'd about,
Most lazar-like, with vile and loathsome crust,
All my smooth body.
```

Seven lines of religious feelings develop from these.

```
Thus was I, sleeping, by a brother's hand
Of life, of crown, of queen, at once
    dispatch'd;
```

> Cut off even in the blossom of my sin,
> Unhousl'd, disappointed, unanel'd;
> No reck'ning made, but sent to my account
> With all my imperfections on my head.
> O, Horrible! Horrible! most horrible!

The Ghost concludes the scene by challenging Hamlet to revenge his murder. The background story in this scene has been disclosed by one character during several long narrative speeches composed of a classic blend of events, feelings, and character descriptions.

In *A Raisin in the Sun,* several characters disclose the past retrospectively and in small fragments. This scene between Walter and his wife, Ruth, occurs near the beginning of the play. It centers on Walter's scheme for buying a liquor store. His project will require $10,000 from his father's life insurance. Intermingled in the argument between Walter and Ruth are background story events, character descriptions, and feelings.

WALTER

You want to know what I was thinking 'bout in the bathroom this morning?

RUTH

No.

WALTER

How come you always got to be so pleasant?

RUTH

What is there to be pleasant 'bout?

WALTER

You want to know what I was thinking 'bout in the bathroom or not?

RUTH

I know what you was thinking 'bout.

WALTER

(*ignoring her*) 'Bout what me an' Willy Harris
was talking about last night.

RUTH

(*immediately—a refrain*) Willy Harris is a good-
for-nothing loud mouth.

WALTER

Anybody who talks to me has got to be a good-
for-nothing loud mouth, ain't he? And what you
know about who is just a good-for-nothing loud
mouth? Charlie Atkins was just a "good-for-
nothing loud-mouth" too, wasn't he? When he
wanted me to go into the dry-cleaning business
with him. And now—he's grossing a hundred
thousand dollars a year. A hundred thousand
dollars a year! You still call him a loud
mouth?

RUTH

(*bitterly*) Oh, Walter Lee.

(*She folds her head on her arms over the table.*)

WALTER

(*rising and coming over to her and standing
over her*) You tired, ain't you? Tired of
everything. Me, the boy, the way we live—this
beat up hole—everything. Ain't you? So tired—
moaning and groaning all the time, but you
wouldn't' do nothing to help, would you? You
couldn't be on my side that long for nothing
could you?

RUTH

Walter, please leave me alone.

                         WALTER

A man needs for a woman to back him up . . .

                         RUTH

Walter—

                         WALTER

Mama would listen to you. You know she listen
to you more than she do me and Bennie. She
think more of you, too. All you have to do is
just sit down with her when you drinking your
coffee one morning and talking 'bout things
like you do—(*He sits down beside her and
demonstrates graphically what he thinks her
methods and tone should be.*)—you just sip your
coffee, see, and say easy like that you been
thinking 'bout that deal Walter Lee is so
interested in, 'bout the store, and all, and
sip some more coffee, like what you saying
ain't really that important to you—and the next
thing you know, she be listening good and
asking you questions and when I come home—I can
tell her the details. This ain't no fly-by-night
proposition, baby. I mean we got it figured out,
me and Willy and Bobo.

                         RUTH

(*with a frown*) Bobo?

                         WALTER

Yeah. You see, this little liquor store we got
in mind cost seventy-five thousand and we figured
the initial investment on the place be 'bout
thirty thousand, see. That be ten thousand
each. Course, there's a couple of hundred you
got to pay so's you don't spend the rest of
your life just waitin' for them clowns to let
your license get approved—

RUTH

You mean graft?

WALTER

(*frowning impatiently*) Don't call it that. See
there, that just goes to show you what women
understand about the world. Baby, don't
nothing happen in this world 'less you pay
somebody off!

RUTH

Walter, leave me alone! (*She raises her head
and stares at him vigorously—then says, more
quietly.*) Eat your eggs, they gonna be cold.

WALTER

(*straightening up from her and looking off*)
That's it. There you are. Man say to his woman:
I got me a dream. His woman say: eat your eggs.
(*sadly, but gaining in power*) Man say: I got
to take hold of this here world, baby! And a
woman will say: Eat your eggs and go to work.
(*passionately now*) Man say: I got to change my
life. I'm choking to death, baby! And his woman
say—(*in utter anguish as he brings his fists
down on his thighs*)—Your eggs is getting cold!

RUTH

(*softly*) Walter, that ain't none of our money.

WALTER

(*not listening at all or even looking at her*)
This morning, I was lookin' in the mirror and
thinking about it . . . I'm thirty-five years old;
I been married eleven years and I got a boy who
sleeps in the living room—(*very, very quietly*)
and all I got to give him is stories about how
rich people live . . .

                              RUTH

Eat your eggs, Walter.

                             WALTER

Damn my eggs . . . damn all the eggs that ever
was!

                              RUTH

Then go to work.

                             WALTER

(*looking at her*) See—I'm trying to talk to you
'bout myself—(*shaking his head with the
repetition*)—and all you can say is eat them
eggs and go to work.

                              RUTH

(*wearily*) Honey, <u>you never say anything new. I
listen to you every day, every night, and every
morning, and you never say nothing new.</u>
(*shrugging*) <u>So you would rather be Mr. Arnold
than be his chauffeur.</u> So—I would rather be
living in Buckingham Palace.

                             WALTER

That's just what is wrong with the colored
women in this world. . . . Don't understand about
building their men up and making 'em feel like
they somebody. Like they can do something.

                              RUTH

(*dryly, but to hurt*) There are colored men who
do things.

                             WALTER

No thanks to the colored woman.

```
Well, being a colored woman, I guess I can't
help myself none.
```

Modern realistic treatment of background story is calculated to create the illusion of everyday life. This means that characters must be able to talk about the past while simultaneously advancing the story occurring on stage. Disclosing the past in this way does provide a surface feeling of credibility, but there is a tradeoff. Since the past is mixed up with the present, it's more difficult to distinguish between them during the rapid unfolding of the action, not to mention during the process of script analysis itself. This is further complicated by the fact that, in the retrospective method, unspoken implications and inferences play a much larger role than they do in historical narrative technique. It was said earlier in this chapter that clustering the background story into long speeches permits the writer to focus more attention on the present unfolding action. This is a substantial writing benefit for plays in which the action is as wideranging as it is in *Angels in America*. It may be the reason Tony Kushner elected to use the traditional method of revealing background story throughout most of the play, as in this passage of past events, character description, feelings, and sense impressions between the Angel and Prior. They are speaking of God's disappearance from heaven.

ANGEL

```
He began to leave US!
Bored with His Angels, Bewitched by Humanity,
In Mortifying imitation of You, his least
   creation,
He would sail off on Voyages, no knowing where
Quake follows wake,
Absence follows absence:
Nasty Chastity and Disorganization:
Loss of Libido, Protomatter Shortfall:
We are His Functionaries; It is
BEYOND US:
Then
April 18, 1906.
In That Day:
```

PRIOR

The Great San Francisco Earthquake. And
also . . .

ANGEL

In that day:

PRIOR

(*Simultaneously*) On April 18, 1906 . . .

ANGEL

Our Lover of the Million Unutterable Names, The
  Aleph Glyph from Which all Words Descend: The
  King of the Universe:
HE Left . . .

PRIOR

Abandoned.

ANGEL

And did not return.
We do not know where HE has gone. HE may
  never . . .
And bitter, Cast-off, We wait, bewildered;
Our finest houses, our sweetest vineyards,
Made dreary and barren, missing Him.

(*Coughs*)

PRIOR

Abandoned.

ANGEL

Yes.

The lesson to be learned about background story is that actors, directors, and designers need to exercise special attentiveness during analysis

and in performance and that audiences need to exercise attentive listening.

SUMMARY

We have been reviewing the topic of background story, noting how it is done and studying the adjustments playwrights have made to accommodate particular needs. We have seen that, since the background story is crowded with significant information, it is essential to know as much about it as possible and sometimes in exhausting detail. Another important part of learning about background story is understanding that for theatre artists it involves much more than the dry theoretical term exposition. Most readers who have followed the discussion so far should see that background story in plays is as dramatic as on-stage action. Often it is more so.

QUESTIONS

Technique   Is the background story disclosed in long speeches? In short statements? In subtle hints and veiled allusions? How reliable are the characters who disclose the background story? Is the background story disclosed near the beginning of the play? Throughout the entire play? Any disclosed near the end of the play? How much background story is there compared to on-stage action? Where does the action of the play begin in relation to the background story? In relation to the end of the action?

Identification   What specific events are disclosed in the background story? How long ago did they occur? What is the original chronology of events? In what order are the events disclosed in the play? Besides events, are there any character descriptions in the background story? Any feelings or sense impressions?

Summary   Write a complete report of each character's background story. Provide a complete report of the background story as told by all the characters.

After Action Analysis, search for the play's Seed, or Subject, hidden within the background story. How does the Seed influence the background story? Why did the playwright choose this specific background story from the whole range of other possibilities? How would the play be different with another background story? In what way does connecting the Seed with the background story help the play grow and develop?

CHAPTER 4

Plot: External and Internal Action

The word *plot* comes from the Old French word *complot*, meaning "a secret scheme." It has an added sense of its parts being closely packed together. Plot has parallel meanings related to secret intrigues or conspiracies and to suspense. Aristotle believed that plot was the first principle and the soul of drama. He described it as the imitation of the action and the arrangement of the incidents. He also said that a plot has a beginning, a middle, and an end and that it presents a single complete action.

Writers from Voltaire to Bertolt Brecht have debated Aristotle's statements about plot, but that is not of concern here. Most audiences, including actors, directors, and designers, expect some kind of plot, even if it is not apparent why they do. Plot means the story line, the sense that things are moving, that the play is getting somewhere, and that the action is moving forward. In this basic sense, plot serves to sustain interest in wanting to learn how everything does or doesn't come together in the end. It causes the questions "What happened?" "What is happening?" and "What is going to happen?"

It is not necessary to define plot more than this, but someone who tried would be obliged to deal with at least four basic principles: (1) External Action, (2) Internal Action, (3) Progressions, and (4) Structure. A plot could be deficient in one of these, but if that happened there would be a sense that something was missing or awry. A play with such an unfinished feeling seldom succeeds, at least on a popular level. External and Internal Action will be the organizing principles of this chapter. Chapter 5 will deal with the plot's progress and arrangement.

EXTERNAL ACTION

The first responsibility of plot is to provide the External Action needed to carry out the story in physical terms. Try to understand the plot on its most basic level, the level of what the characters are seen doing on stage. Stanislavski and his followers refer to this concept as *the first plan*. When external activity is specified in the dialogue, it is considered an elementary part of the plot. In his book, *Creating a Role*, Stanislavski used the term *Physical Action* to describe these basic external activities. He was interested in their role in stimulating the actor's imagination. He believed that for an actor the life of a play begins with Physical Actions then moves on to include Internal, or Psychological, Actions.

Once again when reading only for private study, there is no harm in supplementing the dialogue with the stage directions for information about External Action. In most cases, stage directions are a reasonably accurate record of the original production. If analysis is intended for a production, however, caution should be exercised using the stage directions as authority for anything. Formalist Analysis relies on the dialogue as much as possible. Even when there is no obvious External Action in the dialogue, it can usually be discovered by deduction without consulting other people's suggestions. Most of the interpretive External Action created by professionals does not come from the stage directions anyway but rather from information found in the dialogue.

Entrances and Exits

Entrances and exits in drama are equivalent to attack and release in music: they start and stop the action. The question they answer is, "Who precisely is (or was, or will be) on stage?" In a play, the action normally starts with an entrance and concludes with an exit (or a curtain or blackout, which are the same thing). Entrances and exits differ from one another in their characters and situations, but they all share the same components. Reading the dialogue in the literal sense is helpful to illustrate this lesson, but there is no obligation always to interpret dialogue factually in production.

The following simple example from early in *Oedipus Rex* shows Sophocles presenting an important entrance. Notice the use of repetition for reinforcement.

> CHORUS
>
> He is coming. Creon is coming.

Shakespeare infuses emotion into the following two examples from *Hamlet*. The first is Horatio's warning to Hamlet of the appearance of the Ghost; the second is the Ghost's departure.

> HORATIO
>
> Look, my lord, it comes!
>
> . . .
>
> GHOST
>
> Adieu, adieu, adieu! Remember me.

Molière includes both emotion and information about specific locale in this exit from *Tartuffe*.

> ORGON
>
> I'm so incensed . . . I shall have to go outside
> to recover myself.

Ibsen's talent for innuendo may be seen in the following entrance. Here Gina Ekdal chides her father-in-law for his tardiness while hinting that he has been drinking again. In the second example, Ibsen has concluded a family dispute with an exit that also involves information about character motivation. The third passage shows Ibsen using an exit to provoke a sense of "What's going to happen next?"

> GINA
>
> How late you are today, Grandfather!
>
> . . .

                         GREGERS

When I look back upon your past I seem to see a
battlefield with shattered lives on every hand.

                         WERLE

I begin to think that the chasm that divides us
is too wide.

                         GREGERS

(*bowing with self-command*) So I have observed,
and therefore I take my hat and go.

                         WERLE

You are going? Out of the house?

                         GREGERS

Yes. For at last I see my mission in life.

                         WERLE

What mission?

                         GREGERS

You would only laugh if I told you.

                          . . .

                         GREGERS

Put on your hat and coat, Hjalmar; I want you
to come for a long walk with me.

In this exit from *A Raisin in the Sun*, Mama Younger expresses her feelings about Beneatha's new boyfriend who has just left.

                         MAMA

Lord, that's a pretty thing just went out of
here!

For reasons we will discuss later in this book, Anton Chekhov seldom
wrote entrances or exits in the dialogue. Characters entering and exiting

unannounced is one of the features that promotes that unique sense of aimlessness in his plays. Examples of traditional entrances and exits, however, are not lacking. This passage from *Three Sisters* begins with an unannounced entrance by Andrey Prozorov and Dr. Chebutykin and ends with a statement about their exit. A few moments before, both characters have hurried off stage to avoid an embarrassing situation; now they're escaping to the club for an evening of cards. In this short "on-the-way" scene, the characters reveal meaningful information about themselves.

(*Andrey and Chebutykin come in quietly.*)

CHEBUTYKIN

I never got around to marrying because my life has just passed like lightning, and besides I was madly in love with your mother and she was married already.

ANDREY

One shouldn't get married, indeed one shouldn't. It's a bore.

CHEBUTYKIN

Yes, yes, that's a point of view, but there is such a thing as loneliness. You can argue about it as much as you like, but loneliness is a terrible thing. Though actually of course it doesn't matter.

ANDREY

Let's hurry up and get out of here.

CHEBUTYKIN

What's the rush? There's plenty of time.

ANDREY

I'm afraid my wife might stop me.

CHEBUTYKIN

Oh, I see.

ANDREY

I won't play cards tonight, I'll just sit and
watch. I feel a bit unwell. I get so out of
breath, is there anything I can do for it,
Doctor?

CHEBUTYKIN

Why ask me? I don't know, dear boy. I don't
remember.

ANDREY

Let's go out through the kitchen.

Entrances and exits deserve careful study. Who is coming and going and who is here are the most basic parts of the plot. Arrivals and departures often affect the action of a scene significantly. Moreover, as seen in the passage from *Three Sisters*, the surrounding dialogue can reveal information about character.

Blocking

Blocking is the movement and location of the characters on stage. The ability to visualize blocking while reading is an acquired skill, yet the spatial relationships among the characters are necessary to clarify the story and express emotion. Characters attract and repel each other like polarized magnets. They are close in climactic or affectionate moments and apart at other times. With careful reading, much of this type of blocking may be recognized in the dialogue.

Here are some examples of *indigenous blocking*, or External Action required for the practical execution of the plot. Such instances as these are needed to explain the logic of the events. In the first line, Oedipus provides a picture of the stage positions of the Chorus members as well as some of their costume accessories. The words *strewn* and *before* (in this translation, at least) indicate that the characters are located around the *thymele*, or central altar, which was a standard architectural feature of ancient Greek theatres.

OEDIPUS

```
My children . . .
Why have you strewn yourselves before these
  altars
In supplication, with your boughs and garlands?
```

Hamlet's following line in the mousetrap scene is both a stage direction and a sexual pun. Ophelia is seated on the floor before the Players' makeshift stage. Hamlet asks permission to lay his head on her lap while watching the play.

HAMLET

```
Lady, shall I lie in your lap?
```

In this line from *Tartuffe*, Elmire provides directions to Orgon for hiding under the table. He must avoid being seen by Tartuffe during the next scene. Her persistence shows that Orgon is a reluctant participant.

ELMIRE

```
Help me to bring the table up. Now get under
it . . . You shall see in due course. Get under
there and, mind now, take care that he doesn't
see or hear you.
```

A moment before the next line from *Death of a Salesman*, Biff has discovered his father in a hotel room with another woman. Willy hides her in the bathroom because he doesn't want Biff to see her.

WILLY

```
All right, stay in the bathroom here, and
don't come out. I think there's a law in
Massachusetts, so don't come out.
```

In *A Raisin in the Sun*, Nigerian student, Joseph Asagai, visits Beneatha's apartment. Her family is packing for their move to Clybourne Park. It is not an important entrance in itself, but his line contains hints about the stage picture and blocking as well as a little of the personal charm that makes him so attractive to Beneatha.

```
                    ASAGAI
    I came over . . . I had some free time. I thought
    I might help with the packing. Ah, I like the
    look of packing crates! A household in
    preparation for a journey!
```

In *A Lie of the Mind* there is the following passage between Frankie and Beth that contains blocking as well as an entrance.

```
(Sounds of Mike breathing heavily offstage.)


                    FRANKIE
    What's that? Beth? What's that sound? Is
    someone out there? Beth.
```

```
(Beth continues looking out over the porch.)

    Help me get back on the couch now. There's
    somebody coming.
```

Despite the abundance of External Action in *Angels in America*, little blocking is stated in the dialogue. In this context, the blocking that is stated becomes even more important, as in this sensitive passage between Louis and Joe.

```
(Joe reaches tentatively to touch Louis's face.)


                    LOUIS
    (Pulling back) What are you doing? Don't do
    that.


                    JOE
    (Withdrawing his hand) Sorry. I'm sorry.
```

LOUIS

I'm . . . just not . . . I think, if you touch me,
your hand might fall off or something. Worse
things have happened to people who have touched
me.

JOE

Please.
Oh, boy . . .
Can I . . .
I . . . want . . . to touch you. Can I please just
touch you . . . um, here?

(*He puts his hand on one side of Louis's face. He holds
it there.*)

I'm going to hell for doing this.

LOUIS

Big deal. You think it could be any worse than
New York City?

Use of Properties

A third type of External Action is the use of stage (i.e., furniture) or hand
properties. What makes their use special is their physical reality on
stage. Since properties are among the few things that are real in a performance, they provide a link with the real world and offer opportunities
for informative stage business. Like blocking, the use of properties has
both a logical and a dramatic aspect. Logic is served when characters use
properties to explain the story; drama is released when properties are
used for the expression of feelings.

After Hamlet has spoken with the Ghost, he makes his friends promise not to reveal what they have seen. His line shows that he is using
his sword on which his friends are expected to place their hands
ceremoniously.

HAMLET

```
Swear by my sword
Never to speak of this that you have heard,
```

This line from *The School for Scandal* requires close attention to the context of the improvised auction about to take place. There are three references to properties: (1) a chair used as the auctioneer's pulpit, (2) a parchment with a listing of the family tree, and (3) the same parchment used as an auctioneer's gavel.

CHARLES

```
But come, get to your pulpit, Mr. Auctioneer;
here's a gouty old chair of my grandfather's
will answer the purpose. . . . What parchment
have we here? Oh, our genealogy in full. Here,
Careless, you shall have no common bit of
mahogany, here's the family tree for you, you
rogue! This shall be your hammer. . . .
```

Hjalmar's warning to Hedvig about the pistol in *The Wild Duck* is an External Action that also prepares plot information. Playwrights call this practice *funding* or *foreshadowing*, terms that refer to the accumulation or disclosure of important information prior to an action.

HJALMAR

```
Don't touch that pistol, Hedvig! One of the
barrels is loaded, remember that.
```

In this line from *Mother Courage*, Anna Fierling shows her identity papers to the Sergeant. It's characteristic of Brecht to provide opportunities for character illustration through the use of ordinary, everyday objects like these.

MOTHER COURAGE

```
Here are my papers, Sergeant. There's a whole
missal, picked it up in Alt-Otting to wrap
cucumbers in, and a map of Moravia. . . .
```

The blessing near the end of *The Piano Lesson* involves the use of every-day properties that take on new meaning as part of a religious ceremony.

> AVERY
>
> Seem like that piano's causing all the trouble.
> I can bless that. Berniece, put me some water
> in that bottle . . . Hold this candle. Whatever
> you do, make sure it don't go out.

In *Three Sisters*, Olga removes clothing from a wardrobe and heaps it into Anfisa's arms. Olga is so distracted by the fire in town that she is indifferent to the fact that poor old Anfisa is exhausted. A few moments later Anfisa breaks down in the belief that she will be cast out of the household because she has grown too old to work.

> OLGA
>
> Here, this gray one—take it. . . . And this
> one here. . . . The blouse too . . . And take
> this skirt, Anfisa. . . . What is it, my God,
> Kirsanoffsky Street is burned to the ground.
> . . . Take this. . . . Take this. . . . The poor
> Vershinins were frightened. . . . Their house
> nearly burned up. They must spend the night
> here. . . . We can't let them go home. . . . At poor
> Fedotik's everything got burned, there's
> nothing left. . . .

> ANFISA
>
> You'll have to call Ferapont, Miss. I can't
> carry . . .

Prior Walter experiences a vision of the future when he puts on a pair of bronze spectacles in *Angels in America*. Stage directions play a role here, but the dialogue is the real source of information.

> PRIOR
>
> Oh, look at this. (*He puts them on.*)
> Like, wow, man, totally Paleozoic. This is . . .

(*He stops suddenly. His head jerks up. He is
seeing something.*) OH! OH GOD NO! OH . . . (*He
rips off the spectacles.*) That was terrible. I
don't want to see that.

Properties are meant to be significant when they are described in the dialogue as these are. Playwrights plan their properties to express dramatic effects.

Properties take on ritualistic values in the plays of Sam Shepard. The final scene in *A Lie of the Mind* contains dialogue devoted to Baylor's ceremonial folding of an American flag, the same ceremony that took place at the funeral for Jake's father. The flag folding, which is the visual background for the scene of Jake's reconcilement with Beth, is intended as a symbolic reenactment of that original funeral.

BAYLOR

(*Referring to the rifle.*) What're you doing with
that? . . . What's that wrapped around it?

MIKE

It's just a flag. He [Jake] had it on him. He
had it all wrapped around him. I wanted Beth to
come out so she could—

BAYLOR

It's not just a flag. That's the flag of our
nation. Isn't that the flag of our nation
wrapped around that rifle?

MIKE

Yeah, I guess so. I don't know. I'm tryin' to
tell you somethin' here. The flag's not the
issue!

BAYLOR

You don't know? You don't recognize the flag
anymore? It's the same color it always was.
They haven't changed it, have they? Maybe added

a star or two but otherwise it's exactly the
same. How could you not recognize it?

. . .

Don't let that flag touch the ground!

. . .

Gimme that flag! Hand it over to me! Hand it
over. Meg, come over here and help me fold this
flag. You remember how to fold a flag, don't you?

MEG

I'm not sure. Did I ever fold one before?

BAYLOR

Don't let it touch the ground now. Just back
away from me and we'll stretch it out first.
Don't let it touch the ground whatever you do.

MEG

I won't.

BAYLOR

Now there's a right way to do this and a wrong
way, Meg. I want you to pay attention.

MEG

I am.

BAYLOR

It's important.

. . .

BAYLOR

Now the stars have to end up on the outside. I
remember that much. Who's got the stars?

MEG

I do.

BAYLOR

Okay. Then I've gotta fold toward you. In
little triangles. You just stay put. . . . If
everything works out right we should have all
the stars on the outside and the stripes tucked
in.

MEG

Why do they do it like that?

BAYLOR

I don't know. Just tradition I guess. That's
the way I was taught. Funny how things
come hack to ya' after all those years.
There! Look at that! We did it! We did it, Meg!
I'll be gall-darned if we didn't do it. It's
letter perfect, looks like right outa the
manual.

Astute readers should be asking themselves why, in a play without many
properties, should this particular one undergo so much scrutiny in the
dialogue?

Special Activities

This group of External Actions comprises all the uncommon activities that are not covered under the previous topics. Examples include
stage combat, playing musical instruments, dancing, acrobatics, and
any other movements that may require special knowledge or skill on
the part of the actors. The distinctive attention warranted by lines
describing External Action is also true here. When playwrights make
an effort to describe unusual physical activities in their plays, it is
because they have endowed those activities with playable dramatic
possibilities.

Hamlet's accidental murder of Polonius with a sword is a turning point
in *Hamlet* and must be played as such. Polonius, of course, has been hiding behind the arras to eavesdrop on Hamlet.

POLONIUS

(*behind*) What ho! help, help, help!

HAMLET

(*draws*) How now! a rat?
Dead for a ducat, dead!

(*kills Polonius with a pass through the arras*)

POLONIUS

(*behind*) O, I am slain!

In *The Wild Duck*, Mrs. Sorby's piano playing is the subject of this line. When she returns to the adjoining room, she begins to play cheerful tunes on the piano. The music continues in the background during the next scene in which it serves as an ironic counterpoint to the quarrel between Gregers and his father.

GUEST

Shall we play a duet, Mrs. Sorby?

MRS. SORBY

Yes, suppose we do.

GUESTS

Bravo, bravo!

These three short lines from *The Hairy Ape* contain stage combat. Yank is on a rampage in jail. It takes several guards plus a water hose and a straightjacket to restrain him. There are only a few lines, but they describe a moment that is complicated to stage successfully.

GUARD

Hey, look at dat bar bended! On'y a bug is
strong enough for dat!

YANK

Or a hairy ape, yuh big yellow bum! Look out!
Here I come!

                              GUARD
      Toin on de hose, Ben!—full pressure. And call
      de others—and a straitjacket!

A Nigerian folk dance is the subject of these lines in *A Raisin in the Sun*.

                              RUTH
      What kind of dance is that?

                            BENEATHA
      A folk dance.

                              RUTH
      What kind of folks do that, honey?

                            BENEATHA
      It's from Nigeria. It's a dance of welcome.

Cleaning the floors of the barracks is one of the many special activities
in *Streamers*. The External Action may not seem important, but a closer
study shows that the act of cleaning relates to the main idea of the play.
Cleaning is a mindless ritualized experience in the military. The characters are trained in how to work according to standard procedures, using
Government Issue equipment. It is a small example of the types of dehu-
manizing activities the characters are forced to undergo in the play.

                              BILLY
      I'll go get some buckets and stuff so we can
      clean up, okay? This area's a mess. This area
      ain't standin' tall.

Angels in America contains prominent examples of activities not often
found in plays, notably same-sex sexual intercourse and kissing, sexual
intercourse with an angel, and male and female sexual climax, but also
an enactment of the Jewish prayer for the dead, characters dropping out
of the sky and ascending into heaven, the painful symptoms of AIDS, the
experience of being able to see into the future, and traveling through
space and time by means of hallucination. Near the climax of *Angels in*

America, Prior Walter wrestles with an angel, like Jacob in the famous Old Testament story. The frantic emotional course of their struggle is expressed in the dialogue.

> PRIOR
>
> I will not let thee go except thou bless me.
> Take back your Book. Anti-Migration, that's so
> feeble, I can't believe you couldn't do better
> than that, free me, unfetter me, bless me or
> whatever but I will be let go.

> ANGEL
>
> I I I I Am the
> CONTINENTAL PRICIPALITY OF AMERICA,
> I I I I
> AM THE BIRD OF PREY I WILL NOT BE COMPELLED,
> I . . .
>
> (*There is a great blast of music . . . and a
> ladder reaching up into infinity . . .*)

> ANGEL
>
> Entrance has been gained. Return the text to
> heaven.

> PRIOR
>
> (*Terrified*) Can I come back? I don't want to go
> unless . . .

> ANGEL
>
> (*Angry*) You have prevailed, Prophet. You . . .
> Choose.
> Now release me.
> I have a torn muscle in my thigh.

A knowledge of these and other special physical activities will help readers to appreciate their practical importance as well as their dramatic potential. The benefit is that when readers understand these special activities, they will be able to know how to use them to increase the emotional expressiveness of plays.

INTERNAL ACTION

Plot is often understood as External Action exclusively. According to this argument, plays with strong plots contain plenty of entrances and exits, hazards and rescues, and similar types of clever and interesting physical activities, but this is a misunderstanding. Plot is more than a collection of inventive activities; for besides its external features, it also occurs inside the characters, changing their inner states as well as their outer conditions. This internal dimension of the plot is referred to as *Internal*, or *Psychological*, *Action* to distinguish it from External Action or activity. Stanislavski's followers also call Internal Action *the second plan*.

Internal Action concerns the mental, spiritual, and/or emotional lives of the characters rather than their physical lives. When Internal Action is expressed in the dialogue, it appears in three forms: assertions, plans, and commands. There is nothing unusual or mysterious about these forms. They simply describe the attitude of the character toward what is being said. They are similar to the grammatical principle of mood, whether making an assertion (indicative mood), posing a future plan (subjunctive mood), or giving a command (imperative mood). In the following section, the way Internal Action is expressed in the words of the characters will be examined. Internal Action also has nonverbal characteristics that will be discussed in Chapter 5.

Assertions

Assertions are the simplest forms of Internal Action spoken in the dialogue. In one way or another, they appear on almost every page of a script. The principle behind an assertion needs little explaining. An assertion is a plain statement of fact, a positive declaration that something is true. Saying, for example, "The book is Jill's" or "John has arrived" or "it's five o'clock" is asserting the fact of the book's ownership or of John's whereabouts or the time of day. As a rule, assertions plainly identify people, places, things, or events like these. Several examples follow in which the dialogue is understood literally, but there are times when Internal Actions should not be read this way. Sometimes characters deceive themselves or lie. Even these occasions, however, are instructive because dialogue must be read literally before it can be read in other ways.

In the following lines from *The School for Scandal*, Rowley announces to Sir Peter Teazle the surprise arrival of Sir Oliver Surface in London. When working on a script, it is helpful to highlight the Internal Action so that it stands out from the rest of the dialogue. Therefore here, and in the rest of this chapter, the plot information is shown in bold.

ROWLEY

Sir Oliver is arrived, and at this moment is in town.

Rowley's announcement involves three clear assertions: (1) a person ("Sir Oliver"), (2) an event and time ("is arrived . . . at this moment"), and (3) a place ("in town").

The following moment from *The Wild Duck* consists of an assertion of an important event: that Hedvig Ekdal has shot herself. Note how repetition increases the impact.

RELLING

What's the matter here?

GINA

They say Hedvig shot herself.

HJALMAR

Come and help us!

RELLING

Shot herself!

When assertions involve serious offenses, they grow into accusations. In this selection from *Oedipus Rex*, Oedipus accuses Teiresias of conspiring with Creon to murder King Laius. Angry at this triple accusation of treason, conspiracy, and murder, Teiresias counters by accusing Oedipus of the murder. These two accusations are assertions about three persons and one event.

OEDIPUS

I'll tell you what I think:
You planned it, you had it done, you all but
killed him with your own hands: if you had
eyes, I'd say the crime was yours, and yours
alone.

TEIRESIAS

So? **I charge you,** then,
Abide by the proclamation you have made:
From this day forth
Never speak again to these men or to me;
You yourself are the pollution of this country.

Accusations also appear when Damis condemns Tartuffe for attempting to seduce Elmire: accusations involving a person (Tartuffe) and an event (the seduction). Note that the number of words devoted to plot is quite small. Most of the words in the passage describe Damis's feelings.

DAMIS

We have interesting news for you, father.
Something has just occurred which will astonish
you.

You are well repaid for your kindness! The
gentleman sets a very high value on the
consideration you have shown for him! **He has**
just been demonstrating his passionate concern
for you and he stops at nothing less than
dishonoring your bed. I have just overheard him
making a disgraceful declaration of his guilty
passion for your wife. She in kind-heartedness
and overanxiety to be discreet was all for
keeping it secret but I can't condone such
shameless behavior. I consider it would be a
gross injustice to you to keep it from you.

Notice in *The Piano Lesson* Berneice's insistent accusations that Boy Willie played a part in the death of her husband, Crawley, three years ago.

<blockquote>

BERNIECE

You killed Crawley just as sure as if you pulled the trigger.

. . .

Crawley ain't knew you stole that wood.

. . .

All I know is Crawley would be alive if you hadn't come up and got him.

. . .

Crawley's dead and in the ground and you still walking around here eating. That's all I know. He went off to load some wood with you and ain't never come back.

. . .

He ain't here, is he? He ain't here!

. . .

He ain't here, is he? Is he?

. . .

He ain't here.

. . .

You come up there and got him!

</blockquote>

Three characters and five assertions appear in this passage from *Mother Courage*. First, Swiss Cheese asserts that he did not steal the payroll. Second, the Sergeant asserts that Mother Courage was an accomplice in the theft. Third, Swiss Cheese asserts that she had nothing to do with it. Fourth, Swiss Cheese asserts that he is innocent. Fifth, Mother Courage asserts that she does not know Swiss Cheese. The moment moves quickly, but it is important because it shows Mother Courage denying her own son, even if for justifiable reasons.

<blockquote>

(*Voices are heard from the rear. The two men bring in Swiss Cheese.*)

</blockquote>

SWISS CHEESE

Let me go. **I haven't got anything.** Stop twisting my shoulder, **I'm innocent.**

THE SERGEANT

He belongs here. **You know each other.**

MOTHER COURAGE

What makes you think that?

SWISS CHEESE

I don't know them. I don't even know who they are. I had a meal here, it cost me ten hellers. Maybe you saw me sitting here, it was too salty.

THE SERGEANT

Who are you anyway?

MOTHER COURAGE

We're respectable people. And it's true. He had a meal here. He said it was too salty.

THE SERGEANT

Are you trying to tell me you don't know each other?

MOTHER COURAGE

Why should I know him? I don't know everybody. I don't ask people what their name is or if they're heartless; if they pay, they're not heathens.

Assertions can be composed of announcements, identifications, accusations, and even rhetorical questions, meaning questions that assert or deny something strongly by asking it as a question. In any form, assertions are basic components of the plot. Consider them the internal anchors that hold the plot in place. Actors and directors should see to it that such elementary information is not underplayed in performance.

Plans

A *plan* is any detailed method, formulated beforehand, for doing something. Some plans are very simple, as in "First we'll meet at Mike's house, then we'll go to the movies." Or they may be elaborate, with complex sets of dependent actions leading to a final goal, like the plans for landing an astronaut on the moon. Because plans are a practical, economical method for advancing the plot, their use in plays is everywhere. As the following examples show, playwrights with diverse styles have made use of plans in a wide assortment of dramatic circumstances.

An illustration of a simple and direct plan occurs in *Mother Courage* when Anna Fierling hides the platoon's cash box. She is afraid that her son will be charged with the theft.

> MOTHER COURAGE
> **I'd better get the cash box out of here, I've found a hiding place.** All right, get me a drink. (*Kattrin goes behind the wagon.*) **I'll hide it in the rabbit hole down by the river until I can take it away. Maybe late tonight. I'll go get it and take it to the regiment.**

Hamlet's well-known lines also describe a plan, in this case, one that has profound results. An event in the background story sets up the plan.

> HAMLET
> I have heard
> That guilty creatures, sitting at a play,
> Have by the very cunning of the scene
> Been struck so to the soul that presently
> They have proclaim'd their malefactions;
> **I'll have these players**
> **Play something like the murder of my father**
> **Before mine uncle. I'll observe his looks;**

> I'll tent him to the quick. If'a do blench,
> I know my course.
> **The play's the thing**
> **Wherein I'll catch the conscience of the King.**

Later in the play Claudius arranges a plan with Laertes to use an un-bated foil (that is, without a protective button on the point) tipped with poison to murder Hamlet. Shakespeare is praised for maintaining the rhythm of his verse even when he is describing ordinary actions like those described in these lines.

CLAUDIUS

> But good Laertes,
> Will you do this? **Keep close within your**
> **chamber.**
> **Hamlet return'd shall know you are come home.**
> **We'll put on those shall praise your**
> **excellence,**
> And set a double varnish on the fame
> The Frenchman gave you; **bring you, in fine,**
> **together,**
> **And wager on your heads.** He, being remiss,
> Most generous, and free from all contriving,
> **Will not peruse the foils; so that with ease**
> **Or with a little shuffling, you may choose**
> **A sword unbated, and, in a pass of practice,**
> **Requite him for your father.**

In *Tartuffe*, Dorine prepares an elaborate plan to frustrate Orgon's earlier plan to marry his daughter, Mariane, to Tartuffe. Mariane's boyfriend Valere helps her.

DORINE

> We'll try everything we can. Your father can't
> be serious and it's all sheer rubbish, but **you**
> **had better pretend to fall in with his nonsense**
> **and give the appearance of consenting so that**
> **if it comes to the point you'll more easily be**

able to delay the marriage. If we can only gain time we may easily set everything right. **You can complain of sudden illness that will necessitate delay; another time you can have recourse to bad omens—such as having met a corpse or broken a mirror or dreamt of muddy water.** Finally, the great thing is that they can't make you his wife unless you answer "I will." **But I think, as a precaution, you had better not be found talking together.** (*to Valere*) **Off you go and get all your friends to use their influence with her father to stand by his promise. We must ask his brother to try once again, and see if we can get the stepmother on our side.**

In *The Wild Duck*, Gregers' advice to Hedvig proves to be a misguided plan because it results in her death.

GREGERS

(*coming a little nearer*) **But suppose you were to sacrifice the wild duck of your own free will for his sake?**

HEDVIG

(*rising*) The wild duck!

GREGERS

Suppose you were to make a free-will offering, for his sake, of the dearest treasure you have in the world?

HEDVIG

Do you think that would do any good?

GREGERS

Try it, Hedvig.

HEDVIG

(*softly, with flashing eyes*) Yes, I will try it.

GREGERS

Have you really the courage for it, so you
think?

HEDVIG

**I'll ask grandfather to shoot the wild duck for
me.**

GREGERS

**Yes, do. But not a word to your mother about
it.**

HEDVIG

Why, not?

GREGERS

She doesn't understand us.

HEDVIG

The wild duck! I'll try it tomorrow morning.

Three Sisters is about plans that never materialize. One plan that does
materialize, unfortunately, is Lieutenant Solyony's duel with Baron
Tuzenbach, which is explained to Andrey and Masha in this passage by
Dr. Chebutykin.

CHEBUTYKIN

**Solyony began to pick on the Baron and he lost
his temper and insulted him, and it finally got
to the point where Solyony had to challenge him
to a duel.** (*Looks at his watch.*) **It's time now,
I believe. At half-past twelve, in the forest
over there,** the one we can see from here,
beyond the river. . . . Oh, well, who really
cares. Solyony imagines he's the poet Lermontov

> and he even writes verses. Now a joke is a
> joke, but this is the third duel for him.

Some plans have a larger scope and can form a whole new direction for a character's actions. Acts 1 and 3 of *A Lie of the Mind* are supported by Jake's unspoken plan to atone for the sins of his past and by Beth's unarticulated plan to start a new life. Act 2,3 consists of Lorraine's plans for a new life after she comes to terms with Jake's disposition toward violence. Boy Willie's plan to buy some land with the proceeds from the sale of his sister's piano drives the plot of *The Piano Lesson.* The connecting thread in Part I of *Angels in America* is Roy Cohn's plan to place a confederate (Joe Pitt) in the Justice Department so Cohn can blackmail his enemies.

Plans are productive Internal Actions to study because they appear in the dialogue openly as plans. Their treatment seldom varies. First the characters discuss the tactical details, then they put them into effect. Plans provide demonstrations of how Internal Action advances the plot.

Commands

A *command* is a statement with a built-in feeling of necessity, as in, "This must be done!" The following excerpts demonstrate different kinds of commands.

When Claudius commands Hamlet to leave for England, he is expressing his authority as king.

> CLAUDIUS
> **Hamlet, this deed,** for thine especial safety—
> Which we do tender, as we dearly grieve
> For that which thou hast done—**must send thee
>   hence**
> **With fiery quickness. Therefore prepare thyself;**
> The bark is ready, and the wind at help,
> Th' associates tend, and everything is bent
> **For England.**

HAMLET

For England!

Orgon takes advantage of his paternal authority when he commands his daughter, Mariane, to marry Tartuffe.

ORGON

What have you to say about our guest Tartuffe?

MARIANE

What have I to say?

ORGON

Yes, you! Mind how you answer.

MARIANE

Oh dear! I'll say anything you like about him.

ORGON

That's very sensible. Then **let me hear you say, my dear, that he is a wonderful man, that you love him, and you'd be glad to have me choose him for your husband.** Eh?

Mama Younger expresses another kind of parental authority in this command from *A Raisin in the Sun*. In the preceding moment, her daughter Beneatha has rejected the need for God in her life.

(*Mama absorbs [Beneatha's] speech, studies her daughter and rises slowly and crosses to Beneatha and slaps her powerfully across the face. After, there is only silence and the daughter drops her eyes from her mother's face, and Mama is very tall before her.*)

MAMA

Now—you say after me, in my mother's house there is still God. (*There is a long pause and Beneatha stares at the floor wordlessly. Mama* *repeats the phrase with precision and cool emotion.*) **In my mother's house there is still God.**

BENEATHA

In my mother's house there is still God. (*a long pause*)

MAMA

(*walking away from Beneatha, too disturbed for triumphant posture. Stopping and turning back to her daughter.*) **There are some ideas we ain't going to have in this house.** Not as long as I am the head of this family.

BENEATHA

Yes, ma'am.

The following passage contains military commands as expressed in David Rabe's *Streamers*. The military police have arrived in the cadre room and discover that two soldiers have been murdered.

(*As a Military Police Lieutenant comes running in the door, his .45 automatic drawn, and he levels it at Roger.*)

LIEUTENANT

Freeze, soldier! Not a quick move out of you. Just real slow, straighten your ass up.

(*Roger has gone rigid; the Lieutenant is advancing on him. Tentatively, Roger turns, looks.*)

ROGER

Huh? No.

LIEUTENANT

Get your ass against the lockers.

                                    ROGER

Sir, no. I—

                                  LIEUTENANT

(*hurling Roger away toward the wall lockers*)
MOVE! (*As another M.P., Pfc Hinson, comes in,
followed by Richie, flushed and breathless*)
Hinson, cover this bastard.

                                   HINSON

(*drawing his .45 automatic, moving on Roger*)
Yes, sir.

(*The Lieutenant frisks Roger, who is spread-
eagled at the lockers.*)

                                   RICHIE

What? Oh, sir, no, no. Roger, what's going on?

                                  LIEUTENANT

I'll straighten this shit out.

                                    ROGER

Tell him to get the gun off me, Richie.

                                  LIEUTENANT

SHUT UP!

                                   RICHIE

But, sir, sir, he didn't do it. Not him.

                                  LIEUTENANT

(*Fiercely he shoves Richie out of the way.*)
I told you, all of you, to shut up.

These commands given by Winnie to her husband, Willie, reveal an
important dimension of their relationship in Beckett's play *Happy Days*.
Readers will recall that in this offbeat fantasy, Winnie is buried up to her

waist in an earthen hill and Willie is almost buried out of sight behind her.

>   WINNIE
>
> (*She cranes [her neck] back and down.*) **Go back
> into your hole now, Willie, you've exposed
> yourself enough.** (*Pause.*) **Do as I say, Willie,
> don't lie sprawling there in this hellish sun,
> go back into your hole.** (*Pause.*) **Go on now,
> Willie.** (*Willie invisible [to the audience]
> starts crawling left towards hole.*) That's the
> man. (*She follows his progress with her eyes.*)
> **Not head first, stupid, how are you going to
> turn**? (*Pause.*) **That's it . . . right round . . . now
> . . . back in.** (*Pause.*) Oh I know it's not easy,
> dear, crawling backwards, but it is rewarding
> in the end. (*Pause.*) **You have left your
> Vaseline behind.** (*She watches as he crawls back
> for Vaseline.*) **The lid!** (*She watches as he
> crawls back towards the hole. Irritated.*) **Not
> head first, I tell you!** (*Pause.*) **More to the
> right.** (*Pause.*) **The right, I said.** (*Pause.
> Irritated.*) **Keep your tail down, can't you!**
> (*Pause.*) **Now.** (*Pause.*) **There!** (*All these
> directions loud. Now in her normal voice, still
> turned towards him.*) Can you hear me? (*Pause.*)
> **I beseech you, Willie, just say yes or no, can
> you hear me, just yes or nothing.**

The Angel in *Angels in America* pronounces a series of commands to Prior Walter, who is not enthusiastic about obeying.

>   ANGEL
>
> **Greetings, Prophet!
> The Great Work Begins:
> The Messenger has Arrived.**

>   PRIOR
>
> **Go away.**

ANGEL

Attend:

PRIOR

Oh God there's a thing in the air, a thing, a
thing.

ANGEL

I I I
Am the Bird Of America, the Bald Eagle,
Continental Principality,
LUMEN PHOSPHOR FLUOR CANDLE!
I unfold my leaves, Bright steel,
In salutation open sharp before you:
PRIOR WALTER
Long-descended, well-prepared . . .

PRIOR

No, I'm not prepared, for anything, I have lots
to do, I . . .

ANGEL

American Prophet tonight you become,
American Eye that pierceth Dark,
American Heart all Hot for Truth,
The True Great Vocalist, the Knowing Mind,
Tongue-of-the-Land, Seer-Head!

PRIOR

Oh, Shoo! You're scaring the shit out of me, **get**
the fuck out of my room. Please, oh Please . . .

ANGEL

Now:
Remove from their hiding place the Sacred
Prophetic Implements.

(*Little pause*)

PRIOR

The *what*?

ANGEL

**Remove from their hiding place the Sacred
Prophetic Implements.**

(*Little pause*)
Your dreams have revealed them to you.

PRIOR

What dreams?

ANGEL

You have had dreams revealing to you . . .

PRIOR

**I haven't had a dream I can remember in
months.**

ANGEL

No . . . dreams, you . . . Are you sure?

PRIOR

Yes, Well, the two dead Priors, they . . .

ANGEL

No not the heralds, not them. Other dreams.
Implements, you must have . . . **One moment.**

PRIOR

This, this is a dream, obviously, I'm sick and
so I. . . . Well OK it's a pretty spectacular
dream but it's still just some . . .

ANGEL

Quiet. Prophet. A moment, please, I. . . . The
disorganization is . . .

(*She coughs, looks up*) He says he hasn't had
any . . .

(*Coughs*)
In the kitchen. Under the tiles in the sink.

PRIOR

You want me to . . . tear up the kitchen floor?

ANGEL

**Get a shovel or an axe or some . . . tool for
dislodging tile and grout and unearth the
Sacred Implements.**

PRIOR

No fucking way! The ceiling's bad enough, I'll
lose the lease, I'll lose my security deposit,
I'll wake the downstairs neighbors, their
hysterical dog, I. . . . **Do it yourself.**

ANGEL

(*A really terrifying voice*) **SUBMIT, SUBMIT TO
THE WILL OF HEAVEN!**

Commands push the play forward with events the characters must
strive to carry out. Close reading will also disclose the presence of *driving characters*, strong-willed characters who introduce the plans needed
to drive the plot. Villains, for example, produce plenty of evil plans.

SUMMARY

Both External and Internal Action are important for understanding plot.
External Action includes entrances and exits, blocking, use of properties, and special physical activities that contribute to the basic story.
Internal Action consists of assertions, plans, and commands that
comprise the psychological story. Every assertion, plan, and command
contributes to the forward motion of the plot. Accordingly, actors and

directors will wish to *point* these moments (embellish them theatrically) to make sure that the characters effectively express the plot information. Designers who are sensitized to the function of entrances and exits in the plot may find it easier to determine their most expressive form and placement within the scenic space. In other words, once the External and Internal Actions are known, there is an obligation to illustrate them as powerfully as possible on stage, through performance or design or both. Fortunately, we are aided in this by the emotional dynamics and arrangement of the plot, which will be discussed in the next chapter.

QUESTIONS

External Action   Identify the entrances and exits in the dialogue. How do they contribute to the development of the plot? Are there any movements or positions of the characters in the dialogue? What function do they play in progressing the plot? Are there any practical uses of properties in the dialogue? Are any special activities in the dialogue, like dancing, fighting, cooking, or anything else besides regular blocking or use of properties? Do they advance the plot or do they have some other purpose?

Internal Action   Locate and highlight all the important assertions (including identifications and accusations) about people, places, things, and events that take place in the present action. Any detailed plans for doing something? How do they advance the plot? Any commands issued by a power figure? Any official orders given by someone exercising political or military authority? Any directions or instructions in the form of supervision or teaching? Describe how each of these Internal Actions moves the story ahead.

POSTSCRIPT FOR ACTION ANALYSIS

External and Internal Action and the Seed: After Action Analysis, search for the play's Seed, or Subject, hidden within the External and Internal

Actions. How does the Seed influence the External and Internal Actions? Why did the playwright choose these specific External and Internal Actions from the whole range of possibilities? How would the play be different with other External and Internal Actions? In what way does connecting the Seed with the External and Internal Actions help the play grow and develop?

CHAPTER 5

Plot: Progressions and Structure

There is a progressive growth in a play that is designed to achieve maximum dramatic effect. Actors, directors, and designers concerned with craftsmanship should learn to understand and illustrate this process. For if all the events give the impression of being equally important or their relationship to each other or to the whole play is ignored, the result will be misreading and artistic disorder. The resulting performance will be banal. A production that is "flat," that is, lacking in emotional dynamics, is a sign that too little attention has been given to this issue.

PROGRESSIONS

Plays are written to create the impression that things are moving, that they are getting somewhere. By this we don't always mean a chronological movement but sometimes a psychological one. Even in a play without much obvious External Action, one like *Happy Days* or *Three Sisters*, the plot is always advancing. The feeling of forward motion comes from the dramatist's method of always making the next event more interesting than the last. We're uncomfortable when our interest in the play declines or if there is a feeling of going backwards. We're not even satisfied to maintain the same level of interest. Forward motion is a fundamental necessity of plot.

But a plot does not progress at the same rate throughout the entire play. That would be almost as uninteresting as no forward motion at all. What happens is this: a question is introduced and developed to an emotional peak, and then a new question is introduced that begins to grow toward another peak. Emotional intensity may drop a little after the first peak, but interest will not fade because a new question will emerge and begin moving toward another peak almost immediately. This is how a play moves forward in progressions, which rise, crest, and fall away like waves on the seashore.

Progressions are arranged in groups according to size, called *beats, units, scenes,* and *acts*. Literature employs progressions too, called *sentences, paragraphs, chapters,* and *books*. In drama as in literature, progressions help to create interest, maintain suspense, develop the story logically, and bring everything to a satisfactory conclusion. The study of progressions begins by subdividing the play into a chain of storytelling pieces. After this has been done, it becomes possible to determine the inner logic that connects them. From this process, the dramatic story of the play emerges.

Since progressions are also related to character, some readers may be concerned that we do not discuss character objectives and actions at this point in the book. The principal reason is learning ease. In this chapter, we are interested in the basic storytelling function of progressions, and the main task is to identify them by studying the external features of the story. Some of the descriptions we will use are not actions or objectives in the sense employed by Stanislavski and his followers. Plot may be discussed without always using Stanislavski's vocabulary for analyzing characters. A reasonable explanation of the external activities of the characters is satisfactory at this point and saves time. Chapter 6 will consider how progressions also influence character. There is no pressing need to stick with this strategy. Readers who wish to study character objectives and actions before learning about beats and units can jump ahead to Chapter 6 for that information then return to this chapter.

Beats

The smallest dramatic progressions are called *beats*. In a play, these work like paragraphs in prose, but without their visible identification marks.

Their purpose is identical, namely, to introduce, develop, and conclude a single small topic that adds to the progress of the plot. Any collection of related lines can compose a beat as long as it expresses a single, complete topic (or action, objective, or conflict as we will see in Chapter 6). A typical beat consists of about six lines of dialogue, but many are longer or shorter, and some contain only physical or psychological action with little or no dialogue. The requirements are flexible. The length, internal arrangement, and purpose may vary according to the playwright's intentions and personal style.

Beats are indispensable features of playwriting and can be identified objectively in the script. Different readers analyzing the same play should arrive at the same pattern of beats. Unfortunately, we are so accustomed to seeing dialogue flow uninterrupted on the page that we may not realize how much the practice of grouping by beats helps our understanding. But the effect of dialogue without beats is like a passage of prose without paragraphing. It is almost impossible to make sense of a continuous river of dialogue undivided into beats. Disregarding beats means always having to deal with countless seemingly unrelated lines. Script analysis identifies beats and forces them into the open where they can be used by actors and directors.

At this point, consider two pieces of advice about beats. First, even though beats are present in the script, it is easy to become confused when trying to identify them. Beats are there for a reason, but some playwrights are crafty and inventive with their writing. Even though they should ensure that their subject is always clear, in practice many of them disguise what's happening. After all, plays are meant to be art, not science. A special illusive or indefinite quality is often part of the experience. Readers should make allowances for beats that aim at artistic effects where the playwright's objective is to keep the audience guessing, for the sake of a delayed surprise, for example. Even when authors do not try to conceal their subjects, learning about beats can still be frustrating initially. It is natural to experience confusion at first because learning to recognize beats takes practice. Try not to become trapped in endless mental gymnastics, but make an educated guess, then test the results in rehearsals. The first part of the rehearsal period is normally used to identify and explain the beats in the play anyhow.

Second, in a book on script analysis we are talking about beats in the written part of the play, or *textual beats.* In the vocabulary of some actors and directors, the term beat sometimes also refers to an independent physical acting task—for example, eating a meal or packing a suitcase— within the context of a scene. Understanding textual beats can help in the performance of so-called acting beats, but there is not always a point-to-point correlation.

To understand textual beats, we will look at the opening moments of David Rabe's play, *Streamers*. The setting is the cadre room in an army training camp a few years before the Vietnam conflict became a major war. It is evening. The play begins as Richie has interrupted Martin's latest suicide attempt. Beats are not explicit in a play, so we have illustrated them here with a solid line marked through the script. This is a useful practice for actors and directors to get into the habit of doing. In addition, studying the words of one character at a time can make the topics of conversation and their associated beats easier to comprehend.

```
Beat 1


                          RICHIE
        Honest to God, Martin, I don't know what to say
        anymore. I don't know what to tell you.


                          MARTIN
        (beginning to pace again) I mean it. I just
        can't stand it. Look at me.


                          RICHIE
        I know.


                          MARTIN
        I hate it.


                          RICHIE
        We've got to make up a story. They'll ask you a
        hundred questions.


                          MARTIN
        Do you know how I hate it?
```

RICHIE

Everybody does. Don't you think I hate it, too?

MARTIN

I enlisted, though. I enlisted and I hate it.

RICHIE

I enlisted, too.

MARTIN

I vomit every morning. I get the dry heaves. In the middle of every night.

(*He flops down on the corner of Billy's bed and sits there, slumped forward, shaking his head.*)

Beat 2

RICHIE

You can stop that. You can.

MARTIN

No.

RICHIE

You're just scared. It's just fear.

MARTIN

They're all so mean, they're all so awful. I've got two years to go. Just thinking about it is going to make me sick. I thought it would be different from the way it is.

RICHIE

But you could have died, for God's sake.

(*Richie has turned now; he is facing Martin.*)

                              MARTIN
      I just wanted out.

                              RICHIE
      I might not have found you, though. I might not
      have come up here.

                              MARTIN
      I don't care. I'd be out.

      (*The door opens, and a black man in filthy fatigues—they
      are grease-stained and dark with sweat—stands there. He
      is Carlyle, looking about. Richie, seeing him, rises and
      moves toward him.*)

    This conversation consists of two beats. We said before that an important storytelling function of beats is to disclose a new topic. In the first beat, the topic is Martin's hatred of military life and his appeal for sympathy. This appears in his line, "Do you know how I hate it?" Richie protects Martin from further harm as can be seen in his line, "We've got to make up a story." The beat rises to a small crescendo at the moment Martin flops on Billy's bed, and it ends there. It contains ten lines and concludes with a decisive physical action, flopping on the bed.

    The second beat begins with Richie's line "You can stop that. You can." He warns Martin about the serious consequences. Martin, on the other hand, wishes to show Richie why he needs to get out of the Army so badly. He specifies this in his line beginning, "They're all so mean." The beat lasts for eight lines and ends with Carlyle's entrance. A physical action punctuates this beat also, Carlyle's entrance. To summarize the topics that constitute these two beats:

Beat 1: Martin appeals for sympathy and Richie protects him.
Beat 2: Martin wants out at any cost and Richie warns against it.

There may be other ways to describe these two beats, but at least the reasons for choosing these descriptions should be clear. Notice too this important feature, almost a law of dramatic writing: in each beat, the characters are restricted to one small topic, and after that topic is finished, there is no longer any need to talk about it. The characters may discuss additional issues related to the original topic, but they will never again repeat the topic in the same way or with the same intention. Without this economy, the dialogue we've just studied would have a negligent, unfinished feeling about it. Again, readers should remember that there are other ways to describe beats, and Chapter 6 will present some of them for study. In this chapter, the only concern is their most obvious role in the advancement of the plot.

Units

Beats follow each other without a break but are not lined up end-to-end without connections. They are interrelated and act together with one another in the development of larger progressions called *units*. In other words, while a beat is a group of related lines, a unit is a group of related beats. Compare beats with *musical measures*—groups of related notes, and units with *musical phrases*—groups of related measures. What distinguishes beats from units is their relative influence in a play. A unit is larger and more influential because it contains several beats.

Some writers maintain that units are different from beats because of size difference and all-around importance, while others use the two terms interchangeably. Can these two points of view be reconciled? To clarify the question, it might be helpful to look at the historical picture. Following the practice of Russian formalist critics, Stanislavski employed the procedure of subdividing a play into its component pieces. He explained the process in his book, *An Actor Prepares*, where he spoke of the subdivisions in the Russian edition as *kouski*, meaning *pieces*. He didn't make any further size distinctions except to speak of larger pieces (*bolshe kouski*), medium pieces (*sredni kouski*), and smaller pieces (*menshe kouski*). In her English translation of *An Actor Prepares*, Elizabeth Hapgood designated the larger pieces as *units* and the smaller ones as *bits*. According to Hapgood, the term beat first appeared when Russian teachers of Stanislavski's system in America used the same English terms, only mispronouncing the word *bit*. So initially there was a size distinction. Bits (beats) were finer subdivisions of pieces (units).

Stanislavski was interested in the larger progressions (units), and Hapgood's English terms were chosen to represent his viewpoint. He maintained that analysis of beats might sometimes be necessary to disclose the subtleties within a unit, but he did not believe in dealing with more subdivisions than necessary. The lessons are two: (1) beats are subdivisions of units and (2) it is easier to come to terms with a smaller quantity of larger progressions than a larger quantity of smaller progressions. These are historical distinctions, of course, and they should always be adapted to suit our own needs.

To explain units, we will study the remaining beats that comprise the first unit of *Streamers*.

Beat 3

(*The door opens and a black man in filthy fatigues—they are grease-stained and dark with sweat—stands there. He is Carlyle, looking about. Richie, seeing him, rises and moves toward him.*)

                    RICHIE
    No, Roger isn't here right now.

                    CARLYLE
    Who isn't?

                    RICHIE
    He isn't here.

                    CARLYLE
    They told me a black boy livin' in here. I
    don't see him. (*He looks suspiciously about the
    room.*)

                    RICHIE
    That's what I'm saying. He isn't here. He'll be
    back later. You can come back later. His name
    is Roger.

Beat 4

                    MARTIN
    I slit my wrist.

(Thrusting out the bloody, towel-wrapped wrist toward Carlyle.)

                         RICHIE
     Martin! Jesus!

                         MARTIN
     I did.

                         RICHIE
     He's kidding. He's kidding.

                         CARLYLE
     What's was his name? Martin?

(Carlyle is confused and the confusion has made him angry. He moves toward Martin.)

     You Martin?

                         MARTIN
     Yes.

Beat 5

(As Billy, a white in his mid-twenties, blond and trim, appears in the door, whistling, carrying a slice of pie on a paper napkin. Sensing something, he falters, looks at Carlyle, then Richie.)

                         BILLY
     Hey, what's goin' on?

                         CARLYLE
     (turning, leaving) Nothin, man. Not a thing.

Beat 6

(*Billy looks questioningly at Richie. Then, after placing the piece of pie on the chair beside the door, he crosses to his footlocker.*)

                    RICHIE
    He came here looking for Roger, but he didn't
    even know his name.

                    BILLY
    (*Sitting on his footlocker, he starts taking off his shoes.*) How come you weren't at dinner,
    Rich? I brought you a piece of pie. Hey,
    Martin.

Beat 7

(*Martin thrusts out his towel-wrapped wrist.*)

                    RICHIE
    Oh, for God's sake, Martin!

                    BILLY
    Huh?

                    MARTIN
    I did.

                    RICHIE
    You are disgusting, Martin.

                    MARTIN
    No. It's the truth. I did. I am not disgusting.

                    RICHIE
    Well, maybe it isn't disgusting, but it
    certainty is disappointing.

                              BILLY
        What are you guys talking about?

(*Sitting there, he really doesn't know what is going on.*)

                              MARTIN
        I cut my wrists. I slashed them, and Richie is
        pretending I didn't.

                              RICHIE
        I am not. And you only cut one wrist and you
        didn't slash it.

Beat 8

                              MARTIN
        I can't stand the army anymore, Billy.

(*He is moving now to petition Billy, and Richie steps
between them.*)

                              RICHIE
        Billy, listen to me. This is between Martin and
        me.

                              MARTIN
        It's between me and the army, Richie.

                              RICHIE
        (*Taking Martin by the shoulders as Billy is now
        trying to get near Martin.*) Let's just go
        outside and talk, Martin. You don't know what
        you're saying.

                              BILLY
        Can I see? I mean, did he really do it?

                              RICHIE

          No!

                              MARTIN

          I did.

                              BILLY

          That's awful. Jesus. Maybe you should go to the
          infirmary.

                              RICHIE

          I washed it with peroxide. It's not deep. Just
          let us be. Please. He just needs to straighten
          out his thinking a little, that's all.

                              BILLY

          Well, maybe I could help him?   .

                              MARTIN

          Maybe he could.

Beat 9

                              RICHIE

          (Suddenly pushing at Martin, Richie is angry
          and exasperated. He wants Martin out of the
          room.) Get out of here, Martin. Billy, you do
          some push-ups or something.

          (Having been pushed towards the door, Martin wanders
          out.)

                              BILLY

          No.

                              RICHIE

          I know what Martin needs.

(Richie whirls and rushes into the hall after Martin,
leaving Billy scrambling to get his shoes on.)

>   BILLY
> You're no doctor, are you? I just want to make
> sure he doesn't have to go to the infirmary,
> then I'll leave you alone.

(One shoe on, he grabs up the second and runs out the
door into the hall after them.)

> Martin! Martin, wait up!

(Silence. The door has been left open. Fifteen or twenty
seconds pass. Then someone is heard coming down the
hall. . . .)

From what we know so far, the locus of dramatic interest in the unit seems to be Martin's attempted suicide. We count nine beats in all. In the third beat, Carlyle enters and demands to know where Roger is. The fourth beat is Martin's attempt to gain sympathy from Carlyle by showing him his injured wrist. Billy enters and Carlyle exits in the fifth beat. In the sixth beat, Martin attempts to gain Billy's sympathy. Richie scolds Martin in the seventh beat. In the eighth beat, Billy attempts to help Martin, and in the ninth beat, Richie leaves with Martin. This represents one unit or one full step in the story's progress. The topic of conversation is Martin's attempted suicide. The next unit begins with the tenth beat when someone is heard coming down the hall.

In outline form, the composition of the first unit may be described as follows:

Unit 1: Martin's attempted suicide.
>   Beat 1: Martin appeals to Richie for sympathy.
>   Beat 2: Martin wants to escape.
>   Beat 3: Carlyle enters.
>   Beat 4: Martin appeals to Carlyle for sympathy.
>   Beat 5: Billy enters; Carlyle exits.
>   Beat 6: Martin appeals to Billy for sympathy.

Beat 7: Richie scolds Martin.
Beat 8: Billy offers to help Martin.
Beat 9: Richie departs with Martin.

There may be disagreement about the exact wording of this outline. Some of the items, for example, cannot be considered actions or objectives in the strict sense, just loose descriptions of external activities. It should make the basic principle at stake at least understandable. Each beat has a distinct identity, but it also interacts with other beats in the development of its parent unit, itself distinct from other units. And everything connects together logically under the topic of Martin's attempted suicide.

Like most ordinary garden-variety units in modern realistic plays, this one consists of a little more than one page of printed dialogue in the sort of acting script published by Samuel French or Dramatists Play Service. The playing time is about three minutes. Such a premeditated way of describing units may seem too clinical at first, but there is no need to be concerned about it. There are always exceptions. The length is based on the practical requirements of storytelling in front of an audience. Readers can draw a further lesson from the fact that the unit begins and ends with decisive physical actions, although once again this may not occur in all cases. Because units have no clear identification marks or fixed length and seldom have a clear indication of physical action, they are not always easy to identify. Understanding them at this point may be a challenge, but the effort will be rewarded in production.

Scenes

A *scene* is a progression of related units that is shaped like a small play. This is one reason why scenes are popular choices for acting or directing classes: they're miniature plays. The function of a scene in the plot is equivalent to that of a chapter in a book: to introduce, develop, and conclude a single, large dramatic event. Some plays are subdivided into formal scenes for plain reasons such as a change in locale or the entrance or exit of a major character. In other plays, scenes may be more difficult to perceive because they are not indicated as such in the script. For this reason, occasional confusion about the outermost limits of units or informal scenes should be expected. A scene is similar to a unit since its action is continuous and its locale is constant, but the important difference is that a scene is longer and more substantial than a unit is because it is composed of several units. Moreover, the ending of a scene is stronger and more decisive than is that of a unit because the consequences of the action are greater. In fact, the emotional strength of the ending is what gives a scene its characteristic identity.

In period plays, like *Tartuffe* or *The School for Scandal*, it was common practice to include many formal scenes. Greek tragedies do not contain such divisions, but scenes are identified in them by alternating choral odes with episodes. Modern plays, however, *hold the situation* longer to take more advantage of a scene's dramatic potentials. The result is fewer formal scene divisions and longer scenes.

In any one of the French neoclassical plays, like those by Pierre Corneille or Jean Racine, there seem to be dozens of scenes in each act. Of course, this is not unconditionally true. It was the convention of that era to consider a scene finished when any character entered or left the stage. This so-called *French scene* is not always a scene in the standard sense used here. By this rule, the first unit of *Streamers*, for example, contains three French scenes. They are identified by character groups: (1) Martin and Richie; (2) Martin, Richie, and Carlyle; and (3) Martin, Richie, and Billy. French scenes usually denote beats or units, not always scenes. Even though in *Streamers* the stage is left empty at the end of the first unit, the emptiness does not mark the ending of a complete scene. We know that the scene continues because Billy returns after a few moments and resumes the action with Roger. Despite its obsolescence, the French scene remains a useful device for delimiting beats and units if not traditional scenes. Some directors also find French scenes useful as subdivisions for arranging rehearsal schedules.

To understand how scenes operate together to advance the plot, we might look again at the opening pages of *Streamers*. No scenes are identified as such in Act 1, but based on the logic of the action, the act can be subdivided into five informal scenes. We'll look at the first one, composed of the first four units of the play.

After the first unit, the scene continues when Billy reappears. The general topic of the unit is Billy's frustration with other people's behavior. In the third unit, Richie returns and ridicules his own campy effeminate behavior. The fourth unit begins after Richie leaves. It involves Billy's expression to Roger of concern about Richie's behavior. The first scene ends there. The general topic of conversation is Billy's distrust of people who are different from him. The next unit begins where the previous one ends, and the process is repeated this way until all the units in the play have been collected into their parent scenes.

The four units of this scene complement one another even though they may not appear to do so at first. To understand this, we must reexamine our initial perception of Unit 1 by focusing on Billy instead of on Martin or Richie. Seen from Billy's viewpoint, the first unit deals with his response to Martin's attempted suicide. In outline form, Scene 1 looks like this:

Scene 1: Billy distrusts people who are different from him.
        Unit 1: Billy is stunned by Martin's behavior.
        Unit 2: Billy confides in Roger.
        Unit 3: Billy is suspicious of Richie.

We should be able to understand the logical economy of the scene as it develops through these three units: Billy and Martin, Billy and Roger, Billy and Richie. There is no dramatic need to repeat a subject after it is completed, and therefore each succeeding unit is used to introduce a subject of its own.

In script analysis, it is often necessary to reconsider first impressions as more information becomes known. After reading the remainder of Scene 1, for example, we learned that our initial attention to Richie was incorrect or at least not completely accurate. Rethinking first impressions is perfectly all right and a mark of sound professional analysis. After all, it is natural to sympathize with Martin's attempted suicide here, but it is Billy, not Richie or Martin, who holds the dramatic spotlight in the scene. And the main interest is his suspicion of people with values different from his (although at this point in the play he is no more than dimly aware of his feelings.) Our example shows that the virtues of flexibility and willingness to discard first impressions are crucial for professional script analysis. The initial reading may have been reasonable, but this is a healthy reminder that almost all readings must be considered temporary guesses based on available evidence. There should never be embarrassment about rethinking, above all in analysis. As new evidence emerges, the artistic courage to change course if necessary must be there.

Acts

The largest progression within a play is an *act*, which can either flow continuously or by means of formal or informal scenes. An act is characterized further by the dramatic quality of its ending. The ending of the opening and interior acts of a play will usually leave a clear expectation of something important to come in the next act. The ending of the final act will normally use all the dramatic potentials of the theatre to create a decisive closing impression.

The Roman author Horace was the first to define acts as divisions of a play. His dictum was based on an understanding of the five divisions found in classical Greek tragedy. Because of Horace's influence, the five-act arrangement became the standard for centuries. Shakespeare didn't arrange his plays into acts, that was done for him afterwards by literary editors; however, a number of his plays seem to divide themselves logically into five parts. The practice of writing in four or three acts developed during the nineteenth century, and in the twentieth century, full-length plays with two or even only one long act have become popular. Today, long one-act plays are produced regularly. There are many reasons for this historical tendency. This is the end of a stylistic era. We have seen it all, have no time, have more important things to do, and require more detailed understanding, new techniques, or a deeper penetration of character psychology. Whatever the reason and despite the obvious historical trend, the need to subdivide a play into large, semi-independent masses of action has not disappeared. Playwrights continue to collect scenic progressions into acts or their equivalents.

The next logical step with *Streamers* is to assemble the related scenes into acts. Since the analytical routine is the same as has been described before, let's pass over the intermediate explanations and just collect the scenes into their parent acts. At this advanced point in analyzing progressions, individual details can be suppressed and situations described in broad terms to see the big picture. Once again, there is no need to be too concerned with verbal nuances, only with describing the advancement of the plot.

Act 1: Billy encounters the real world ("I'm not like *them!*")
    Scene 1: Martin's despair
    Scene 2: Richie's homosexuality

Scene 3: Carlyle's threats
Scene 4: Billy's warning
Scene 5: Cokes and Rooney's war stories
Scene 6: The story of Billy's friend
Scene 7: Carlyle's fear
Act 2: Billy revolts ("I must put a stop to *them!*")
    Scene 1: Carlyle's threat
        1: Billy's conscience
        2: Carlyle's proposal
        3: Going to town
    Scene 2: Billy's defense
        1: Carlyle's warning
        2: Billy's defiance
        3: Carlyle's attack on Billy
        4: Carlyle's attack on Rooney
        5: The military police
        6: Cokes' lament

After studying the entire play, it becomes clear that the center of attention is indeed Billy. The play may be seen as the story of a naive idealist who encounters the mindless violence of his society. In effect Billy declares, "*I am not like them,*" and in doing so he is alarmed to find out that, "*I am like them.*" As the action breakdown shows, the dramatist has selected and arranged the material to emphasize Billy's central importance in the play. Readers should be able to understand the thinking behind these descriptions even though they may not agree with them in every case. Acts are coherent groups of related scenes. To understand their role in storytelling completely, it's necessary to understand how each scene contributes to its parent act just as each unit contributes to its parent scene, each beat to its unit, and each line to its beat.

STRUCTURE

The arrangement of the parts of the plot and their relationship to each other and to the whole play is called the *structure.* Just as literary critics sometimes speak of the *gestalt,* the unified pattern, of the whole work, we can speak of the beats, units, scenes, and acts comprising the harmonious structure of a play. Regardless of the individual arrangement of these parts, each continues to perform its assigned function in the whole play. The main structural difference from one play to the next lies in the amount of emphasis devoted to each of its constituent parts.

Some textbooks about drama suggest that the structure of the plot consists of *rising action* (complications or obstacles), *climax,* and *falling action* (resolution, dénouement, or closure). German critic Gustav Freytag described this arrangement as a pyramid, the so-called *Freytag pyramid.* In his explanation, the tension of the plot rises through complications to a climax (the apex of the pyramid) after which it subsides until the end. The rising and falling may consist of several parts or of a single scene, but the climax, according to Freytag's arrangement (here we would say the most important climax) is a single big scene somewhere in the middle of the play.

Freytag points out that Shakespeare often used a regular pyramidal structure like this. In *Hamlet,* for example, he placed what Freytag argues is the most powerful scene straight in the middle of a five-part structure. The first half of the play shows Hamlet searching for conclusive proof of Claudius' guilt. Then, after the mousetrap scene, Hamlet sets in motion the second half of the play, which leads to the deaths of Ophelia, Polonius, Rosencrantz and Guildenstern, Gertrude, Laertes, Claudius, and Hamlet himself.

Despite the appeal of Freytag's theory in classrooms, there is no law that requires such a symmetrical structure. Readers determined to search for it at all costs may overlook all the climaxes except the one that might be in the middle of the play. A more practical approach would be to consider the typical dramatic structure not as a symmetrical pyramid but rather as a line ascending upward at an angle, interrupted by one or more less important climaxes in each act, and terminating with the most important climax. *Oedipus Rex, Tartuffe, Death of a Salesman, A Raisin in the Sun,* and *The Piano Lesson* are all examples of plays with such uneven rising structures. Their most important climaxes appear at or near the end of the final act. Certain modern plays, like *Happy Days, Three Sisters, A Lie of the Mind,* and perhaps *Angels in America,* employ an unusual structure that is flat, or at least free of traditional climaxes, but more about this later. The structure of most dramatic works reveals several moments of high tension whose placement varies from one play to another.

Point of Attack

Now that we have considered the general nature of structure, we will explore the individual parts of the rising and falling action. Their nature and organization help determine the relative amount of restriction or freedom in the development of the story.

The first part of the rising action to consider is the *point of attack*, the moment when the play begins in relation to the background story at one end and the climax at the other. When the on-stage action begins later in the background story and closer to the climax, the play is said to have a late point of attack. *The Wild Duck* has such an arrangement. The on-stage action reveals only the last two days of a story that began more than nineteen years before. A play with a late point of attack, like *The Wild Duck*, compresses a great deal of background story and on-stage action into a brief performance time frame. Because of this compression, plot freedom is constrained because it is packed with both present and past action. *The Wild Duck* is a modern realistic play, but the use of a late point of attack is not restricted to the modern era or to the style of realism. *Oedipus Rex*, *Tartuffe*, and *Three Sisters* also demonstrate late points of attack.

Conversely, a play shows an early point of attack when there is little background story and a long stretch of on-stage dramatic time between the opening curtain and the major climax. The background story for *Hamlet* begins a few weeks before the start of the play, while the on-stage action covers a period of several months. Once again, the treatment of the point of attack is independent of the play's historical period or style. *The Hairy Ape, Mother Courage,* and *Angels in America* also have early points of attack. Because of the longer on-stage dramatic time involved, the plot is freer, its feel more is roomy. There is less moment-to-moment tension and a looser arrangement than is found in plays with a late point of attack. The manner of treatment of the point of attack is characteristic of the temperaments of individual playwrights and of the writing fashion in vogue when they wrote.

Inciting Action

The *inciting action* is the single event that sparks the main action of the entire play. It occurs at the point when the leading character is set in motion or where a feeling arises in the character that sets the action in motion. It becomes the chief driving force for all the succeeding action of the play. In *Hamlet,* the inciting action occurs in the fifth scene when the Ghost informs Hamlet about the murder and challenges him to revenge. The inciting action in *Oedipus Rex* occurs in the Prologue when Creon informs Oedipus of the Oracle's warning. In *The School for Scandal* it happens in 1,2 when Sir Oliver Surface returns to London. In *The Hairy Ape,* the inciting action occurs in 1,3 when Yank meets Mildred for the first time. The inciting action of *The Piano Lesson* occurs at the moment when Boy Willie first appears. The inciting action may appear in a variety of different positions near the beginning of the play and may take on different forms. It may be short or long; it may be an incident, an idea, a wish, or a plan in the mind of the leading character. The main action can begin only after the inciting action takes place. It forms the transition between the introductory material and the body of the play, and its location in the overall structure helps to shape the emotional dynamics of the play.

One writer asserts that sometimes the inciting action may even occur while the protagonist is offstage. If so, it is a missed opportunity for the dramatist because the inciting action is one of the most powerful events in the play. Or perhaps the real inciting action has been misunderstood. In *A Lie of the Mind,* for example, some readers might consider the inciting action to be Jake's shocking abuse of Beth that has landed her in the hospital with brain damage. This is obviously a significant action. It happens before the play begins, however, and here is considered background story. The real inciting action is the telephone call between Jake and Mike that kick starts the play.

Obstacles

On the stage as in life, all planned human behavior encounters difficulties as it tries to reach its goal. Characters meet others who have opposing wishes, or they run into opposing events, or they may even give up their goals themselves. *Obstacles,* sometimes called *complications* by scholars, are the counter movements in the plot created by these conflicting motives and events. Note that, according to this definition, obstacles must be about common points of disagreement shared by at least two characters. Without a shared disagreement, there is no opportunity for an obstacle. It is the obstacles that produce the increasing levels of tension in the play. The plot thickens and becomes more complex, and the internal tensions begin to surface. Disparate parts of the play begin to connect, and it feels as if the play has movement. Obstacles appear in a variety of different forms and illustrations, and they tend to become more interesting and exciting as the play progresses.

To explain we will review the obstacles found in 1,1 of *A Raisin in the Sun*. The action takes place in the living room of the Youngers' apartment on Chicago's South Side, an African-American neighborhood. It is Friday morning. On stage are Walter Younger, his wife and son, and his mother and sister. The obstacles in the scene proceed in seven steps. As Ruth is awakening the family, the first obstacle appears when she objects to Walter's question about the impending arrival of the life insurance check. Her criticism of Walter for staying up late with his friends the night before forms the second obstacle. Obstacle number three occurs when Ruth refuses to give Travis an extra 50¢ for school, and Walter disagrees with her. Next, there is another obstacle involving Ruth's objection to Walter's incessant talk about becoming a big success. Beneatha's appearance provides the pretext for the fifth obstacle when Walter objects to her (costly) ambition to become a doctor. The sixth obstacle is a short discussion between Ruth and Mama about her own plans for the money. Mama's objection to Beneatha's disavowal of God is the seventh and final obstacle of the scene.

This opening scene furnishes the largest part of the information needed by actors to understand the characters, situation, and background story for what is to follow. It also introduces the main action, which is Walter's dream for the future as represented by his wish to buy a liquor store with the insurance money. Each of the seven obstacles adds to the total level of tension in the scene. This scene is a model of realistic craftsmanship and will reward patient analysis.

Climaxes

A *climax* is a prominent peak of emotional intensity in the play. It is the point when the obstacles appear strongest and most decisive. Climaxes are the zeniths of big accentuated scenes, and they may be considered major or minor. As a rule, the highest peak of emotional intensity in the play is considered the *major climax*. It is surrounded on either side by connecting scenes that form the rising and falling action, and it dominates any other climax. The major climax can appear at an assortment of distances from the end of the play. In A *Raisin in the Sun* it appears in the final scene with Walter, Mr. Lindner, and the family. The end of the play after that occupies two and a half pages of dialogue. In *Oedipus Rex* it occurs near the end of Episode 4, and the last two scenes are devoted to the catastrophe (scene of physical violence) and the resolution. *The Wild Duck* has its major climax very near the end of the play just after Hedvig kills herself. In *Streamers,* the major climax occurs midway through 2,2 when Billy condemns Carlyle. Berniece sitting down to play the piano to exorcise Sutter's ghost is the major climax of *The Piano Lesson.* Prior's demand for a blessing from the Angels is the major climax of *Angels in America.* In these examples and many others readers can point to, playwrights use all their writing skills to ensure that the major climaxes are the most dramatic and memorable moments in the play.

One major climax may work all right for scholars, but for actors, directors and designers the idea of one major climax is almost too static. In the theatre, it is better to consider that every play actually exhibits *three major climaxes* that mark the beginning, middle, and end of the action. This way of thinking emphasizes the forward movement of the action, which is a distinguishing feature of a good professional performance. In *Hamlet*, for example, the beginning, the first major climax, occurs when the Ghost reveals the circumstances of his murder to Hamlet. The middle, the second major climax, occurs during the mousetrap scene in the middle of the play. With its tense, complicated interplay among Hamlet and Claudius, the Players, and the members of the court, it is one of the most effective scenes in the theatre. The end of this play, or third major climax, occurs in the final scene when Hamlet slays Claudius. *The School for Scandal* contains five acts, but it has three major climaxes. The first major climax occurs in 1,1, when Lady Sneerwell sets her plan in motion to break up the mutual attachment between Charles Surface and Maria. The second major climax is the famous "screen scene" in 5,2, which is considered a good model of comedy writing. The third major climax occurs in the final scene of the play when Joseph Surface is exposed as a scoundrel. In *Three Sisters*, the first major climax is the scene where Andrey admits that his wife, Natasha, is an insipid person and his marriage is a failure. The second major climax is the departure of Vershinin and Masha's resultant despair. The third major climax is the collapse of Irina's hopes for a new life when Baron Tuzenbach is killed in a duel. Later on in the book we will see that under certain conditions the climaxes in *Three Sisters* can be interpreted differently.

In addition to its three major climaxes, a play also contains various *minor climaxes* that occur every time a significant adjustment takes place in the course of events. Minor climaxes show characters making hard decisions about vital things in their lives, but not necessarily life-changing decisions as major climaxes are. There are minor climaxes in the scene we examined earlier from *A Raisin in the Sun.* In one minor climax, Beneatha reminds Walter that the insurance money belongs to their mother and that nothing he can say or do will tempt her to invest it in a liquor store. At this sharp reminder, Walter storms out of the apartment. If Walter had remained, he would have been obliged to confront his mother about the money immediately, and the remainder of the play would have been different. As it is, he departs and the critical issue of who will control the life insurance money remains unresolved for the time being. Another minor climax occurs when Beneatha's liberal views about God challenge Mama's religious convictions. Mama wins this confrontation by slapping her daughter hard across the face and demanding an apology. This physical action shows that Mama is capable of defending her values. If she had walked away from Beneatha instead of challenging her, Walter's later confrontation with her about the insurance money would have been weaker by comparison. These two minor climaxes show characters forced to deal with vital issues in their lives: Walter's reckless ambition and Mama's intense morality. Notice, too, that each of these minor climaxes is marked by a decisive physical action: slamming a door, slapping a face.

Recognition, Reversal, and Catastrophe

Before we move on to the remaining elements of structure, it might be helpful to pause and examine certain characteristics of climaxes in a little more detail. The word *climax* is a composite term used to describe two distinct processes that unfold together in performance: recognition and reversal.

Recognition, according to Aristotle, is a change from ignorance to knowledge on the part of the main character, the so-called protagonist. At the third major climax of *A Raisin in the Sun*, for example, Walter Younger finally recognizes that he has not earned his family's respect but their contempt. He has failed as a husband, father, and human being. The most effective kind of recognition is accompanied by a *reversal* (radical change in fortune). In Walter Younger's case, the reversal is from bad fortune to good. After a considerable amount of inner turmoil, he achieves self-respect by sacrificing his personal dream of financial success to gain his family's respect. In view of Walter's newly won status in the family, the lost insurance money is no longer an important issue for him.

In *Death of a Salesman*, Willy Loman's recognition is similar in spirit to Walter Younger's, but his reversal works in the opposite direction. Willy discovers that he has been a failure as a father, but then, instead of changing his point of view the way Walter does, he decides to sacrifice his life for his son for the sake of the life insurance money. Reversals from good fortune to bad (that is, from life to death) like Willy Loman's are accompanied by an event called a *catastrophe*. Willy's suicide is a catastrophe in the technical sense as are Oedipus' self-mutilation and Hamlet's death. Although Walter does lose the money, there is no technical catastrophe in *A Raisin in the Sun* because there is no violence. In any event, the intense emotions that characterize a third major climax are the direct result of sympathies and antagonisms generated by recognition and reversal. Incidentally, in both plays above, we are again reminded of getting or losing money as a major given circumstance.

Simple and Complex Plots

Aristotle described plots with traditional climaxes (those containing recognitions and reversals) as *complex*. He believed that complex plots were inherently dramatic and therefore most effective in the theatre. He described plots without climaxes (that is, those without recognitions and reversals) as *simple*. Although Aristotle believed that simple plots were undramatic, nevertheless many playwrights, even classical Greek playwrights, have made effective use of them. The plots of *Mother Courage*, *Happy Days*, and *Three Sisters*, for example, are technically simple because they do not contain the usual recognitions or reversals in their leading characters, yet no one would accuse them of being undramatic.

Among modern playwrights, Bertolt Brecht, Samuel Beckett, and Anton Chekhov have employed simple plots. They chose to substitute other dramatic values in their plays for the emotional excitement provided by traditional climaxes. Brecht employed narration, poetry, music, and emphatic social commentary. Beckett used pantomime, detailed character drawing, unusual moods, and sharp thematics. Chekhov used detailed character description, lyrical moods, contradictory actions, multiple plots, and multiple points of dramatic focus. Plays with complex plots have no built-in advantage over those with simple plots. In the hands of a skilled playwright, either kind can be effective. The main difference lies in the presence or absence of recognition and reversal.

Resolution

The *resolution* (falling action) includes all the events following the third major climax. Sometimes this is also called the *dénouement* (unraveling) of the obstacles or complications. The resolution is characterized by a gradual quieting of the tension and a return of the original opposing forces to a state of near equilibrium or adjustment. The resolution in *Oedipus Rex* begins after the Messenger recounts the double catastrophe of Jocasta's suicide and Oedipus' self-mutilation. It consists of the final lament of Oedipus and his banishment by Creon. The resolution in *Hamlet* is accomplished with the arrival of Fortinbras and the removal of Hamlet's body from the stage. Still shorter is the resolution in *Tartuffe*. It consists of the Officer's announcement of Tartuffe's arrest and the return of the estate to Orgon. Also brief is the resolution in *A Lie of the Mind*, which consists of the folding of the flag concluded by a fleeting moment of affection between Baylor and his wife, Meg. The final scene, or requiem, is the resolution in *Death of a Salesman*. It also acts as a kind of *epilogue* (formal concluding scene) to the play. The resolution in *Streamers* consists of Sergeant Cokes' drunken tale of violence and his singing of "Beautiful Dreamer." It could also be considered an epilogue. The resolution in *Angels in America* consists of everything that happens after Prior receives the blessing of the Angels, leading to the Epilogue at Bethesda Fountain in Central Park.

SUMMARY

In the study of plot, readers are inclined to devote most of their attention to understanding the basic external and internal actions, but as we have shown, this is not all that goes into crafting a successful plot. Besides identifying these actions, readers will also need to explore their progress and arrangement. Initially it may be tricky to catch the flow of dramatic progressions and to develop a sense of how they relate to each other and to the whole play. The temptation is to read plays merely as sequential arrangements of scenes without much regard for their internal connections. But analyzing the progressions and structure is essential for professional-level competence and therefore should not be undervalued. Regardless of the kind of play or what it means, dramatic interest depends not only on the story but also on how it is told.

QUESTIONS

Progressions   Take time to subdivide the action of the play (or scene) into units (or beats if necessary) and ask: What is the story logic and how does each beat and unit contribute to it? How is the action divided into scenes (informal, formal, and French) and acts? Describe how each of these larger progressions contributes to the logical development of the story.

Structure   What is the motivating force that sparks the story (inciting action or first major climax)? What are the obstacles (complications)? What are the three highest points of emotional intensity in the play (three major climaxes)? What are the other points of emotional intensity (minor climaxes) in the play? What is the overall pattern of emotional intensity (formed by the collective major and minor climaxes)? Does the leading character or any character undergo a psychological recognition (complex plot)? If so, describe it. If not, why not (simple plot)? Is there an important change of fortune (reversal) for the leading character? If so, what is it? Does the reversal lead to better or worse fortune? What important actions, if any, occur after the highest peak of emotional intensity (resolution)? How can the decline in tension be described at this point in the play?

After Action Analysis, search for the play's Seed, or Subject, latent within the Progressions and Structure. How does the Seed influence the Progressions and Structure? Why did the playwright choose these specific Progressions and Structure from the whole range of other possibilities? How would the play be different with other Progressions and Structures? In what way does connecting the Seed with the Progressions and Structure help the play grow and develop?

CHAPTER 6

Character

The term *character* has taken on various meanings over time. It developed from a Middle English root associated with something fixed and permanent, like an identifying mark or a sign on a building. During Shakespeare's time, character was still considered a permanent feature. It was said to stem from certain bodily fluids called *humours* that once were thought to shape a person's disposition. In the nineteenth century, character continued to mean a fixed state of development, though with added moral implications as in, "She had character." This meaning was associated with moral strength, self-discipline, and, most important to the Victorians, a sound reputation. The modern meaning of character is more comprehensive. Today we consider character the entire pattern of behaviors that identify a person. This is the definition we will examine in this chapter. In drama, character is not a static object fixed forever in time but rather a dynamic pattern of features that develops over the course of the play. Some writers think this suggests that characters can change during a play, while others claim they only reveal hidden traits. It's an interesting puzzle, but it need not detain us here. To recognize that character is composed of a shifting pattern of mixed elements is satisfactory for practical purposes.

Although sometimes stage characters are studied as if they were real people, they are truly artificial because they are objects created by playwrights. It's risky to depend too much on psychoanalytical methods, for example, to understand them. Psychoanalysis is a method of examining mental disorders, and its main purpose is medical treatment of those disorders. Its methods sometimes can be useful in artistic circumstances, but character analysis is an artistic enterprise, not a medical one. Dramatic characters may be performed by real people and their emotional lives may be similar to those of real people, but the resemblance stops there. Compared to real people, stage characters are very predictable. In life, few people are as relentlessly absorbed with a single overpowering goal as are characters in plays. The compact expressiveness of drama involves reduction to essentials. To portray character, the whole array of ordinary human behavior is condensed to a few selected features.

This chapter will study character under eight headings: (1) *Objectives* equip the characters with goals to aim for. (2) *Qualities* are the behaviors they use to pursue those goals. (3) *Conflict* describes the tensions in situations between conflicting characters, and (4) *willpower* is the amount of force they use in the pursuit of their objectives. (5) *Values* are the intangible things the characters consider good and bad. (6) *Personality traits* are those strokes of individuality that show how characters look, feel, and think. The topic of (7) *complexity* represents how much characters are conscious of their situations. Under (8) *relationships* are the primary and secondary associations characters develop with one another. These topics provide the general lines of inquiry that can be used to understand dramatic character. Some actors think of them as individual *layers* that combine to form the complete character. Rehearsing layer by layer is a useful way to come to terms with a character without having to deal with everything at one time.

OBJECTIVES

Character desires Stanislavski and his followers called *objectives*, or *goals*. Boleslavsky and the members of the Group Theatre (formed by Harold Clurman, Lee Strasberg, and Cheryl Crawford in 1929) and their students and followers have used the term *spine* or *intention*. *Want* is another variation. The terms may vary, but they all mean the same thing: the character's basic desire or plan of action. Objectives are part of the soul, the inner life of the character. They stem from religious, social, political, or artistic feelings, from dreams of personal glory or empire, or from whatever controls the inner life of the character.

A single objective for an entire play can be a very extensive undertaking, however. It may be so large that it is impossible to complete all at once. For this reason, it is necessary to subdivide it into minor objectives that are easier to understand and accomplish. This turns out to be practical because objectives are tied to the progressions that already exist in the plot. The largest objective, called by Stanislavski the *super-objective*, is the one that arises from the whole play and governs its limits. Minor objectives are tied to beats, units, scenes, and acts and define their limits.

Objectives should not be complex, abstract, or literary statements. On the contrary, everyone, professionals and nonprofessionals alike, should learn to describe them in the form of simple human drives. In *An Actor Prepares*, Stanislavski suggested a number of guidelines for discovering, if not explaining, objectives. As usual, his guidelines are practical and easy to understand. Five of the most important are: (1) Objectives should come from the characters' goals, (2) be directed at the other characters (as opposed to oneself or the audience), (3) describe the inner life of the character as opposed to the outward physical life, (4) relate to the main idea of the play, and (5) be framed in the form of an infinitive phrase from an active (transitive), concrete verb.

It is important that the last guideline be very clear. From Stanislavski's point of view it was necessary for the actor to know the character's objectives from the start. He asserted that objectives must lure the character into physical action while challenging the actor's imagination. Burnet Hobgood has reminded us that Stanislavski was helped in this understanding of objectives by a grammatical feature in the Russian language called *verbal aspect*, which doesn't exist in English. When Stanislavski described objectives, he always used verbs in the perfective aspect, which in Russian signifies future action. Stanislavski's model objective goes, "I want to [verb] in order to [statement of purpose]," and the verb and its corresponding purpose are selected to explain the character under study. In English, the use of the infinitive indicates a similar sense of the future. By far the most common form of an infinitive in English is with the word "to," as in "to walk," "to cry," "to eat," "to fear." This is known as the *to-infinitive*. Stanislavski's grammatical practice supports his assertion that objectives express something the character believes will happen or is about to happen *in the future*. It helps to explain why he insisted that characters should be understood as striving to reach objectives that always lie ahead of them.

Objectives are best understood in relation to a specific play, so we'll study *A Raisin in the Sun*. In order to learn Walter Younger's super-objective for the play, first find out what he wants to do with his life. In a scene in Act 1, he tells his wife Ruth that he has been planning to use the life insurance money to invest in a liquor store. "I got me a dream," he says, "I got *to take hold of this here world . . . I got to change my life.*" When Ruth expresses doubts, he responds, "This morning, I was lookin' in the mirror and thinking about it . . . I'm thirty-five years old; I been married eleven years and I got a boy who sleeps in the living room—and all I got to give him is stories about how rich white people live." From these lines and other evidence in the play we might agree that Walter's super-objective is *to buy a liquor store* or *to achieve success.* This would be correct, but most readers would agree that it leaves out a large part of Walter's character, notably his love for his family. A stronger super-objective would be *to win the respect of his family.* Several other workable alternatives are possible, but in any case, this is an acceptable choice because it conditions everything Walter does in the play.

Walter's dream is an ambitious one. To accomplish it, he must subdivide it into more manageable pieces, the minor objectives that are tied to the individual progressions in the play. For example, in Walter's first unit, he gives Travis extra spending money despite Ruth's protests. His objective for this unit might be *to appear generous* or *to win Travis's admiration.* In his next unit, Walter turns to Ruth *to disclose his personal frustrations* or *to obtain Ruth's sympathy.* When his sister Beneatha enters, Walter wishes *to belittle her* or *to destroy her expensive dream of becoming a doctor.* In the important scene with his mother later in the act, Walter reveals how desperate he is to achieve his super-objective. Mama is a moral person, and objects to the prospect of anyone in her family owning a liquor store. Walter forces a confrontation with her over the issue. His objective here is *to ridicule his mother's doubts* or *to take the insurance money away from her.* Each minor objective defines its own unique progression while also adhering to Stanislavski's basic guidelines. Walter's minor objectives follow from his super-objective; they are directed at specific characters and not at the world in general, and they relate to his inner life.

As mentioned earlier, successful super-objectives should also relate to the main idea of the play. Chapter 7 will explain the concept of the *main idea*, sometimes called the *super-objective* or *spine* of the play. For this discussion a convenient example will serve for demonstration. The main idea of *A Raisin in the Sun* is *the struggle for a dream* or *to struggle for a dream*. It is easy to understand how Walter's minor objectives relate to these statements. For the description to be convincing for the whole play, however, the super-objectives of all the other characters should relate to it just as well. And they do relate to it because everyone in the play is struggling for a dream. Ruth's main objective is *to support Walter* or *to save their marriage*; Mama's is *to help her children*; and Beneatha's is *to become a doctor* or *to obtain an education*. Although each of these super-objectives contains its own separate feelings and thoughts, each also relates to the main idea of the play: the struggle for a dream.

Director-critic Harold Clurman was always one of the strongest advocates of the use of objectives by actors and directors. In his writing, he cautioned actors against always looking for minor personality traits, which is a frequent temptation. He believed the actor's most important analytical task should be to find the character's super-objective, the basic drive that determines the character's behavior in the whole play and throughout the acts, scenes, units, and beats of which the play is composed. He pointed out that, even though many of the characters will experience similar feelings of anger, joy, or sadness, it is their super-objective that explains these changing feelings and thoughts by showing that they are all related to a single permanent goal.

QUALITIES

Qualities are the behaviors that characters use to achieve their objectives. Sometimes they are called *tactics*. We might think of how a sailboat changes its course to adjust to opposing winds. To make headway, the captain employs a zigzag pattern in which each course of the boat is different from other ones or from the preceding one; so also a character uses different qualities to adjust to opposition from other characters when that character is working toward an objective. Characters employ not just one quality but rather a whole range of qualities, shifting from one to another to achieve their objectives. Readers familiar with the acting principles of Michael Chekhov will recognize the term qualities as an important part of his teaching. According to Chekhov, objectives express *what* happens and qualities express *how* it happens. In any event, qualities are inherent in the objectives already present in the play. Since qualities modify objectives the way adverbs modify verbs, qualities are often described using adverbs, such as happily, powerfully, wearily, proudly, skeptically, forcefully, etc.

Qualities can be illustrated in the units studied in *A Raisin in the Sun*. Recall that Walter's main objective is to buy a liquor store or to gain the respect of his family. It follows that he also has a major quality or a dominant way of behaving that stems from his super-objective. He believes that he deserves the insurance money because his dreams are praiseworthy, his frustrations are real, and his scheme is a sure thing. It's clear that his attempts to behave *fairly* or *reasonably* do not persuade his family, so he adopts different behaviors in an attempt to win them over. His major quality for the play is *forcefully* or maybe *belligerently*. Within this dominant quality, Walter adopts a variety of minor qualities to deal with the different obstacles with which he finds himself confronted. He behaves *boastfully* before his son Travis, *reproachfully* with his wife Ruth, *mockingly* with his sister Beneatha, and *defiantly* with his mother. These zigzag behaviors of Walter's are the qualities he feels are necessary to adopt to achieve his objectives.

Here we are treating qualities that are written in a play itself. But qualities can also stem from the personality and imagination of the actors playing the roles. In fact, Michael Chekhov based his system of actor training on the principle that a character's qualities ought to come from the actor's imagination and not the playwright's. Not all actors possess the brilliant imagination of Michael Chekhov, of course. What is more, some plays are more adaptable than others in their character qualities. Period plays, for some reason, seem to permit more flexibility in their qualities than do modern plays. On the other hand, screenplays and television scripts tend to offer more freedom in the choice of qualities than stage plays do (in general, broadly speaking, with exceptions and caveats). Maybe this is why Michael Chekhov's teachings have been adopted successfully by so many film and television actors.

ROLE CONFLICTS

Since the subject of conflict comes up so often in discussions about plays, it is important to examine it closely. The word *conflict* stems from a Latin root meaning to strike together, from which comes its current meaning of a battle, quarrel, or struggle for supremacy between opposing forces. Does conflict appear in every play? If it is defined as open arguments between characters, the answer is no. There are few open arguments, for example, in *The Wild Duck*, *Happy Days*, or *Mother Courage*. Moreover, in these plays and in many others the characters do not even seem to struggle conspicuously to escape from their surroundings. Looking for traditional big conflict in situations like these is unrewarding.

Instead of being a single narrow concept, conflict appears in many different forms. There may be conflict between one character and another, between character and environment, between character and destiny or the forces of nature, between character and ideas, or even among forces inside a character. All these are legitimate types of conflicts, but not all of them produce the same kinds of tensions. Conflict from intellectual abstractions such as environment, society, or destiny, for example, produces intellectual tensions. These conflicts are useful for critics and academicians because they provide the intellectual material needed for scholarly work. They can also be useful for directors and designers in their creative work as will be seen in Chapter 7.

To achieve the kind of appeal necessary for acting, however, conflict must be more than an intellectual abstraction. It must be tangible and have a human face. In other words, it must involve the behavior and emotions of the characters. This kind of conflict stems from concrete conditions in the given circumstances and is grounded in the world of the play. It is the most productive kind of conflict in the rehearsal hall because it provides the inner tensions that stir actors' creative imaginations. Conflicts in this concrete sense may be divided into two classes: (1) *role conflicts* stemming from characters' opposing views of each other and (2) *conflicts of objectives* stemming from their opposing goals. Role conflicts and conflicts of objectives are parts of the characters' outer selves; they help to shape the way characters relate to each other. That is why the subject of conflict occurs both in this chapter and in Chapter 7.

Role conflicts arise from characters' opposing views of each other. Sometimes they are called *conflicts of attitude* or *rite-role conflicts*. They come from conditions in the given circumstances that cause one character to start a disagreement and that cause the opposing character's counter adjustments. The reader's task is to search the given circumstances for the right conditions and to think about them as the characters would. There may be a number of different role conflicts among the characters, each defined by its own conditions in the given circumstances.

For an explanation of how role conflict comes from the given circumstances, return to the scene between Walter and Ruth in *A Raisin in the Sun*. The given circumstances for the scene are: The year is 1959. The Youngers are an African-American family. They live in a crowded apartment building on the segregated South Side of Chicago. Thanks to the sturdy moral temperaments of Walter, Sr. and Mama Younger, the family has managed to endure most of the hardships African Americans encountered in the United States during the 1950s. To make ends meet, everyone in the family has to work hard at low-paying jobs without any future.

About 11 years ago, Walter Younger, Jr. married Ruth, and now they have a son, Travis. They have lived in the same small apartment with Walter's father, mother, and sister Beneatha since they were married. Walter's father died about a month ago, and Mama is about to receive his life insurance, amounting to $10,000, and a very large sum for the financially deprived Younger family. Walter feels humiliated at the prospect of becoming the head of the family without any future ahead of him. The most important given circumstance for him is the scheme he concocted with his friends to buy a liquor store with his father's life insurance money. He feels that this project will give him a chance to become a successful husband and provider for the family. (Note once again the importance of economic given circumstances in this play.)

Ruth is disappointed in Walter. When she married him, she was excited about their hopes and dreams for the future. Now she's become disillusioned with his endless scheming and lack of ambition. She has concluded that Walter no longer cares for her or the family. The crucial facts are that Ruth is pregnant with their second child and has not told Walter about it. Moreover, she feels that under the circumstances she must have an abortion, a prospect that disturbs her.

This summarizes the relevant given circumstances. After that it's necessary to identify the character that controls the situation. The dialogue shows that Walter is the controlling character in this scene. He insists on pressing Ruth with his plans for the liquor store while she is trying to get the family ready for work and school. Ruth doesn't want to listen to Walter. Therefore she is the one who starts the conflict and continues it. Without her resistance to Walter's plan, there would be no conflict. Walter leads the attack and Ruth resists.

Now that the positions of the two characters are clear, the heart of the role conflict becomes clear. Walter's given circumstances show why he is seeking help from Ruth in spite of her resistance. No one in the family is closer to Mama than Ruth is. She is not only Mama's daughter-in-law but also her close friend and confidante. Walter needs Ruth to intercede with his mother on his behalf for the life insurance money. This is his side of the conflict. But his request upsets Ruth. Because of all the frustrations she has endured, she no longer shares her husband's hopes and dreams as she once did. In fact, she does not even consider him her husband anymore. All she's concerned about now is the baby and the disturbing possibility of an abortion.

The role conflict emerges. Walter sees himself as a good husband and father, and he expects Ruth to be a loyal, supporting wife. In contrast, Ruth feels that she no longer has anything in common with Walter because she considers him a failure. Their images of each other and themselves are in complete disagreement. The concrete cause that sparks the conflict is the insurance money. It constitutes the *shared point of dispute* that brings their conflicting views of each other into the open. Without the disagreement over the insurance money, the role conflict would stay hidden inside the characters.

CONFLICTS OF OBJECTIVES

A second category of conflict comes from the ideas of the nineteenth-century French critic Ferdinand Brunetière. His so-called *law of conflict* states that drama is defined by the obstacles encountered as a character is attempting to fulfill his objectives. The key issue in this understanding of conflict is obstacles, or complications. Characters have objectives, direct everything toward fulfilling those objectives, and try to bring everything in their lives into harmony with them. Obstacles in Brunetière's sense are the opposing objectives of other characters that stand in the way of this process. In Stanislavski's terms, the chain of opposing objectives forms the *counter through-action*. Minor and major climaxes occur at those points where one character's through-action crosses the counter through-action formed by the opposing objectives of another character. These clashes in turn produce the scenes that make plays exciting. Aside from the emphasis on obstacles, *conflicts of objectives* share the same prerequisites as role conflicts do.

To prove this statement, we'll examine *A Raisin in the Sun* one more time. Walter wants to buy a liquor store in order to gain respect, and the question is how he will succeed. He is prevented from fulfilling his super-objective by Mama's super-objective, which is to invest the insurance money in the best way so that her children can fulfill their dreams. Their encounter fulfills the same requirements treated under role conflict. It arises from the given circumstances and is concrete rather than abstract; Walter controls the conflict and Mama resists it; the objectives clash; and the money constitutes a shared point of dispute. Walter overcomes his mother's opposition, but he is defeated then by his friend Willy, whose super-objective is to get hold of the insurance money by deception in order to steal it. Does Walter's encounter with Willy also fulfill the requirements of a conflict of objectives? It arises from the given circumstances; it involves a concrete dispute between Walter and Willy; Willy begins the conflict and Walter resists it; their objectives clash; and finally the shared point of dispute is again the money. It's not hard to find examples of opposing objectives in other plays. The real effort is seeing their built-in opposition.

Of the two categories of conflicts we just explained, conflicts of objectives are used more often because they are more easily grasped and explained. Role conflicts may impose a more severe analytical test, but the reward is a larger assortment of acting options. Searching for either type of conflict will supply many alternatives. Assuming the conflicts have been accurately perceived, the final choice depends on the creative imagination of the artistic team and on what they decide to emphasize in production.

WILLPOWER

Will has been described as a strong wish, a firm intention, a power of choosing, a determination to do, and an inner force used to undertake conscious, purposeful action. The key words here are *strong, firm, power, determination,* and *force.* Will is associated with power because it is the driving force of drama. Strong-willed characters make things happen. Plays depend on them to keep the action moving. Some characters may not have strong wills, but if the leading character is also devoid of a strong will, the results may be unsatisfactory unless other compensations are provided. Because conflict always requires resistance, characters without strong wills are unable to create conflicts because they are incapable of resisting. They may participate in conflicts, but they seldom seem to instigate or influence them. They can't struggle against their situations, and they are often the victims of the more willful characters who control them.

Modern artistic sensibilities seem to sympathize with victims more than heroes, but it's not always easy to come to terms with passive, victimized characters. Before sympathizing with them, it's necessary to try to understand the reasons for their relative inactivity. Instructive examples of such characters appear in *Mother Courage* and *Hamlet*. In *Mother Courage* there is Anna Fierling, the canteen woman who earns a living by following after armies on the march and selling necessities to them at inflated prices. The strength of her will shows up in the first scene of the play when she loses her son Eilif to the Recruiting Officer. She has been distracted by the chance to make a quick profit selling a belt buckle. We know that Anna is a shrewd and single-minded businesswoman, yet she does nothing when her son is taken from her, a fact that Brecht emphasizes in stage directions that state, "she stands motionless."

Anna is unable to prevent her second son, Swiss Cheese, from being sacrificed to the war either. She compromises with the same Recruiting Officer by permitting him to enlist as a paymaster. She claims that at least he won't have to fight, but she knows he's simple-minded and will get himself into trouble because he can't count. She's troubled by these concerns, but she justifies her decision on the grounds that the war has been good for her business. Soon she finds that Swiss Cheese has panicked during an enemy offensive and unwittingly fled with the cash box. When he's arrested, Anna haggles over the bribe to save his life. Meanwhile Swiss Cheese is taken before a firing squad and shot. She observes, "Maybe I bargained too long," and the stage directions indicate once again that she "remains seated." Afterward Anna refuses to acknowledge the body of her son rather than risk arrest herself. Later on she attempts to file an official complaint about it, but after thinking it over, she changes her mind.

In another scene, Anna's son, Eilif, arrives to say good-bye before being taken away to be executed for a petty crime. Just then the cease-fire is cut short by the renewed outbreak of war. Anna is so excited by the chance to make money that she misses the chance to save Eilif's life. Further on in the play, Anna finds herself in town on business when her remaining child, the mute Kattrin, is shot sounding an alarm to warn the town of an enemy attack. "Maybe it wouldn't have happened if you hadn't gone to town to swindle people," a peasant says to her. "I've got to get back in business," she replies. Then she hails a passing regiment and shouts "Hey, take me with you!" and the play ends.

Someone in Anna's predicament should invoke sympathy, but Brecht attempts to dispel this natural inclination. He shows Anna Fierling as a character who lacks a mother's most basic power to protect her children. This would be a formula for certain failure in the theatre, but there are deliberate compensations that stimulate interest and sympathy. Brecht tries to show that Anna's helplessness is not her fault. The play argues that her power for good has been exhausted by the brutal economics of war. Compelled to choose between peaceful poverty and wartime affluence, she chooses the latter. She believes she can keep her family together despite the war by employing her business instincts. We are meant to feel that this choice hurts her even though she doesn't know why. Anna Fierling never learns that she is mistaken. For many readers, Anna's story is a vivid illustration of social and economic injustice.

Besides these thematic considerations, Anna Fierling's apparent inactivity is further offset by other features in the play. The back-and-forth changes in the course of the war, for example, unsettle everyone. Also Anna's daughter, Kattrin, and the prostitute, Yvette, show remarkable strength of will and even heroism. Other offsetting features are the earthy humor and homespun intelligence of the characters, and the play's unusual production style, which employs signs, banners, musical interludes, poetry, and direct address to the audience. All these features give the play compelling social relevance, variety of feeling, and a special kind of excitement that compensate for the absence of traditional willpower in the leading character.

Another seemingly weak character who is attractive to modern audiences is Hamlet. A sensitive person, he is burdened with the responsibility of revenging his warrior-father's murder. Hamlet has already neglected one of his royal responsibilities by standing aside while his uncle usurped the throne that is rightfully his. Nor did he do anything to prevent his mother's overhasty and incestuous marriage to his uncle. By these examples of inaction, Hamlet seems to show weakness and even cowardice. At his first appearance in the play, Hamlet refuses to take part in the coronation ceremonies for the new king. His display of temperament in the scene is interpreted by the court as spitefulness stemming from immaturity and emotional instability. His strong conscience soon regains control over his grief, and he scolds himself for his inertia. He gets a chance to make up for his initial inaction when the Ghost appears and challenges him to take revenge, but here too Hamlet seems to miss one chance after another to carry out his duty. Instead of concentrating on revenge, he is trying to come to terms with the moral implications of the events in which he is participating. It is Claudius who provides the force behind the play's conflict when he becomes worried about Hamlet's moodiness, interpreting it as suspicion of his own guilt.

Hamlet is sensitive, introspective, and outwardly inactive, at least as compared to Claudius, Laertes, and Fortinbras. Despite appearances, however, his will is not weak, nor is he a coward. On the inside, where it counts, he's the strongest character in the play. It's his over-scrupulous conscience that drives him to undertake seemingly foolish schemes to test his uncle's guilt and to gratify his own moral quest. This is what makes him so attractive to us. We feel somehow that he has the strength of will to do something extraordinary. To test himself, he disregards Horatio's warnings and accepts Claudius' challenge to duel with Laertes. In effect, Hamlet challenges Claudius to kill him.

Hamlet has enjoyed success on the modern stage in spite of, or perhaps because of, its externally weak leading character. It is the compensating features in the play, which provide the attractions. For one thing, Hamlet is likable. He loves his mother and honors his father. He has a sense of humor. He is a gentleman, a poet, a scholar, and a well-trained swordsman and soldier. He is not cowardly inside but morally brave, and of course he's always driven to understand the true morality of the situation. Many of the other characters in the play are also interesting in themselves. There are the strong-willed characters of Claudius, Laertes, and Fortinbras, whose crusades for power offset Hamlet's philosophical ennui. It is the combination of all these features plus the comic interludes and the language that make the play dramatic.

Nevertheless, *Hamlet* and *Mother Courage* are exceptions that prove the rule. In most cases, strong wills are essential to create the conflicts that make plays dramatically compelling in the accepted sense. The leading characters in *Oedipus Rex* (Oedpius), *Tartuffe* (Tartuffe and Orgon), *The School for Scandal* (Joseph Surface), and *The Piano Lesson* (Boy Willie), for example, are models of such strong wills. They are characterized by their determination to impose their wills on everyone else, regardless of the outcome. They drive forward the action in their plays and force things to happen. The leading characters in *The Wild Duck* (Hjalmar Ekdal), *Death of a Salesman* (Willy Loman), *Streamers* (Billy), *Three Sisters* (Irina), and *Angels in America* (Prior Walter) are technically weak. What are the compensating features that furnish the dramatic interest in these plays?

VALUES

Values are what characters stand for or against in the world of the play and their ideas of good and bad and right and wrong. To achieve their objectives, characters embrace the values that gratify them and reject, or at least struggle against, those that do not do so. Values tell characters how they can best get where they want to go. They affect their personal, family, and social lives, their work, and their leisure. They define their reasons for choosing to be who they are. Values arise from personal beliefs about such things as conscience, public- and family-mindedness, ambition, success, and physical pleasure. In some characters, these beliefs will form a pattern of virtues, while in others they may be vices. The deciding issue is whether the values are real convictions or merely tactics adopted for short-term ends.

Madame Pernelle, Orgon's mother in *Tartuffe*, is an example of a character whose values are designed more for social utility than they are for true morality. On the surface her values are honorable. She advocates proper behavior, religious observance, modesty in dress, and respect for authority. She reveals her values in the opening scene when she reproaches the family for what she interprets as their immoral behavior. This is another way of saying that she disagrees with their values. She even criticizes Elmire's clothes, which she believes are too showy for her position in society. Madame Pernelle also criticizes Cleante, Elmire's brother, and Orgon's brother-in-law, whose religious skepticism offends her. In spite of her protests, however, the most important value for Madame Pernelle is not virtue but the appearance of virtue, otherwise known as respectability. Her values are a behavior she has adopted to enable her to appear virtuous to other people, a fact that she naturally tries to conceal.

Values also play an important role in *Death of a Salesman*. As a traveling salesman, Willy believes in the traditional values held by many Americans during the period following World War II. He believes in material prosperity, that the world is a fair place, and that good friends and hard work will lead to success. Early in Act I, Willy tells Linda that he expects the same values in his son, Biff. He wants Biff to accomplish something in the all-American world of business. Although Biff has been on his own for ten years, Willy worries that he "has yet to take thirty-five dollars a week!" Willy believes that in "the greatest country in the world," someone with Biff's "personal attractiveness" and who is such a "hard worker" should be successful. Driven by his absolute faith in the necessity of success in business, Willy is determined to help Biff get a job selling. In the first flashback scene, where Biff and Happy are young boys, Willy reminds them of the values he believes to be important in life, "the man who makes an appearance in the business world, the man who creates personal interest, is the man who gets ahead. Be liked and you will never want."

But if money and friends were Willy's only values, he would not be a very sympathetic character. He values other things, too. First, he loves nature. Besides his garden, one of the things he enjoys most is the New England scenery he sees on his travels. Respecting people as individuals is also important to him, but he senses that this value is disappearing in America and being displaced by financial self-interest. He complains that selling is not as attractive as it once was for someone like him: "The competition is maddening!" Willy also values loyalty, hard work, and friendship, but perhaps most important of all, he values his family. He reveals to Linda that his deepest concern is the possibility of not being able to support them as a father should.

Willy's sensitivity, kindness, sense of duty, and love for his family coexist with his selfishness. That he does not value material success in itself but rather what he believes it can do for his family is clear. His single-minded faith in the religion of business is at odds with his humane family values. In the end, the materialistic values he advocates are discredited. Willy dies for his son, yet Biff only has contempt for his father. It is the neglected son, Happy, who dedicates himself to upholding his father's values. The central issue in *Death of a Salesman* is in large measure the conflict of values between a father and son.

Characters declare their belief in what is right and wrong throughout *The Piano Lesson*, another play about the clash of cultural values. Doaker Charles, a railroad cook, expresses his values with a railroad simile.

> DOAKER
>
> If everybody stay in one place I believe this
> would be a better world. Now what I done
> learned after twenty-seven years of railroading
> is this . . . if the train stays on the track . . .
> it's going to get where it's going. It might
> not be where you're going. If it ain't, then
> all you got to do is sit and wait cause the
> train's coming back to get you. The train don't
> never stop. It'll come back every time.

Which is to say, stick to what you know how to do, mind your own business, and go along with the way things are. Doaker's values are contested by his nephew, Boy Willie, who is from a younger generation and sees things differently.

> BOY WILLIE
>
> See now . . . I'll tell you something about me. I
> done strung along and strung along. Going this
> way and that. Whatever way would lead me to a
> moment of peace. That's all I want. To be easy
> with everything. But I wasn't born to that. I
> was born to a time of fire.
>
> The world ain't wanted no part of me. I could
> see that since I was about seven. The world say
> it's better off without me. See, Berniece
> accept that. She trying to come up where she
> can prove something to the world. Hell, the
> world a better place cause of me. I don't see
> it like Berniece. I got a heart that beats here
> and it beats just as loud as the next fellow's.
> Don't care if he black or white. Sometimes it

beats louder. When it beats louder, then
everybody can hear it. Some people get scared
of that. Like Berniece. Some people get scared
to hear a nigger's heart beating. They think
you ought to lay low with that heart. Make it
beat quiet and go along with everything the way
it is. But my mama ain't birthed me for
nothing. So what I got to do? I got to mark my
passing on the road. Just like you write on a
tree, "Boy Willie was here."

In this speech, Boy Willie has also accurately, if coldly, characterized his sister's values. Berniece thinks she understands her values when, earlier in the play, Avery asks her, "Who you got to love you, Berniece?"

> BERNIECE
> You trying to tell me a woman can't be nothing
> without a man. But you alright, huh? You can
> just walk out of here without me—without a
> woman—and still be a man. That's alright. Ain't
> nobody going to ask you, "Avery, who you got
> to love you?" That's alright for you. But
> everybody gonna be worried about Berniece. "How
> Berniece gonna take care of herself? How she
> gonna raise that child without a man? Wonder
> what she do with herself. How she gonna live
> like that?" Everybody got all kinds of
> questions for Berniece. Everybody telling me I
> can't be a woman unless I got a man. Well, tell
> me, Avery—you know—how much woman am I?

Avery understands that Berniece's way of thinking is more apparent than real, an expression of hurt more than anger. He is speaking about love, not power, he says.

> AVERY
> How long you gonna carry [your deceased
> husband] Crawley with you, Berniece? It's been

over for three years. At some point you got to
let go and go on. Life's got all kinds of
twists and turns. That don't mean you got to
stop living. That don't mean you cut yourself
off from life. You can't go on through life
carrying Crawley's ghost with you. . . .

What is you [waiting] for, Berniece? You just
gonna drift along from day to day. Life is more
than making it from one day to another. You
gonna look up one day and it's all gonna be
past you. Life's gonna be gone out of your
hands—there won't be enough to make nothing
with. I'm standing here now, Berniece—but I
don't know how much longer I'm gonna be
standing here waiting on you.

Berniece is cutting herself off from the past and all the pain it represents to her. She is someone, perhaps like Willy Loman or the Prozorov siblings, who doesn't comprehend what she really values. It takes someone who loves her, an Avery or a Boy Willie, to break through her façade and encourage her authentic self to emerge. August Wilson's conception of authentic black values are the "lesson" of *The Piano Lesson*, and the number of lines devoted to talk about the characters' values are the evidence.

PERSONALITY TRAITS

The word *personality* comes from the Latin *persona*, meaning mask or appearance, ergo the meaning of personality as the manner in which a character is perceived by others, the way he relates to others. Personality has certain definable features called *traits* that include outward appearance. Traits may change in a character depending on the situation, but there is a pattern that shows up under a variety of circumstances. This pattern allows for the collection of a personality profile. For some actors, personality traits are the choices that control how the character looks, sits, stands, walks, gestures, speaks, and behaves with other characters.

Personality traits classify characters into one or more categories, or types. One of the earliest known personality authorities was Hippocrates, the Greek physician responsible for promoting ethical behavior in medicine through the Hippocratic oath. He proposed that the highest amount among four bodily fluids, or humors, determined one's personality type: blood (cheerful, active), phlegm (apathetic, sluggish), black bile (sad, brooding), and yellow bile (irritable, excitable). His personality theory was widely accepted in the West up until the eighteenth century. Although Hippocrates' theory is obsolete, speculation about personality remains fashionable because personality traits are relatively easy to understand and apply in daily life as well as in dramatic literature. One modern version of character types is based upon the work of Carl Jung (a student of Sigmund Freud), in which people are classified on four dimensions: extraversion-introversion, sensing-intuition, thinking-feeling, and judgment-perception. Other familiar examples are narcissistic, perfectionist, aggressive, submissive, non-compliant, compliant, active, sociable, risk-taking, impulsive, expressive, reflective, responsible, confident, happy, anxious, obsessive, autonomous, hypochondriac, guilty, etc.

Personality traits, like other features of play analysis, should be described as simply and clearly as possible. Although the list is potentially endless, the process of determining them is not difficult. First, list all the traits the character shows in the play. At this point, it helps to think broadly better than narrowly. Next, reduce the list to manageable proportions by combining related traits and identifying those of central importance. The result will be a concise profile of personality traits. The most challenging part of the task is learning how to recognize personality traits from what characters say and do. Because personality is something all of us gossip about every day, close observation of human nature is required to distinguish clichés from real human behavior.

Willy Loman is a valuable character on whom to apply this process. He reveals several of his most important personality traits in the opening scene. There Willy is *impatient*, *indecisive*, *impulsive*, and *unkind*; "I said nothing happened. Didn't you hear me?" When he explains why he returned home unexpectedly, he is *worn out*; "I'm tired to death . . . I couldn't make it. I just couldn't make it." His explanation is also *absent-minded*, "I suddenly couldn't drive anymore. . . . Suddenly I realize I'm goin' sixty miles an hours and I don't remember the last five minutes. I'm—I can't seem to—keep my mind to it." The mental confusion that underscores his line, "I have such thoughts, I have such strange thoughts," shows *anxiety*. His rejection of Linda's appeal to him to ask for a desk job reveals *confidence*; "They don't need me in New York. I'm the New England man. I'm vital in New England." Another important trait is *cynicism*, which appears when Linda reminds him that Biff and Happy haven't been home for some time, "Figure it out. Work a lifetime to pay off a house. You finally own it, and there's nobody to live in it." There's also evidence of *loyalty* and *faithfulness*, traits reflected in his public values. More traits appear as the action unfolds, but these traits provide the raw material for Willy's personality profile.

For an example of personality traits in a historical play, consider Hamlet again. His objectives, dramatic actions, willpower, and values have already been discussed. What else can be learned about him? In the first court scene, he shows sensitivity as well as loyalty and devotion to his father. He displays a sharp wit and a lethal sense of irony. In his soliloquies, he shows his habit of intense self-criticism, his penetrating intuition, a mercurial nature, and profound curiosity. His frequent classical references and love of aphorisms indicate that he is intelligent and interested in classical learning. When meeting old friends or being introduced to new ones, Hamlet shows courtesy and sometimes a sunny disposition. He also has a reputation for being a skilled swordsman. Ophelia sums up the general view of at least the public dimensions of Hamlet's personality:

```
                    OPHELIA
    . . . The courtier's, soldier's, scholar's, eye,
       tongue, sword;
    Th' expectancy and rose of the fair state,
    Th' observ'd of all observers.
```

The number and variety of traits in Hamlet's personality make clear why he remains one of the theatre's most appealing characters.

What are the personality traits that distinguish the four Prozorov siblings in *Three Sisters*? Olga is generous, gracious, considerate, and intelligent. As the oldest sibling, she has assumed parental responsibility for keeping up everyone's collective spirits. This has come at the expense of her personal happiness, as expressed by her frequent migraine headaches. Irina is youngest of the four, excitable, sentimental, intelligent, spoiled and self-centered, and anxious about her future. The disintegration of her sentimental view of love forms the through-action of the play. Masha is thoughtful and intelligent, embittered about her failed marriage, and desperate for companionship and affection. Their brother Andrey is cultured, scholarly, kind, introverted, poetical, naive, and insecure. Note their common personality traits of intelligence and good breeding, which is puzzling since they cannot understand themselves or stand up for their own interests.

COMPLEXITY

Characters are interesting to us in relation to how much they know about their circumstances. Their awareness or lack of it is what connects them with the play and determines their importance in the overall dramatic scheme. This capacity for self-knowledge indicates their *complexity*. It is governed by what the characters respond to and by how they respond, whether ignorant, apathetic, and compliant or perceptive, intense, and self-conscious. The most complex character, the one who shows the most power to know himself or herself, is usually the main character. The others are arranged around this character in different degrees of complexity depending on their capacity for self-knowledge. This arrangement is not a defect in the writing but rather a technical necessity resulting from the inherent economy of dramatic composition.

The least complex characters are *types*. They display a single state of mind and are recognized as particular "types" of people found in everyday life. In this group are domineering spouses, slow-witted or quick-witted servants, absent-minded professors, and so forth. A few examples in the study plays are Cokes and Rooney, the braggart soldiers in *Streamers*; Howard Wagner, the heartless businessman in *Death of a Salesman*; and Osric, the foppish dandy in *Hamlet*. Character types show a minimum capacity for self-knowledge and reveal very little about themselves apart from the narrow limitations of their type. They may be interesting, but their dramatic significance stems from their influence on other characters.

The middle degree of complexity includes characters who are more self-aware than types but who are still not as knowledgeable about the whole situation as they might be. Intermediate characters such as Linda and Happy Loman, Mama and Ruth Younger, Gertrude and Ophelia, Natasha Ivanovna, and Doaker Charles are some of the most attractive roles in dramatic literature. By searching the given circumstances for playable potentials, talented actors in these roles often create the impression that their characters are more complex than they are in the script.

The most complex characters are those who are capable of knowing what is happening to them and who allow us to share in their knowledge. As a rule, there is only one character with this degree of complexity in a play, the main character. He or she forms the organizing principle for the play, and most of the action is devoted to this character. There are exceptions to this unitary principle but not as many as some may think. Walter Younger is the single main character in *A Raisin in the Sun* as are Anna Fierling in *Mother Courage*, Yank in *The Hairy Ape*, Prior Walter in *Angels in America*, and Berniece in *The Piano Lesson*. Their capacity for self-knowledge is one of the features that makes them sympathetic and identifies them at once as main characters.

Most plays may be considered biographies of one individual as these are, but sometimes a play may contain more than one complex character, more than one character capable of self-knowledge. Identifying the main character in such plays is not always easy. Is *Death of a Salesman* about Willy or Biff? Is *The Wild Duck* about Gregers or Hjalmar? Is *Tartuffe* about Tartuffe or Orgon? Is *A Lie of the Mind* about Jake, Beth, or even Lorraine? Who is the main character in *Three Sisters*, or indeed is there one in the accepted sense? Some of the issues involved in identifying the main character are discussed below. In any case, although there is only a single main character, there may be more than one character capable of self-awareness. We'll learn more about this issue later on.

RELATIONSHIPS

The focus of dramatic interest of a play is the conflict between the leading character and his or her chief opponent. Citing Aristotle, writers call these characters the *protagonist* and the *antagonist*. The relationship formed by them comprises the *main relationship* in the play. Oedipus and Teiresias provide the main relationship in *Oedipus Rex*, Hamlet and Claudius in *Hamlet*, Walter and Mama in *A Raisin in the Sun*, Willy and Biff in *Death of a Salesman*, Berniece and Boy Willie in *The Piano*

Lesson, and Prior and Louis in *Angels in America*. The relationships between these opposing pairs is purposely designed to be the center of dramatic attention. Incidentally, the fact that some plays contain only one character does not dispose of the concept of a main relationship. In such cases, the antagonist may be off-stage (the wife in Anton Chekhov's monodrama *On the Harmfulness of Tobacco*, for example) or may be a different part of the main character (like young Krapp in Samuel Beckett's play *Krapp's Last Tape*).

The protagonist and antagonist's relations with other characters can be considered minor relationships. Although these can be as interesting as the main relationship, they are nonetheless subsidiary to it for reasons of dramatic focus. They exist to underscore the main relationship thematically, and only enough of the minor relationship is furnished to fulfill this function. For example, Oedipus has minor relationships with Creon and Jocasta; these relationships, however, are a direct outcome of his main relationship with Teiresias. Walter Younger and his mother have minor relationships with Ruth, Beneatha, and Bobo. Walter and Mama are not continuously on stage together, but their relationship is developed by implication through these minor relationships.

There are differences of opinion about main relationships. Modern artistic conventions presume that our understanding of plays is not permanently fixed. Productions need to be single-minded, of course, but interpretations are expected to be diverse. Within limits, the inherent meanings of plays may change from one generation to the next as society changes. This is true as well in the choice of a main relationship, which should be a central issue in any new interpretation of a classic. In Tyrone Guthrie and Laurence Olivier's famous Old Vic production of *Hamlet* in 1937, the main relationship was Hamlet and his mother. Guthrie professed to demonstrate how the Oedipus complex operated through them. Sigmund Freud's theories were still novel enough in 1937 for the interpretation to cause considerable controversy. Some said that the production was *revisionist*, meaning that it was intentionally unconventional, made for the sake of shock value.

It is true that some of the unconventional main relationships in recent revivals of older plays are probably revisionist in intent. But theatre is not science. There is no law against a fresh understanding of the main relationship if it is based on an honest appraisal of the script and consistent with the sense of the production. A fair understanding of *Hamlet*, for example, might suggest other choices for the main relationship—Hamlet and his deceased father, Hamlet and Horatio, Hamlet and Laertes, Hamlet and Fortinbras, or (according to playwright Tom Stoppard) not Hamlet and anyone else, but Rosencrantz and Guildenstern. What about the relationship between Walter and his deceased father in *A Raisin in the Sun*? Or between Jake and his deceased father, or Jake and his brother Mike, or Jake and his mother Lorraine in *A Lie of the Mind*? All of these are unconventional choices and yet all are based on a fair assessment of the information provided in the plays themselves. The key to identifying the main relationship is honest understanding based on a conscientious analysis of the script.

SUMMARY

Objectives are the specific goals that characters strive to achieve. They help make sense of a character's different feelings and thoughts by relating them to a single commanding desire. Qualities are the behaviors that characters employ to achieve their objectives. Role conflicts consist of the tensions that arise from characters' opposing views of each other. Conflicts of objectives result from their opposing goals.

The degree of force with which characters pursue their goals is their willpower. Although historical drama depends on strong-willed characters to make things happen, in modern plays many weak-willed characters and those with vacillating wills can often be found. When the leading character is weak-willed, there are usually compensating factors to sustain the play's interest. The characters' choices of the good and bad things in life define their values. A character's situation in relation to other characters and his or her point of view to the world of the play is determined by his or her values. Personality traits are a character's physical and vocal identification marks together with the impulses and inhibitions that reveal his or her individuality and how he or she relates to others. To focus attention, playwrights compose their characters in progressive levels of complexity. Ordinarily, the more self-aware a character is, the more important that character is in the play. The main character is the one who is most self-aware, or at least potentially so, although there are exceptions. Playwrights also arrange character relationships to further concentrate dramatic attention. The conflict between the main character and his or her main opponent is the main relationship. Other relationships are considered minor but contribute to the main relationship in some identifiable way.

All these features are carefully crafted by the playwright and form the collective pattern that we call character. Strictly speaking, dramatists create characters that exist only in the script. It is actors who create living *characterizations* from the raw material provided by written characters.

QUESTIONS

Objectives   What is the character's super-objective in the play? What are the minor objectives for each scene, unit, and beat? (Super-objectives should be expressed using infinitive forms of active, concrete verbs.) How do the minor objectives for each character unite to form the through-action for that character's super-objective? How do the super-objectives for each character unite in the super-objective of the play?

Qualities   What is the character's main quality or behavior in the play? What are the secondary qualities for the beats, units, and scenes under study? For all the beats, units, and scenes in the play? Can a quality be discovered for each line of dialogue as well?

Conflicts   For the unit or scene under study, what are the characters' opposing views of one another (role conflicts)? For the play as a whole? Do the characters' super-objectives and minor objectives clash with those of other characters (conflicts of objectives)? Where do those clashes appear?

Willpower   How much power does the character possess to carry out his or her objectives? Why? Is the character's willpower steady, does it vacillate or gain or lose force in certain circumstanes? If so, where in the play does it do so? Why?

Values   What does the character stand for and against? What does the character consider to be right and wrong? Good and bad? How do the character's values relate to those of the other characters? To the world of the play?

Personality Traits   What is the character's energy level? Is it consistent or does it vary from one scene to another? How old is the character? What occupation? How does the character look? How does the character move? How does the character sound? What is the character's mental and emotional outlook? What are the character's internal impulses and inhibitions?

Complexity   How self-aware is the character? Is the character a type or an intermediate or a fully complex individual? Why? Who is the most complex (main) character? Why? Who are the minor characters? Why?

Relationships   What is the main character relationship? Why? Could any other relationship be interpreted as the main relationship? Why? What are the minor character relationships? Why? How do they augment the main relationship?

POSTSCRIPT FOR ACTION ANALYSIS

After Action Analysis, search for the play's Seed, or Subject, hidden within the characters. How does the Seed influence the characters? Why did the playwright choose these specific characters from the whole range of other possibilities? How would the play be different with other characters? In what way does connecting the Seed with the characters help the play grow and develop?

POSTSCRIPT FOR THE SCORE OF A ROLE

The *Score of a Role* was one of Stanislavski's last contributions to his system of acting. Even as Action Analysis of a play is more or less equivalent to the Score of a Play, Action Analysis of a character is much the same as what he called the Score of a Role. As a result, the process of developing the Score of a Role closely corresponds to that described in Chapter 1, except that it is applied only to a single character. Actors will find the Score of the Role one of the most useful ways to take hold of a character as a whole. A Score is not a substitute for Formalist Analysis with all of its details and layers, but a Score usually provides enough groundwork to start rehearsals with.

To give a demonstration of the Score of a Role, we will analyze the character of Ophelia from *Hamlet*. Setting down the Score in the form of an outline reinforces the logic of its keystone, the Seed. Chapter 1 provided explanations for each concept and the procedure for establishing it. The practical value of the Score of a Role should become self-evident from the following account.

Sequence of Events: External Events

The Score of a Role is concerned with only those events in which the character appears on stage, whether speaking lines or silent. Ophelia is not in every scene of *Hamlet*; few characters are in any play. She plays a part in only six External Events:

1,2: Claudius takes over the throne
1,3: Laertes departs for France
2,1: Reynaldo departs for France
3,1: Claudius eavesdrops on Hamlet and Ophelia
3,2: The "mousetrap scene"
4,5: Laertes returns to Elsinore

This is how we defined the External Events in Chapter 1, when dealing with Action Analysis for the whole play. To establish the Score of the Role for Opehlia, we should revise the descriptions to center on her. The following descriptions do so while using the same kind of brevity and simplicity promoted in Chapter 1.

1,2: Ophelia attends the accession of Claudius
1,3: Laertes says good-bye to Ophelia
2,1: Ophelia seeks help from Polonius
3,1: Ophelia returns Hamlet's gifts
3,2: Ophelia meets Hamlet in public
4,5: Ophelia presents flowers to Claudius and Gertrude

Reviewing the Facts

We can see the broad outline of Ophelia's role emerging already. Consider: her father stops loving her, her brother abandons her, her lover rejects her, her father forces her to give up the only person she loves, her lover torments her in public, she escapes into the past where she used to be happy.

Seed

Previously, we determined that the Seed of *Hamlet* is *idealism*. Since by definition the Seed must influence all the characters, it follows that idealism also influences Ophelia. Her idealism is embodied in Hamlet, Laertes, and Polonius, each of whom she loves and each of whom turns on her and becomes her tormentor.

Sequence of Events: Internal Events

One by one, Ophelia's ideals are destroyed. The Internal Events illustrate the assaults on her idealism.

1,2, External: Ophelia attends the accession of Claudius

1,2, Internal: Ophelia sees that Polonius supports Claudius and that Hamlet is distressed. Two of her ideals have suddenly become distorted.

1,3, External: Laertes says good-bye to Ophelia

1,3, Internal: Laertes, another of her ideals, deserts her

2,1, External: Ophelia seeks help from Polonius

2,1, Internal: She vainly seeks her Father's help when Hamlet, her most sacred ideal, rejects her

3,1, External: Ophelia returns Hamlet's gifts

3,1, Internal: Her father forces her to lie to Hamlet and Hamlet abuses her for lying

3,2, External: Ophelia meets Hamlet in public

3,2, Internal: Hamlet, once her ideal gentleman-courtier-lover, publicly torments her

4,5, External: Ophelia presents flowers to Claudius and Gertrude
4,5, Internal: Ophelia bids farewell to this ruthless world and returns to
   the ideal world where she remembers being happy

Three Major Climaxes

A role has a beginning, a middle, and an end just as a play does. With
only six events to deal with, these points in Ophelia's character are relatively easy to recognize. The First Major Climax occurs when her world,
composed of her father, her brother, and Hamlet, changes with the accession of Claudius to the throne. The Second Major Climax, the middle or
tipping point of her development, is 3,1, where she is forced to act in
opposition to everything she holds good and true by lying to Hamlet
about her love for him. The Third Major Climax, the end, is her farewell
to this world in 4,5.

Theme

The Theme of the play is *impossible idealism*, but that description applies
to Hamlet more than to Ophelia. Her idealism is not of the impossible
variety. She asks only that Hamlet, Laertes, and Polonius love and understand her as they used to do. Moreover, she does not attempt to impose
her idealism on others. It is the others who assault her with their distorted
brands of idealism. Her fate may be compared with that of Hedvig in *The
Wild Duck*. Thus, Ophelia's variant of the Theme might be described as
the destruction of innocent idealism.

Super-Objective

To ascertain Ophelia's Super-Objective, ask, "What does she want from
life?" Let's make several tries at it. She wants Hamlet to love her; she
wants to obey her father; she wants to please her brother; she wants
things the way they were before Claudius took over; she wants a happy
life once again. What unites these alternatives is Ophelia's belief that
something has gone terribly wrong, but that despite her best efforts, she

cannot discover what it is. Maybe she has done something wrong, something to make everyone suddenly hate and abuse her? Therefore, her Super-Objective could be *to find out what she has done wrong*. There may be other choices for Ophelia's Super-Objective, but this description is supported by a great deal of evidence in the play and offers a unifying line of development for her character. The submissive goal *to find out* is also consistent with her subordinate role. Ophelia is not in a position to influence significantly the actions of others.

Through-Action

The Through-Action is an account of a particular character performing a particular action under particular conditions. Who is Ophelia? The innocent daughter of a newly appointed government official. What is she doing? Trying to come to terms with her new world. Where is she doing it? In the corrupt court of Denmark. Hence, the Through-Action, *the innocent daughter of a crooked government official tries to come to terms with the corrupt environment in which she is forced live*. Ophelia is the daughter of a criminal who is forced to choose whether she wants to live in his morally corrupt world.

Counter Through-Action

Hamlet's chief opponent in the play is Claudius, who is the cause of the corruption in the court. His relationship with Claudius forms the *Main Relationship* of the play. But Claudius does not directly influence Ophelia's behavior. Her actions are influenced by Polonius, Laertes, and, above all, by Hamlet—all three of whom assault her innocence in one way or another. Most readers would probably agree that Hamlet is the character who influences her most and is the one in whom she is most disappointed. Hamlet occupies the other position in Ophelia's Main Relationship. Accordingly, the Counter Through-Action for Ophelia's character may be described as *a passionately idealistic prince (unwittingly) destroys the woman he loves in a reckless attempt to purge the court of corruption*.

CHAPTER 7

Idea

The word *idea* comes from Greek meaning the inner form of a thing as opposed to its physical reality. From this root comes the current meaning of a thought or a mental image. Idea is also related to the word *ideal*, meaning a model or an original pattern. To some extent, idea has been discussed already in connection with given circumstances, background story, plot, and character. Earlier chapters, however, treated each feature's contribution to idea, not the element itself. This chapter will concentrate on idea as a basic element of drama.

Many people think of idea in drama in connection with *idea plays*, sometimes called *problem plays, thesis plays, propaganda plays*, or *social dramas*. Idea plays began in France during the early nineteenth century with the works of Alexander Dumas the younger, Henri Bisque, and Eugene Brie. The tradition was expanded by Ibsen and Shaw and by later dramatists. They are a part of today's theatre tradition. Idea plays treat controversial issues from a didactic, or instructional, point of view and offer, or at least imply, a solution. Sometimes idea plays call attention to shortcomings alleged in society; at other times, their intention is more radical. Shaw originated the *discussion play*, a kind of idea play in which current social, political, or economic issues are debated as part of the play's action.

Although idea and discussion plays aim at social reform, the concept of idea under discussion now is broader than these two types of plays. Idea here means the thought pattern expressed by the whole play. Some writers refer to this as the *theme, super-objective, spine, meaning, outlook,* or *world view* of the play. Idea is present in all plays in one form or another, but we should stress that dramatic ideas are not always as significant as those found in *Oedipus Rex, Hamlet, Angels in America,* or *Happy Days.* Idea is most important in serious plays and satires. Idea appears in comedies, too, but in such plays, character and plot are more important. Idea is least important in farce and old-fashioned melodrama; the absurdists, however, even managed to invest farce with intellectual significance.

According to critic Francis Fergusson in *The Idea of a Theatre,* the idea "points to the object which the dramatist is trying to show us, and we must in some sense grasp that if we are to understand his complex art." In other words, idea controls the direction play analysis and subsequent artistic work should take. Learning to deal with idea is also a good mental exercise because it tests the quality of our thinking about the play. Idea lays the foundation for intelligible discussions about plays and is essential for communication among the members of the artistic team.

Differences of opinion about the concept of idea illuminate one of the major differences between studying plays for purposes of performance and for other purposes. For despite idea's centrality in script analysis, it cannot be everything in a production. The intellectual issue a play expresses seldom provides enough entertainment value by itself. In *Mother Courage, Happy Days, Three Sisters, Angels in America,* or *The Hairy Ape,* the idea may be stimulating, but the play's characters and unusual style are what entertain audiences. In other words, idea may hold a play together, but normally it is not the chief entertainment value. Idea illuminates characters and plot, which in turn provide the entertainment value. That is why actors, directors, and designers should guard against the notion that playwrights are philosophers and that plays are meant to demonstrate intellectual issues. Idea is not imposed on a play by the author but rather formed from within it. Idea determines what a play is about on its deepest level, forming the organizing principle of the entire work.

Plays express idea in many ways, but there are two general methods, *direct* and *indirect.* The idea in *Death of a Salesman* is expressed directly because it is stated in the words of the characters. The same may be said of *Tartuffe, The Piano Lesson, Angels in America,* and *Hamlet.* On the other hand, the idea in *Streamers* is expressed through the implications of the plot and characters. The same is true for *Happy Days, A Lie of the Mind,* and *Three Sisters.* Intellectual discussion is not usually found in these plays. Nevertheless, the use of one method does not exclude the use of the other at the same time or in the same play.

IDEA IN THE WORDS

The standard verbal devices for conveying literary meaning include the titles, discussions, aphorisms, allusions, set speeches, and imagery and symbolism. In some plays the need to talk about idea is so strong that the plot seems a pretext for a discussion of intellectual issues—for example, in the plays of George Bernard Shaw or Tom Stoppard. Characters talk about ideas in such a way that their words can almost be removed intact from the dialogue and used for a composition on the intellectual issues in the play. But playwrights are subtler than this. Discussion or comments about ideas are embedded in conversations so that a feeling of continuous everyday speech is maintained. Dramatists may turn their attention to intellectual issues, but they seldom overlook the principal need for dialogue to advance the plot and reveal character.

Titles

Very often playwrights embed ideas in titles. The title of *A Raisin in the Sun* is a line from a poem by Langston Hughes about frustrated idealism. The titles of *The Wild Duck, Happy Days, A Lie of the Mind, The Piano Lesson,* and *Streamers* indicate the dramatic idea by implication. The important task with implications, of course, is interpreting them within their proper contexts. Often the title points to the main character of the play as in *Oedipus Rex, Three Sisters,* and *Hamlet.* A title that refers to both the main character and the idea is *Death of a Salesman.* Willy Loman, the salesman, is the main character of the play, but the title also points by implication to the dramatic idea. We would expect a title like "The Death of . . ." to refer to an important person such as a member of royalty or a famous artist. However, a salesman is an ordinary person, an illustration of the American common man. Thus Miller's decision to use the word *salesman* (i.e., ordinary businessman) instead of someone more important is a clue to the idea of the play. The titles of *The Hairy Ape*, *The School for Scandal*, and *Angels in America* were probably chosen as much for their curiosity value as their ability to connect with the dramatic idea.

Discussions

Characters sometimes step back from the plot and engage in discussions about an assortment of ideas. When this happens, the principle of artistic unity ensures that the discussion topics will relate in some way to the main idea of the play. As was mentioned earlier, pointed debates are a characteristic of discussion plays, but shorter debates, or discussions, may occur in any kind of play. In *Oedipus Rex*, Sophocles included discussions about the capriciousness of the gods, the nature of political power, the role of chance in human affairs, and the credibility of oracles. Shakespeare is not an intellectual dramatist, but he included discussions about a wide assortment of ideas in *Hamlet*. Some of them are grief, love, duty, afterlife, revenge, divine Providence, indecision, ennui, ambition, suicide, the art of acting, the responsibilities of public office, divine forgiveness, honor, and guilt. The working-class characters in *Mother Courage* discuss their opinions about the war, economics, means and ends, military strategy, religion, and politics. *Angels in America* contains many discussions about politics and religion. *The Piano Lesson* contains discussions about moral issues presented in the form of homespun anecdotes.

Discussions exist in serious plays as well as in comedies. Discussions about religious principles and tolerance in *Tartuffe* have already been pointed out. In *The School for Scandal*, there are discussions about reputation, literary fashions, and relations among the classes. *Three Sisters* contains discussions about how best to conduct one's life, which may or may not be reflected in the lives of the characters that offer it. Discussions may not always point directly to the main idea, but they can lead the way to it through careful consideration of the given circumstances in which they occur.

Aphorisms

The term *aphorism* comes from a Greek word meaning a concise statement of a principle, truth, or sentiment. We use the word in script analysis to cover proverbs, precepts, maxims, rejoinders, epigrams, famous sayings, mottoes, self-evident truths, sententious generalizations, and intellectual inversions—all the brief, quotable statements that compress human experience into a concise generality. For example, architect Miës van der Rohe's observation, "God is in the details," is an aphorism, as is Thoreau's statement, "It is never too late to give up your prejudices." Both statements consolidate personal experience about life into short statements. Unlike discussions, aphorisms are not mini-debates or reports of specific matters. They are brief remarks about general principles.

Sophocles introduced a number of aphorisms into *Oedipus Rex*. Some of the most notable are:

```
—There is no fairer duty than that of helping
 others in distress.
—No man can judge the rough unknown or trust in
 second sight, for wisdom changes hands among
 the wise.
—Time, and time alone, will show the just man,
 though scoundrels are discovered in a day.
```

Hamlet's enjoyment of aphorisms is one of his personality traits:

```
—Frailty, thy name is woman.
—Foul deeds will rise, though all the earth
 o'erwhelm them, to men's eyes.
—That one can smile and smile and be a villain.
—To be or not to be, that is the question.
```

Hamlet takes so much pleasure in aphorisms that he writes them down in his table book, a personal accessory Elizabethan gentlemen kept handy for this purpose: "My tables—meet it is I set it down / That one may smile, and smile, and be a villain."

The value of aphorisms in revealing idea depends on the intellectual acuteness and credibility of the character that is speaking. When unscrupulous characters speak aphorisms, they can express an opposite meaning from what is intended. For instance, in *Hamlet*, Polonius is also fond of aphorisms. His famous farewell advice to Laertes is often cited out of context as a model aphorism of moral behavior. Knowing what a hypocrite Polonius is, however, it is hard to take him seriously when he says things like "To thine own self be true, and it must follow, as the night the day, thou, canst not then be false to any man."

Irony also characterizes the use of aphorisms in modern plays. In *Mother Courage*, Brecht uses epigrams that sound like simple folk sayings:

```
—If you want the war to work for you, you've
 got to give the war its due.
—On the whole, you can say that victory amid
 defeat cost us plain people plenty.
—The best thing for us is when politics gets
 bogged down.
```

An interesting aphorism appears in *Angels in America* when Rabbi Isador Chemelwitz declines to hear Louis confess his guilty feelings about leaving Prior. The epigram is underlined.

```
              RABBI ISADOR CHEMELWITZ
. . . You want to confess, better you should find
a priest.


                      LOUIS
But I'm not a Catholic, I'm a Jew.


              RABBI ISADOR CHEMELWITZ
Worse luck for you bubbalah. Catholics believe
in forgiveness; Jews believe in guilt.
```

Discerning readers may find in this aphorism an analogue for the two different world views expressed in Part I and Part II of this play. Dramatists employ aphorisms to highlight certain ideas that help to form a pattern of meaning throughout the play.

Allusions

An *allusion* is a reference to another work of literature or to a person or an event outside of the play. It is a way of sending a signal about the idea to the culturally literate members of the audience. Not everyone may recognize allusions. On the other hand, those who do spot them are rewarded with the thrill of additional hidden insights. Historically, the most common allusions came from the Bible, Torah and Koran, and classical literature, history, and mythology. In the present day, there may be a variety of hidden references in a play, including many that refer to current affairs and popular culture.

One playwright acknowledged for his use of allusions is Samuel Beckett. His play *Happy Days* contains many examples. Sometimes they are set off from the dialogue like aphorisms and at other times they are integrated into the dialogue and require very close reading to uncover. Scholars have discovered over two dozen sources for the allusions in *Happy Days*, ranging from the works of classical Greek playwright Menander to songs by Viennese composer Franz Lehar. Even the physical action of the play is an allusion. The reference is to Dante's *Inferno*, where characters in one level of hell lie half-buried in the earth as punishment for their sins. All the allusions relate in some way to the nearness of death and the transitory nature of earthly things, issues that are connected to the main idea of the play.

In *Angels in America,* Tony Kushner was fond of using allusions from all kinds of highbrow and lowbrow sources, including politics, religion, camp homosexual culture, and popular culture, to cite some of the obvious examples.

—*Annie Hall*	—Clinique
—Bayeaux tapestry	—*Come Back, Little Sheba*
—Belle Reeve	—Conran's
—Berlin Wall	—D Train
—Big Mac	—*Democracy in America*
—CBS Mike Wallace	—Ed Koch
—Cecil B. Demille	—Ed Meese
—Central Park	—Ethel Rosenberg
—Chernobyl	—George Schultz
—Christian martyr	—Grace Jones

—Henry Kissinger	—Morticia Addams
—*in vitro*	—Newt Gingrich
—J. Edgar Hoover	—Ollie North
—Jacob and the Angel	—Pepto Bismol
—Jesse Helms	—Perestroika
—Jessie Jackson	—prodigal son
—Joe McCarthy	—*Profiles in Courage*
—Kaddish	—*Rosemary's Baby*
—*King Lear*	—the Rosenberg case
—land of the free, home of the brave	—Roy Cohn
—Lazarus	—San Francisco
—Legionnaire's disease	—Stephen Spielberg
—Louis Farrakhan	—Tab
—Macy's	—The Ramble
—Mikhail Gorbachev	—*The Twilight Zone*

Perhaps separately these references don't mean much to readers who understand them, but collectively they fulfill a particular artistic purpose that harmonizes with the thematic heart of the play.

Allusions may be difficult for some readers to catch, but they are meant to be more than mind games. In the hands of a skilled playwright, allusions enrich plays with their associations. The Yellow Dog talked about so often in *The Piano Lesson* is a piece of Southern folklore that refers to an ill-tempered dog that turns on its own master. This moral precept could have a bearing on our understanding of the play. More specifically, on our understanding of Berniece, who behaves as though she is rejecting her own heritage. Comparable to other conventions described in this chapter, allusions such as this one can lend themselves to a coherent pattern of meaning that points to the main idea if not completely illuminating it. Moreover, allusions are a practical test of artistic awareness because their understanding depends on our cultural literacy, or knowledge of our common cultural heritage.

Set Speeches

Set speeches are extended speeches in which important issues in the play are emphasized. They stand out from the surrounding dialogue because they are longer and because they are so rationally composed and orchestrated, like operatic arias or arguments in a formal debate. There may be one or several set speeches (or none) in a play on a variety of subjects or viewpoints. In all cases, however, they embody at that moment the thematic essence of the scene or play. Because of their self-conscious craftsmanship, set speeches appear more often in nonrealistic period dramas where poetic language is used. Laertes' admonition to Ophelia in 1,3 of *Hamlet,* in which he warns her against expecting too much from Hamlet's affection, is an example of a set speech. In the context of saying good-bye to his sister, he concisely explains the responsibilities of kingship for Hamlet. Laertes' speech lifts the story out of the realm of individual personalities and reinforces the social and political significance of the play. There are three set speeches in *Tartuffe.* The first two appear together in Act 1, when Cleante describes the ideal traits of a religious person, and the third takes place at the end of the play when the Officer pays tribute to the wisdom and generosity of the king.

Set speeches present plausibility problems in modern realistic plays, but Arthur Miller managed to include one by Charley in the Requiem scene of *Death of a Salesman,* and David Rabe included several in *Streamers.* Louis Ironson's role in *Angels in America* contains several set speeches about political liberalism. In the same play, Aleksii Antediluvianovich Prelapsarionov's remarks at the beginning of Part II form a set speech. Because set speeches are intended to call attention to important intellectual issues in the play, they are reliable sources of information about the main idea. Moreover, as windows into the core of the play, they also provide excellent acting opportunities for clever actors. They're longer than adjacent speeches, are orchestrated to achieve particular emotional effects, and emphasize crucial issues in the play.

Imagery

What has already been written in literature textbooks about imagery (and the next topic, symbolism) doesn't need to be repeated here. It is enough to point out that imagery refers to figurative words used to represent people, places, or things; feelings or ideas; or sensory experiences. By expressing issues in sensory form, imagery increases the resources for understanding plays. Critics have found that the image of light, for example, is important in *Oedipus Rex*. G. Wilson Knight *(The Wheel of Fire)* and Caroline Spurgeon *(Shakespeare's Imagery and What It Tells Us)* have found that imagery plays a role in Shakespeare's plays. *Hamlet*, for example, contains many images of decay. Various post-apocalyptic images are found in *Happy Days*, and imagery about bodily functions is seen in *Mother Courage*. Images of frontier America can be found in *A Lie of the Mind*. Imagery creates sensory patterns of meaning that help to illuminate the play as a whole. Studying the imagery may not be as immediately productive as analyzing other features, but it can clarify thinking and help resolve confusions that might otherwise exist. Perhaps the main practical value lies in the ability of imagery to influence designers' imaginations in harmony with the main intellectual issues of a play.

Symbolism

A *symbol* is something that represents something other than itself. The word *symbol* comes from a Greek verb meaning to throw together; its noun form means a mark or a sign. Symbols vary in complexity and purpose, but here we will consider two kinds. *Intentional symbols* are those in which there is a direct equation (that is, scales equal justice, owl equals wisdom) either because of a commonly accepted meaning or because of being designated as a symbol in the play. In contrast, *incidental symbols* are imposed on the play from outside, that is, from readers. They are of minor or casual interest and have little practical value in script analysis.

Normally, the author who uses intentional symbols slips them in cunningly. If they stand out from the context, they may distract from the play and make it too much like a sermon or a book report. In the hands of a skilled playwright, intentional symbols can enrich by association, like allusions or imagery, except more noticeable and therefore more potent. By evoking abstract ideas and feelings in concrete form, intentional symbols function as connections between the play and the outside world. They can often reveal more about the main idea, and reveal it more emphatically, than any other literary element.

The wild duck in the play of the same name is an example of an intentional symbol. We learn from the play that when a Scandinavian wild duck is wounded, it doesn't try to escape but dives into the water and clings to the weeds on the bottom. Readers also learn that a wild duck is easily tamed and despite its name thrives in captivity. Notice that Gregers, the radical idealist, is the one who designates the wild duck as a symbol of Hjalmar when he says to him in Act 2, "I almost think you have something of the wild duck in you." The symbol of the wild duck reinforces behavior patterns that Gregers thinks he sees in Hjalmar. According to Gregers, the wild duck represents Hjalmar's inability to cope with the misfortunes in his life. He also believes that Hjalmar has forsaken his youthful ideals for a comfortable existence. The meaning of the wild duck is clear because the playwright has made it part of the story.

Other intentional symbols are the ape in *The Hairy Ape,* Mama's potted plant in *A Raisin in the Sun,* the pregnant ant in *Happy Days,* Anna Fierling's canteen wagon in *Mother Courage,* the spinning top that Fedotik presents to Irina in *Three Sisters,* the piano in *The Piano Lesson,* Bethesda Fountain in *Angels in America,* and the name Oedipus (wounded foot) in *Oedipus Rex.* As was said before, symbolism should be treated carefully as a device for expressing idea. It may be an appealing exercise to impose symbols onto a play, but there is a risk that the result may express merely marginal notions. By definition, intentional symbols are legitimately present in the play, therefore they are more helpful in script analysis than are symbols that are imposed externally.

Prologue and Epilogue

The prologue and epilogue are other literary devices used for directly presenting idea. The *prologue* (literally, the speech before) introduces background story and sets up what the play is about. The *epilogue* (the speech after) summarizes idea by restating it at the end of the play within a larger context. In a classical Greek tragedy such as *Oedipus Rex,* the prologue and epilogue frame the action according to accepted tragic form. They highlight the main idea by their characteristics as formal parts of the play and through the words of the Chorus. The Requiem at the end of *Death of a Salesman* is a formal epilogue that has a similar function. The nature of the funeral scene leads us to expect a summing up, which we find in the words of Linda, Biff, Happy, and Charley. *Angels in America* has a formal epilogue, which helps to concentrate the idea in this lengthy play made up of so many dissimilar elements.

IDEA IN THE CHARACTERS

Another way idea may be expressed is through conventional kinds of characters. Expressing idea in this way involves definite technical restrictions, however, because characters cannot speak for the meaning too much without hurting the play's plausibility. They can only say what is permitted within the limits of their own identities and while addressing other characters. With these limitations in mind, playwrights have developed conventional characters that can embody idea without straining logic or risking entertainment value. These conventional characters do not appear in every play. Moreover, when they do appear there is no rule against a single character fulfilling several playwriting functions at the same time.

We should not depend too much on conventional characters to learn about idea, for that comes close to one of the reading fallacies discussed in the Introduction. Interest in the ideas that characters express and the technical functions some characters carry out should not lead to misunderstanding the characters as characters. Some characters may give emphasis to idea, but in the best plays, they are never just mouthpieces for the playwright. Characters behave as characters because they are governed first by artistic considerations and only later by technical requirements.

Narrator or Chorus

The narrator or chorus tells a story to the audience and participates in it with the other characters. Because they always know more about the circumstances than do the other characters, they can be looked to for information about idea. In *Mother Courage*, Anna Fierling, Eilif, Yvette, and the Chaplain step out of the action several times and speak or sing to the audience as narrators. They explain the play in musical numbers like

"The Song of the Old Wife and the Soldier," "The Song of Fraternization," and "The Song of the Great Capitulation." Choruses in Greek tragedies also play the dual roles of narrators during the choral odes and ordinary characters during the episodes. In Part II of *Angels in America*, Aleksii Antedilluvianovich Prelapsarionov addresses his colleagues in the Kremlin Hall of Deputies in a way that functions like a narrator, and Prior Walter steps forward and speaks to the audience at the end of the play. When the narrator or chorus interrupts the action to talk about ideas, the purpose is usually to explain something about the meaning.

Raisonneur

Another character that knows more than the other characters is the *raisonneur*, a type of narrator, but one who always remains within the action. Although participating in the action, the *raisonneur* has little direct effect on it, thus furnishing this character with objectivity and credibility. The *raisonneur* is often a doubter, wishing to offer sound advice or to convince through reason. A classic example of a *raisonneur* is Cleante in *Tartuffe*. He always remains within the action, yet his skeptical personality encourages him to editorialize without obviously appearing to do so. Although he has no major influence on the plot, he expresses his opinions about intellectual issues in the play. Dr. Relling in *The Wild Duck* is another example of a *raisonneur*. After his introduction during the lunch scene in Act 3, he appears in the plot four more times. He objects to Mrs. Sorby's marriage plans, admonishes Gregers' misplaced idealism, locates the missing Hjalmar, and provides medical help for Hedvig. Relling says that he is "cultivating the life illusion" in others. Despite an inclination to moralize, *raisonneurs* like Relling are most effective in performance when they are understood as part of the world of the play and not merely as sermonizers. For example, as a character Cleante expresses outrage when Orgon treats his religious skepticism as the rantings of an atheist. Similarly, Dr. Relling becomes angry when Gregers Werle accuses him of being indifferent to the welfare of his friend Hjalmar. Their words are part of their characters, not merely stuck on to explain the meaning.

Confidant

A *confidant* (or feminine *confidante*) is a character with the technical function of sympathizing with the private feelings and thoughts of the main character. Like a *raisonneur*, this character has little direct influence on the action even though remaining within it continuously. Since others confide in this character, however, the confidant is more often a trusted friend than a skeptical observer, a well-adjusted character without serious personal conflicts. An actorly objective for a confidant might be to help the main character adjust to a difficult situation. In this capacity, a confidant provides an opportunity for talking about matters that are important to the main character.

Charley, Willy Loman's next-door neighbor in *Death of a Salesman*, is a typical confidant. Aside from Willy's brother Ben, he is the one with whom Willy shares his private feelings. In Act 1, Charley listens sympathetically and helps Willy to take his mind off his troubles. In Act 2, he gives Willy practical help with offers of money and a job. Other examples of confidants are Horatio in Hamlet, Ruth in *A Raisin in the Sun* (she's Mama's confidant), Roger in *Streamers,* Belize and Hannah in *Angels in America,* and Sally in *A Lie of the Mind.* By definition, confidants function outside the main action most of the time. This apparent weakness is compensated for by their strong desire to help. By offering the main character a chance to talk in safety about private matters, confidants provide support and encouragement unobtainable from anyone else in the play.

Norm Character

Literary critics borrowed the term *norm* or *normative character* from the social sciences. It describes someone who is prudently adjusted to the dominant social standards in the world of the play. The norm character is another example of a character that knows more about the situation than do the other characters, but in this case superior awareness results more from personal insight than from direct information. Norm characters do not appear in every play. As a rule, they appear in comedy, in which their common sense serves as a technical reference point against which to compare the eccentric behavior of other characters. Comic writers know that eccentricity is more clearly illuminated if it is displayed against a background of cheerful common sense.

In *Tartuffe*, the norm character is Orgon's wife, Elmire. Despite Madame Pernelle's harsh opinion of her, Elmire is prudently adjusted to the peculiar social standards of her society. She is independent-minded, good-natured, tolerant, and wise in the ways of the world. For her, religion is a private matter, not a commodity for public discussion. Although Elmire disapproves of Tartuffe, she does not overreact by publicly condemning him, an act she knows would almost certainly backfire. Instead, her objective is to save Orgon by exposing Tartuffe as a fraud. This is part of her main objective, which might be to rescue Orgon from the influence of his mother.

In *The School for Scandal*, Rowley performs the dual functions of norm character and confidant, as does Charley in *Death of a Salesman*. Mrs. Sorby is the norm character in *The Wild Duck*, as is Joseph Asagai in *A Raisin in the Sun*. For sound dramatic reasons, norm characters are of central importance in their plays. A crucial point is that they are too intelligent to be pressured by social conventions. And since they don't take themselves too seriously, they frequently display a well-developed sense of humor. They should be understood as attractive characters, not colorless or insipid, or else the comedy may misfire.

Having reviewed the ways playwrights present idea directly through the words, we should be careful of assuming that the words spoken by a character invariably reveal the main idea. This does not mean that characters never say anything trustworthy. It's that they have their own personalities, and what they say is shaped by their situation from moment to moment. Although their words may be appropriate in one instance, they may not explain the entire play.

IDEA IN THE PLOT

Thornton Wilder, author of *Our Town*, said that playwriting springs from an instinctive linkage between idea and action. Although dramatists may present the idea directly in the words of the characters, a successful play works mainly through action, not verbal statements. Plays are not philosophical essays. There is seldom much obvious talk in them about ideas. And no matter how intellectual a play may seem on the surface, its main idea is presented most convincingly through the plot, the pattern of the actions. Plot is part of the expressive system of drama. Just as dialogue and character conventions can express idea, so too can technical conventions in the plot. This section will study those conventions in an effort to understand how dramatists express idea through them.

Parallelism

Playwrights who feel the need to express a series of equivalent or similar ideas sometimes use a plot device called *parallelism*. When characters have matching counterparts in other characters, the issues connecting them will be reinforced by means of repetition and contrast. Shakespeare used parallelism to point up idea in his plays. An analysis of *Hamlet*, for example, reveals a number of parallelisms linking the characters of Hamlet, Fortinbras, and Laertes. Hamlet's and Fortinbras' fathers were both deceased warrior-kings. Both Hamlet and Fortinbras are princes as well as rightful heirs to their thrones, yet neither holds the throne in his own country. Hamlet and Fortinbras' uncles are usurpers who have gained their thrones by dishonest means. Moreover, there are or were close personal relationships between the three sets of fathers and sons: Hamlet and King Hamlet, Fortinbras and King Fortinbras, and Laertes and Polonius. Certain actions of Hamlet, Fortinbras, and Laertes are also parallel. Hamlet has embarked on a course of revenge for his father's murder. For equivalent reasons, Fortinbras threatens to retake lands his father lost in Denmark and Poland, and Laertes threatens to revenge the murder of Polonius. Such character parallelisms are considered *foils*, meaning characters that are presented as contrasts to another character to point to or show to advantage some aspect of the other character. From these and other connections, it seems clear that technically Laertes, Fortinbras, and Hamlet are foils for one another.

When there are enough similarities to make certain that parallelisms exist in the play and are not projected into it from outside sources, clues about idea can be uncovered. Although all three parallel foils in *Hamlet* aim to revenge the deaths of their fathers, Fortinbras and Laertes are fully committed to their tasks. Hamlet's hesitation is a sign that he's more like a poet or philosopher than a soldier. The contrasts between the personality traits and willpower of these three characters provide clues to the main idea of the play. The parallelisms also emphasize the complex personality traits Hamlet displays compared to those few traits displayed by Fortinbras and Laertes.

Parallelism in modern plays appears in subtle forms. In *The Wild Duck*, the activities of the Werle and Ekdal families constitute parallelisms. The main idea expresses itself through Gregers and Hjalmar's contrasting ideals and through their relationships with their parents, above all with their fathers. The parallelisms in *Death of a Salesman* also reiterate the relations between fathers and sons. The sub-plots in this play are of minor importance, but Miller has shown enough about them to reinforce certain key issues connected with the main idea.

The two families in *A Lie of the Mind* form parallelisms, for their links are brought to our attention by the alternating construction of the plot. The question is, what about the two families should the reader compare or contrast and how does it help us to understand the play? The same question arises with *Angels in America* in the obvious parallelism between Harper and Joe Pitt on one hand and Prior Walter and Louis Ironson on the other. Of course readers shouldn't look for parallelisms all the time or in every play, but whenever parallelisms can be established, readers are justified in studying them for clues about idea.

Conflict

Chapter 6 explained that some kinds of conflict produce intellectual tensions that may be useful for directors and designers in their artistic work. In this context, artistic work means work on the play for production. Intellectual conflict stems from the opposition of the customs or beliefs of a society against a different social order or perhaps against no social order at all. The tensions between different social systems, between character and environment, character and destiny, or character and the forces of nature are inherently interesting. When intellectual conflict of this kind appears in the plot, the resulting tensions illuminate ideas.

Consider the ideas that can be drawn from the intellectual conflicts in the plot of *Streamers*. At first sight, mindless violence appears to be the main interest in the play, but after deeper analysis, this violence begins to illuminate one of modern society's most pressing intellectual dilemmas: the decline of moral values. Billy believes in the orthodox values he grew up with in the American Midwest, but society has changed since he was a boy and so has its values. The play offers no glimpse of what the new values might be, but it does show the moral disarray that characterizes modern American society and the fate that awaits a naive idealist who clings to an extinct set of beliefs (like Hamlet?). Gregers in *The Wild Duck* is an impractical dreamer just as Billy is. His idealism causes serious harm to others (again, like Hamlet?), but Gregers survives, albeit to influence society in problematic ways. Billy destroys the lives of others as well as his own. Moreover, by his stubborn refusal to deal with reality, he contributes to the kind of moral anarchy that so horrified him.

The opposition between Billy's stubborn, old-fashioned morality and modern society's so-called amorality is a source of the intellectual conflict in the play. Combined with the supporting issues of racial tensions, sexuality, and militarism, *Streamers* offers a rich supply of intellectual tensions. With its frequent discussions of religion and politics, *Angels in America* also offers rich opportunities for intellectual conflicts. Abstract conflicts like these are too general to be of more than minor interest for actors, but they can be directly useful for directors and designers. By setting the play in a context larger than itself, intellectual conflicts contribute to those aspects of staging and design that depend on seeing the play in its imaginative entirety.

Climax

Director Elia Kazan observed that the climax of a play is the most concrete illustration of its main idea. All the parts of the play converge at this point, and everything appears in its most vivid theatrical form. The quality of a play's climax is judged by how it fulfills these functions. All the essential forces of the play are found at work in the climax.

This may be explained by studying an effective climax in detail. In *The Wild Duck*, the climax begins almost at the end of the play when the characters learn that Hedvig has shot herself. She killed herself, but it's the various responses to her death that are illuminating. Old Ekdal attributes her death to forest demons. He flees into the garret to comfort himself with his pets and with liquor. Reverend Molvik is always drunk anyway. He mumbles a few prayers over Hedvig's body, but his gesture is embarrassing rather than consoling. Hjalmar Ekdal, Hedvig's father, reacts in typical fashion by thinking of himself first. When Dr. Relling tries to comfort Hjalmar by assuring him that Hedvig's death was painless, Hjalmar cries melodramatically, "And I! I hunted her from me like an animal . . . She crept terrified into the garret and died for love of me!" Idealist Gregers Werle looks at Hedvig's death as a symbolic validation of his mission in life. "Hedvig has not died in vain," he moralizes to Dr. Relling, "Did you not see how sorrow set free what is noble in him [Hjalmar]?" Relling scoffs at this. He warns Gregers that even Hedvig's suicide will not change Hjalmar's natural selfishness, but Gregers refuses to believe it. "If you are right and I am wrong," he replies, "then life is not worth living." But Relling, the *raissoneur*, sees things more skeptically. He recognizes that Hedvig's death has become for Hjalmar little more than an opportunity for extravagant declamation, self-admiration, and self-pity. In addition, he knows that Hedvig would not have died if Gregers hadn't misled Hjalmar with his foolish notions of "the claim of the ideal."

The death of an innocent child is a heartbreaking event. It should bring out feelings of unaffected sorrow and remorse in the characters. The family picture Ibsen provides at the climax of *The Wild Duck*, however, is one of drunkenness, petty vanity, and thoughtless insensitivity. Gregers had hoped to inspire Hjalmar with passionate idealism; instead, he has had the opposite effect. This climax shows in concrete form that Gregers is a dangerous failed idealist. Although Relling provides a few remarks about the situation, Ibsen has chosen to express the idea of the play through the actions and attitudes of the characters. Notice that Dr. Relling can only talk about others' indifference to suffering; long ago he lost the ability to feel anything himself.

The climax of *A Lie of the Mind* is another useful model. Three moments late in the play offer possibilities for the major climax: the moment when Lorraine learns from her daughter Sally that her son Jake murdered his father; when Baylor kisses Meg, thereby reversing their uncaring relationship; and when Jake relinquishes his wife Beth to the care of his brother Mike. Sam Shepard described this play as "a love ballad . . . a little legend about love." Which moment best expresses that statement? Studying the major climax can help to give us an idea about how idea works in plays. This is how to understand that idea in drama is not an abstract concept but rather the philosophy of the play in action.

Some readers think it is necessary to see a play in concrete physical terms, then rise above it one way or another into an abstract world of meaning. Dramatic ideas, however, are too complicated to be expressed by abstract thinking alone. Rather by using selection and compression, playwrights transform ideas into concrete physical experience. They do this by putting audiences through a controlled series of events intended to make them feel as the characters do in similar given circumstances. Every word in the play exists for this reason, and every detail and incident has been prepared with this end in view. The result is that, even though the dramatist isn't there in person, the main idea is understood by the actors, director, designers, and audience as an obvious conclusion. This main idea is a result of the entire presented experience of the play. Incidentally, the main idea should not be confused with the production concept. The main idea is an issue that relates to the written script. The *production concept,* on the other hand, is an original idea, design, or plan for producing a play. Of course, a production concept should be based on a sound understanding of a play's main idea, but this does not always happen in practice.

To be studied in itself, the main idea must be changed from its original concrete expression in the play into literary form. This is accomplished by applying a process of radical reduction to the entire play to disclose its underlying form. An automobile, for example, stripped to its bare frame is still an automobile; though most of the details have been removed, it still retains its underlying form. The other parts are extensions and elaborations of the basic framework. Similarly, the main idea represents the underlying framework of the play that unites all the details, the *internal structure* or *second plan* of the play. This process of extreme reduction is more than academic, it is professionally essential. By stating the idea in simple, condensed form it remains close to its original unified illustration in the play. As soon as minor qualifications— more words—are added, information enters that may obscure the main idea's basic unity. Moreover, whenever the formulation of the main idea is confused or contains too many qualifications, there is a strong chance that some basic misunderstanding exists about the play.

Of course, radical reduction comes after the fact, when the play has already been written. Most playwrights don't create their works backward; that is, they don't begin with an intellectual conception of the play's meaning then work backward to the finished play. In the initial stages of work at least, they usually have an incomplete awareness of what they've written, at least in intellectual terms. Nonetheless, this fact doesn't mean their plays lack coherent main ideas, nor does it lessen the importance of the main idea for the artistic needs of actors, directors, and designers.

Although there are no fixed rules governing how to state the main idea in reduced form, it can usually be expressed in one of four ways: (1) super-objective, (2) action summary, (3) thesis sentence, or (4) theme. No single method has any particular advantage over the others, and any or all of them may be used for just about any play.

The *super-objective* (some writers say *spine*) is Stanislavski's method of describing a play's main idea. It seems to be the most common form, even for those who are not influenced by Stanislavski. Therefore we'll begin with it and since we already know about character objectives, the principle is not that difficult to understand. According to Stanislavski, all of the individual minor and major character objectives in a play should come together under the command of a single, unified objective called the super-objective of the play. We might think of the relation between the super-objective and all the supporting objectives as the popular Russian nesting dolls (*matrushka* dolls), each of which is found to contain a smaller one.

Naturally, like other objectives, the super-objective is seldom directly observable in the play but must be deduced from the action. It is the reader's responsibility to search for the logic that frames all the character objectives to relate them to the super-objective. Any character objective, no matter how small, that does not relate to the super-objective is considered incorrect or at least incomplete. To repeat an earlier discussion, it is important to choose an infinitive form of an active, concrete verb for character objectives to energize the action in the right direction. The same principle applies in the formulation of a super-objective.

How does the process actually work? To produce *Hamlet*, for example, the super-objective of the play might be *to search for a father's murderer* or *to revenge a king's death*. It is possible to imagine how all the character objectives could relate to these choices because a great deal of information in the play supports them. Strictly speaking, however, they are incomplete. The problem is that, by treating the play as a murder mystery or a revenge play, the other issues in it will have only accidental importance. The play's social, political, moral, and religious implications will be afterthoughts. If the super-objective were *to rescue Denmark,* the through-action would be more developed. Hamlet's love for his fellow citizens and his country would receive the emphasis. The social ideas would also grow in importance, giving the whole play larger social and political significance. The play can be enriched still further if the super-objective is *to reawaken everyone's conscience.* This is a paraphrase of the formulation Edward Gordon Craig and Stanislavski devised for their production at the Moscow Art Theatre in 1924. It proved to be effective for them because it unified the character objectives under an appropriate commanding idea without omitting anything they believed to be significant in the play. Hamlet's goals became greater, and the whole play became less personal than it was when he was occupied with only his father or his country. The implications behind this super-objective are no longer merely social or political but universal in scope. Moreover, the poetic dimensions of the play now take on enormous significance, an important issue for Craig because of his affection for symbolism in design.

We can see that the super-objectives were described in three ways: (1) personal (to search for a father's murderer), (2) social and political (to save a country), and (3) universal (to breathe life back into morality). Each choice had a great deal in the play to support it, but each was also progressively broader in scope and carried more meaning to the play. In the classroom, the exact wording of the super-objective is up to the individual reader. In production, however, the director is usually responsible for communicating the super-objective to the production team. The scope of the super-objective can be within any range of meaning the director desires—personal, sociopolitical, or universal—as long as the choice is supported by information in the play itself.

The same two-step procedure can be used to develop the other types of statements that describe the main idea. First, develop a concise literary statement that describes the important conditions in the play. Then present all the information in the play so that it is understood in a manner that relates to that description. In some plays, readers may choose to state the main idea as an action summary, without bothering about Stanislavski's requirements. Actor Laurence Olivier used this approach when he described his film version of *Hamlet* as "the story of a man who could not make up his mind." Olivier's choice highlights the philosophical dimensions of the play with emphasis on its moments of philsophical anguish. Readers who are more socially or politically inclined may choose to express the main idea as a *thesis sentence,* a single declarative sentence that asserts a lesson about the subject of the play forcefully. For example, Ibsen wrote *The Wild Duck* to demonstrate that *impractical idealists always go wrong,* or Brecht may have written *Mother Courage* to show that *capitalism destroys human feeling. Three Sisters* may be a demonstration that *love always gives back much less than we expect,* and *Angels in America* a presentation of evidence that *political freedom that fails to grow will not last.* All four examples show that a thesis sentence is often useful for highlighting social or political issues. In contrast to a thesis sentence, a *theme* is not an arguable message but rather an expression of the main idea in more universal terms. For example, the theme of *The Hairy Ape* might be *a struggle for identity* or that of *Oedipus Rex, a quest for truth.* Theme statements seem to work best when they are expressing the broad philosophical and poetic aspects of a play. Chapter 1 presents a different but related explanation of Theme.

All these formulations are legitimate appraisals of the main idea for their respective plays. The logic behind them should be plain. The statement of the main idea is an effort to describe in condensed form the basic conflict at the center of the play. Regardless of the formulation, the cardinal principle is to state the main idea in a single declarative statement. Main ideas stated as questions ("Is idealism worthwhile?") or calls to action ("Let's fight to preserve our ideals!") can obscure the issue. They have a reluctant or ambivalent feeling about them. The main idea will be clear if its formulation confidently asserts or denies something about the meaning of the play.

Developing a statement of the main idea tests artistic awareness because it forces the artistic team to determine at the beginning of the process just what it is they want to say. It will stimulate thoughts about acting, directing, and design. Often it takes considerable practice to acquire the skills needed to define the main idea accurately. The growth of this skill can be nurtured by making it a habit to describe the main idea for any plays read or seen. As was said earlier in this chapter, sometimes the playwright helps by stating the main idea somewhere in the dialogue. The task is to find that statement. In most cases, however, the main idea is not stated anywhere and so must be extracted from the action of the whole play. The ability to draw out implications this way is one of the last skills acquired in learning how to analyze a play. If actors, directors, and designers cannot learn to extract the main idea in some convincing way, it is unlikely they will be consistently successful in their artistic work.

SUMMARY

This chapter concerned itself with some of the ways in which the main idea may be found in plays. It takes considerable experience to develop the ability to understand and describe a play's idea with clarity and simplicity. Nevertheless it is a skill that must be acquired if students expect to communicate successfully with others involved in the artistic process, as well as with the audience. Sometimes the clearest understanding of the main idea may not occur until late in the process of analysis or even during rehearsals. Sometimes the main idea does not become completely clear until after the play has opened, and it can at last be comprehended whole as it was originally intended. Nevertheless, for professionals the search always continues. Most of the audience will never judge the play on the basis of its main idea but rather as drama and feeling. But one way or another, for reasons already discussed, the main idea shows the way for actors, directors, and designers. The main idea gives each play its unique identity. It is the starting point and focusing device that propels the artistic team toward its final result. Regardless of whether a particular statement about the idea is definitive, the practice of determining the main idea is one of the major goals of play analysis.

QUESTIONS

Words   Does the title reflect the meaning? If so, does it do so directly, indirectly, or ironically? Any discussions about ideas in the dialogue? If so, who is involved? What specific ideas are discussed? Are there any examples of aphorisms? If so, who speaks them? What ideas do they illustrate? Any literary, religious, or cultural allusions? If so, who speaks them? What are the sources? What ideas do they illustrate? Any speeches putting forward specific ideas (set speeches)? If so, who says them? What ideas do they illuminate? Are there any images or intentional symbols in the dialogue? If so, what are they? What ideas do they suggest? Is there a prologue or an epilogue? If so, how does it point up the main idea of the play?

Characters   Is there a narrator or chorus? If so, when and how do they express the main idea? Is there a skeptical character that offers advice or tries to reason with others *(raisonneur)*? If so, how does the character express the main idea? Is there someone in whom the leading character confides private feelings (confidant[e])? If so, how does that character relate to the main idea? In a comedy, is there a character that has maturely adjusted to the behavior code of the world of the play (norm character)? If so, how does that character illustrate the main idea?

Plot   Are there any characters or situations that repeat or highlight others (parallelisms or foils)? If so, how do they relate to the main idea? Are there any intellectual conflicts involving the social order, destiny, or the forces of nature? Can any intentional symbolism be found in the dialogue or action? If so, how does it relate to the main idea? How does the major climax embody the central idea?

Statement of the Main Idea   What is the main idea of the play? Frame the description in the form of an action summary, a super-objective, a thesis sentence, or a theme. Justify the response with detailed information from the play itself.

POSTSCRIPT FOR ACTION ANALYSIS

This chapter on Idea completes our investigation of the formalist origins of Action Analysis (Chapter 1), of which the theoretical underpinnings should by now be fully evident. The Sequence of Events and Three Major Climaxes stem from External and Internal Action (Chapter 4) and Progressions and Structure (Chapter 5). Reviewing the Facts stems from the Given Circumstances (Chapter 2) and Background Story (Chapter 3). Through-Action and Counter Through-Action are outcomes of the study of Character (Chapter 6). And Idea (Chapter 7) can be seen as a comprehensive treatment of the concepts of the Seed, Theme, and Super-Objective.

The following chapters continue to explore the method of Formalist Analysis; however, they deal with subtler and more complex issues than Action Analysis was intended to address. Because Action Analysis depends by definition on the study of action, by itself it can provide few practical insights into Dialogue (Chapter 8), Tempo, Rhythm, and Mood (Chapter 9), or Style (Chapter 10). Formalist Analysis is equipped to sort out advanced subjects such as these. The going will be slower because it involves a microscopic look at numerous fine points in the play. If it is true, as architect Ludwig Mies van der Rohe famously stated, that "God is in the details," then advanced Formalist Analysis may be a factor in the magic of inspiration.

CHAPTER 8

Dialogue

Dialogue consists of the passages of talk in the play. It involves all the conversations, monologues, soliloquies, narration, choral odes, songs, and anything else spoken by the characters. It does not include stage directions. Enough has already been said in earlier chapters to show how important it is to study the dialogue for information about the given circumstances, background story, plot, character, and idea. Yet even when the dialogue is clear about all this information, it still deserves to be studied for its own self. In addition to being the play's primary means of communication, dialogue is also the playwright's sole means of creative expression. It can be merely workmanlike or it can display a high degree of virtuosity.

Although most readers don't pay much attention to the language as such in a play, it does exert a subtle influence. The language may evoke comments such as,

—The dialogue is easy to understand.
—The words come from the characters naturally.
—The play uses lots of short words.
—I was so bored by the long and complicated sentences that I skipped whole passages.

Most of these opinions are too general to be genuinely useful. Analysis needs to be more specific in order to teach anything that can be helpful in the rehearsal hall. When critics use the term *diction*, they mean the technical and artistic qualities of language, and the selection and arrangement of words, phrases, sentences, lines, and speeches. This chapter treats dialogue as diction, starting with the basic technical building blocks and progressing to more creative qualities. Some features are relative and opinions about them vary, but most dialogue can be studied in the same open-minded way already recommended in this book.

Often the analysis of dialogue uncovers a hidden complication. Readers cannot hope to understand the language in a play if they have not mastered the basics of grammar, syntax, punctuation, sentences, paragraphs, and so forth. Before starting to work, they may need to review the fundamentals. Although the rules of diction can be subtle and complex, their subtlety and complexity appears in the way dramatists stretch the rules. Readers should know immediately which rules are being stretched and why. It's not a good idea to worry about these issues in a script analysis textbook. Script analysis is challenging enough without also having to worry about the fundamentals of English. Fortunately, the subject is not that difficult. Any serious student can cover the basics with a good guidebook and a little help from the right tutor. Two such books are *The Elements of Grammar* by Margaret D. Shertzer and *The Elements of Style* by William Strunk, Jr. and E.B. White. Both are short, accurate, practical, and widely available.

WORDS

There may be many characters in a play, and they may speak in various ways, but each normally preserves a certain manner of speech identified as that character's own and no one else's. Since characters speak in their own voices, the words they use potentially tell a great deal about them. This is achieved partly by the choice of words; characters can be measured partly by certain features of the specific words they use.

Abstract and Concrete

One of the first values to search for in words is the quality of abstraction or concreteness. Abstract words describe qualities, concepts, or ideas— things that cannot be perceived by the senses—such as love, honor, experience, heritage, democracy, or materialism. Creon in *Oedipus Rex* and Cleante in *Tartuffe* use words like power, knowledge, justice, hypocrisy, and self-sacrifice. Characters who use a surplus of abstract words describing intellectual concepts like these often appear reserved, aloof, or affected. By contrast concrete words describe things that can be seen and touched, like flowers, smiles, thumbtacks, or hammers. They are vivid and emphatic, and the characters who use them display analogous personality traits. Oedipus and Orgon speak in specific terms like this. They express their hasty judgments and rash decrees using strong, concrete language that differs considerably from Creon's and Cleante's cautious abstractions.

Formal and Informal

Another value in conversational speech is the level of formality or informality of the words. Formal speech makes generous use of elevated words of the kind often found in scholarly books (mediocrity, ubiquitous, Weltanschauung, verisimilitude) and also literary words (however, nonetheless, consequently, moreover). Formal language aims at precision, but in doing so it intentionally restricts feeling. Simple informal language, for many sorts of characters, can be more effective emotionally.

Comparing the words of Joseph Surface with those of his brother Charles in *The School for Scandal* we can see an illustration of these principles. Joseph's frequent use of *indeed, certainly*, and *however*, and similarly formal wording, tells us that he is pretentious, he puts literary style first. By contrast, his brother Charles' *bumper, blockhead,* and *wench*, and similar kinds of humble, everyday words, grow unaffectedly out of his egalitarian feelings. He doesn't worry about how he sounds to others. The Angel uses an amusing mixture of formal and informal words when addressing Prior in *Angels in America*. The homespun characters in *A Lie of the Mind* generally use informal words to express themselves.

Closely affiliated with formal and informal qualities is the syllabic composition of words. Polysyllabic words frequently stem from Latin, traditionally the language of scholars. Joseph Asagai is the Nigerian exchange student who is Beneatha Younger's boyfriend in *A Raisin in the Sun*. He enjoys displaying his new American education with polysyllabic words like *mutilated, accommodate,* and *assimilate.* On the other hand, the uneducated characters in Brecht's *Mother Courage* frequently speak in short, abrupt sentences (in translation): "Halt, you scum!" "He's pulled a black cross. He's through." "You've left your hat." Broadly speaking, formal, multisyllabic words tend to be associated with emotional restraint while short, informal words imply emotional freedom.

Jargon and Slang

Jargon (professionals' specialized vocabulary) and *slang* (nonstandard everyday speech) have special appeal in dramatic dialogue because they sound unusual, vivid, and colorful. Our recognition of such language as entertaining is just as important as is the realism it lends to certain situations. *Mother Courage* and *Streamers* acquire some of their entertainment value from the use of military jargon and everyday slang. They employ *good-bad speech,* meaning bad speech that is intentionally written to achieve expressive effects. The obscenities in *Angels in America* have shock value, of course, but they also serve to keep the political thematics of the play operating on a basic human level. Characters in *The Hairy Ape* speak the jargon of life at sea, and in *A Raisin in the Sun* and *The Piano Lesson,* they often speak in the slang of African-American folk culture. Our national culture is enriched by jargon and slang from these social groups and from many more besides. On stage, jargon and slang help to identify characters within a particular social context.

Connotation

Recall from the Introduction that to connote means to suggest or convey associations in addition to the explicit (denoted) dictionary meaning. Connotative words, therefore, are words that convey more than their literal meaning. For example, the simple sentence, "There's a spider," will often create a shiver of disgust, whereas the statement, "There is an insect," may not. This happens because for many people *spider* is automatically associated with creepy feelings of disgust. Dramatists like to use connotative words because they add emotion to the dialogue without adding more words.

Some words are almost purely connotative, having little or no objective meaning at all. Linguists describe them as *snarl* and *purr* words. They may look like normal words, but their literal meanings are often of only secondary importance. Words like *damn!* or *ouch!* or *wow!* are little more than snarls that express pure feelings. Since emotion plays such a large part in dramatic dialogue, play readers should always be alert for the connotative as well as the literal meanings of words.

For example, the obscenity in *Streamers*, *A Lie of the Mind*, and *Angels in America* may offend some readers, but it is actually very effective connotative dialogue. It may not seem especially dramatic, but no one will deny that obscenity expresses thoughts and feelings impressively. It shocks, but it communicates feelings too. Many of Winnie's and Willie's words in *Happy Days* are richly connotative. In the right context, simple, isolated expressions like *what*, *no*, *yes*, or *God* suggest surprisingly rich and complex feelings. When Winnie discovers an ant carrying a little white ball (that is, an egg, which suggests hope for the future), her subsequent dialogue of six simple words with Willie forms an ironic play on words involving sex, biology, entomology, and philosophy.

SENTENCES

The next rhetorical device is the sentence, the primary verbal tool of play. Some very interesting observations can be made about a play by studying various features of the sentences. Literary examination can reveal dramatic possibilities that are particularly useful for actors and directors.

Length

Sentence length reveals useful particulars about character. Readers can begin to arrive at some understanding of an author's or character's sentence length simply by counting the words and sentences in a continuous section of the play and then dividing the total number of words by the number of sentences. After estimating the average number of words for each sentence, more important considerations can be worked at, namely, what is the relation between sentence length, dramatic context, and character?

An illustration of the value of sentence length for character analysis occurs in the scene between Polonius and Reynaldo in 1,2 of *Hamlet* in which Polonius directs Reynaldo to keep an eye on Laertes while he is in France. In this short scene Polonius speaks seven times as many words as Reynaldo, his sentences are over four times longer, and he uses a large number of abstract words. Of course, we would expect Polonius to say more in this scene because he is giving the instructions, but even so, the calculations tell us that Polonius talks too much in a misplaced attempt to sound important. Reynaldo speaks in short sentences, trying to bring the frustrating conversation to a rapid conclusion.

In *Streamers* sentence length offers some opportunities for playable dramatic values. Martin, Richie, Carlyle, Billy, and Roger appear in the first informal scene of Act 1. The average sentence length for all the characters in the scene is only six words. True, in modern plays, characters generally say what must be said using the fewest words possible. These sentences, however, are much shorter than we might expect even for a modern play. What's more, many of them are only fragments. This might indicate the absence of formal education as well as strong emotion. Together with the army jargon, abusive slang, and connotative words, the short length of the sentences enhances the highly charged emotional quality of this savage play.

Long sentences may be carried along by hysterical emotion or reflect a halting, insecure feeling of anxiety. They may also be sustained by the complexity of their thoughts or the richness of their images, as in the case of Shakespeare. Short sentences and sentence fragments create different effects. They can be tough, penetrating, and incisive, or they can suggest weariness or dullness. Readers should learn to recognize both extremes and all the variations in between.

Type

Sentences can be grammatically simple, compound, complex, or compound-complex; rhetorically loose, periodic, balanced, or antithetical; or functional statements, questions, commands, or exclamations. The types of sentences used in a play and the proportions of the various types to one another can reveal some potentially playable features. Dialogue in older, historical plays is often self-consciously composed like music.

Sentences show noticeable patterns; they flow obviously from one point to another and are accentuated by prominent stops. There is frequently enough expressive matter in them to make up several sentences in modern plays. By contrast, most sentences used in modern dialogue do not deliberately call attention to themselves. They are comparatively short, and they stop when the sense is complete. Yet within these two broad limits, there may still be many types of sentences. This is not the place for a discussion of the basics of grammar, rhetoric, or syntax, however. The lesson here is that once the types of sentences are defined, the associations between them can be studied. Their proportion to one another as well as their relationship to the dramatic context can be examined.

To illustrate this point, consider the sentences in a passage from one historical and one modern play. The first passage is from *The School for Scandal*. Rowley is persuading Sir Peter Teazle that he is mistaken in his opinions of Charles and Joseph Surface.

ROWLEY

You know, Sir Peter, I have always taken the
liberty to differ with you on the subject of
these two young gentlemen. I only wish you may
not be deceived in your opinion of the elder.
For Charles, my life on't! he will retrieve
his errors yet. Their worthy father, once my
honored master, was, at his years, nearly as
wild a spark; yet when he died, he did not
leave a more benevolent heart to lament his
loss.

SIR PETER

You are wrong, Master Rowley. On their father's
death, you know, I acted as a kind of guardian
to them both till their uncle Sir Oliver's
liberality gave them an early independence. Of
course no person could have more opportunity of
judging their hearts, and I was never mistaken
in my life. Joseph is indeed a model for the
young men of the age. He is a man of sentiment
and acts up to the sentiments he professes;

but, for the other, take my word for't, if he
had any grain of virtue by descent, he has
dissipated it with the rest of his inheritance.
Ah! my old friend Sir Oliver will be deeply
mortified when he finds how part of his bounty
has been misapplied.

The modern example involves a similar situation in *The Wild Duck*.
Dr. Relling is attempting to refute Gregers Werle's opinion of the character of Hjalmar Ekdal.

GREGERS

What is your explanation of the spiritual
tumult that is now going on inside Hjalmar
Ekdal?

RELLING

A lot of spiritual tumult I've noticed in him.

GREGERS

What! Not at such a crisis, when his whole life
has been placed on a new foundation? How can
you think that such an individuality as
Hjalmar's—

RELLING

Oh, individuality—he! If he ever had any
tendency to the abnormal developments you call
individuality, I can assure you it was rooted
out of him while he was still in his teens.

GREGERS

That would be strange indeed—considering the
loving care with which he was brought up.

RELLING

By those two high-flown, hysterical maiden
aunts, you mean?

GREGERS

Let me tell you that they were women who never
forgot the claim of the ideal—but of course you
will only jeer at me again.

RELLING

No, I'm in no humor for that. I know all about
those ladies, for he has ladled out no end
of rhetoric on the subject of his "two soul
mothers." But I don't think he has much to
thank them for. Ekdal's misfortune is that in
his own circle he has always been looked upon
as a shining light.

GREGERS

Not without reason, surely. Look at the depth
of his mind!

RELLING

I have never discovered it. That his father
believed in it I don't so much wonder; the old
lieutenant has been an ass all his days.

The passage from *The School for Scandal* contains many generalized or indefinite words and a variety of sentence types. The sentences are comparatively long and include an assortment of dependent and independent clauses. The tempo of the dialogue is slow and measured. In the selection from *The Wild Duck* there is a greater percentage of concrete words, fewer different types of sentences, and shorter sentences with fewer dependent and independent clauses. The dialogue in the second passage also shows occasional broken sentences, missing links, and nonstandard grammar. The characters speak rapidly, and the stresses are crowded together unevenly ("Oh, individuality—he!"). The types of sentences in the first passage reveal that Rowley and Sir Peter disagree in a reasonable and gentlemanly manner. The sentences in the second selection show that Gregers and Dr. Relling disagree with more emotion. Also notice that in both selections the important information normally comes at the end of a sentence. Of course here we're comparing an English play with a Norwegian play translated into English, but the practical consequences still apply. Most plays in the United States are read and performed in English. Actors obviously must attend to the features of the sentences in the English translation they are using.

Rhythm

Prose rhythm is a challenge to analyze. Although there is no reliable method for objectively measuring the rhythm of prose sentences, rhythm probably plays a large part in producing emotional effects. Scanning sentences for rhythm in the manner of poetry may not be a very valuable exercise if it is practiced for very long. The rhythmic sound of prose sentences must be heard to be appreciated. It's no doubt better for play readers to get into the habit of reading aloud. Oral reading allows for hearing the difference between harmonious and clashing rhythms and between agreeable and awkward sound combinations.

For illustrative purposes, try to scan the rhythm of a prose passage and compare it with the two selections just examined. Now turn to this famous prose speech from *Hamlet* that has been scanned for rhythmical accents. Stressed words are underlined and rhythmic pauses are indicated by double bars.

HAMLET

<u>Speak</u> the <u>speech</u>, // I pray you, // as I
<u>pronounc'd</u> it to you, // <u>trippingly</u> on the
tongue; // but if you <u>mouth</u> it, // as many of
our <u>players</u> do, // I had as lief the <u>town</u> <u>crier</u>
spoke my lines. // Nor do not saw the <u>air</u> too
much with your hand, // thus, // but use all
<u>gently</u>; // for in the very <u>torrent</u>, // <u>tempest</u>,
// and, as I may say, <u>whirlwind</u> of your
<u>passion</u>, // you must acquire and beget a
<u>temperance</u> // that may give it smoothness. //
O, it <u>offends</u> me to the <u>soul</u> // to hear a
<u>robustious</u> <u>periwig-pated</u> <u>fellow</u> // <u>tear</u> a
passion to <u>tatters</u>, // to very <u>rags</u>, // to
<u>split</u> the ears of the <u>groundlings</u>, // who, //

```
for the most part, // are capable of nothing //
but inexplicable dumb shows and noise. // I
would have such a fellow whipp'd for o'erdoing
termagent; // it out-herods Herod. // Pray you
// avoid it. //
```

For comparison, here is a prose selection from *Death of a Salesman*:

```
                    BIFF
I am not a leader of men, Willy, // and neither
are you. // You were never anything but a hard-
working drummer // who landed to the ash can //
like all the rest of them! // I'm one dollar an
hour, Willy! // I tried seven states // and
couldn't raise it. // A buck an hour. // Do you
gather my meaning! // I'm not bringing home any
prizes anymore, // and you're going to stop
waiting for me to bring them home! //
```

There may be other ways to scan these passages, but at least this way shows how certain important words are stressed. In this last selection, the rhythmic pulse is different from the prose passages that were examined earlier. The language in *Hamlet* is formal and rhetorical like that in *The School for Scandal*, but it is clearly more lyrical than its eighteenth-century counterpart: When the formal rhythms of *Hamlet* are compared to the irregular rhythms of the sentences from *Death of a Salesman*, the contrast is even more striking. The sentences in all three passages require a sense of rhythm from the actors to express their musical potential completely.

SPEECHES

Routine stage speech uses short, simple sentences, sometimes broken or telegraphic, but the extra length and expressiveness required when speaking about misfortunes, adversities, or key ideas demands longer strings of sentences. Dramatic dialogue becomes more extended and intense when crucial questions are discussed. Accordingly, speeches—

lines composed of more than a few sentences—should be treated carefully. Their punctuation, linking, internal organization, and relationship to adjoining dialogue can communicate meaning almost as powerfully as do the words themselves. Despite appearances, speeches are not just lengthy emotional expressions, but instead purposely orchestrated to achieve dramatic effects.

Punctuation

Each punctuation mark has distinctive characteristics requiring both comprehension from readers and special intonations from actors for correct interpretation. Periods, commas, exclamation points, question marks, ellipses, and single and double dashes all have unique meanings. The vocal drop which normally accompanies a period indicates the end of a thought or feeling. The vocal rise of a question mark demands a reply. Commas and semicolons are warnings that call for pauses of certain durations. A colon demands our attention to what follows it. An exclamation point signals approval or disagreement. Dashes indicate an interrupted thought. Ellipses hint at something left unsaid. Director and Shakespeare scholar B. Iden Payne often reminded his students that punctuation in dramatic dialogue is not only *grammatical*, but also *dramatical*. By this he meant that playwrights employ punctuation not solely for reasons of good grammar but also to signal dramatic action. Notice the difference, for example, between the punctuation in Shakespeare's original quartos, which were written for actors, and the later editions, which were "corrected" by scholars. The emotional connotations related to punctuation are meant to help actors feel the texture of the dialogue more vividly.

We might study this passage from *A Raisin in the Sun* for a profitable illustration of the expressive use of punctuation. Readers will recall that Walter Younger is angry about his friend Willy's theft of the $10,000 in insurance money that Walter was planning to use to buy a liquor store. In an effort to replace the money, Walter has cynically agreed to accept a realtor's payoff to keep his family from moving into a white neighborhood. This humiliates Walter and his family.

WALTER

What's the matter with you all! I didn't make
this world! It was given to me this way! Hell,
yes, I want me some yachts someday! Yes, I want
to hang some real pearls 'round my wife's neck.
Ain't she supposed to wear pearls? Somebody
tell me—, who decides which women is suppose to
wear pearls in this world. I tell you I am a
man—and I think my wife should wear pearls in
this world!

MAMA

Baby, how you going to feel on the inside?

WALTER

Fine! . . . Going to feel fine . . . a man . . .

MAMA

You won't have nothing left then, Walter Lee.

WALTER

I'm going to feel fine, Mama. I'm going to look
that son-of-a-bitch in the eyes and say—and
say, "All right, Mr. Lindner—that's your
neighborhood out there. You got the right to
keep it like you want. You got the right to
have it like you want. Just write the check
and—the house is yours." And, and I am going to
say—And you—you people just put the money in my
hand and you won't have to live next to this
bunch of stinking niggers! . . . Maybe— maybe
I'll just get down on my black knees . . .
Captain, Mistuh, Bossman. A-hee-hee-hee!
Yassssuh! Great White Father, just gi'ussen de
money, fo' God's sake, and we's ain't gwine
come out deh and dirty up yo' white folks
neighborhood . . .

To stress the emotion in this passage, Lorraine Hansberry has used exclamation points, commas, ellipses, and dashes (plus folk speech and prose rhythm) in dramatic fashion. As Walter uncovers more and more of his feelings, each punctuation mark becomes more meaningful. The exclamation points in the first line show his open anger. At the word *man*, he begins to hesitate, and his speech becomes increasingly halting and agitated. He falters several times during the last speech as the humiliation settles into his consciousness. His voice breaks, he stumbles and falls to his knees. Then he breaks down. The speech ends with an embarrassing silence. Hansberry has provided *dramatical* punctuation in the dialogue to emphasize the stages in the progress of Walter's thoughts and feelings. Hansberry's punctuation throughout is dramatical more than grammatical, more than a signal of African-American folk speech. For evidence compare it with the dialogue in *The Piano Lesson*, which is also folk speech and has virtually no dashes or caesuras even though it contains many more long speeches.

Linking

The idea of linking comes logically after sentences and punctuation. We know from composition classes that linking in prose is performed by antecedents and tenses, phrases and clauses, and other forms of backward and forward reference to knit sentences together. Linking is a basic principle of prose writing. When there is no linking or when it is weakly done, meaning falters. Linking is also an important feature of dramatic dialogue because it helps maintain the feeling of forward motion necessary for good dramatic structure. Moreover, dialogue linking is one of the basic principles of line-to-line communication between characters, which some writers call *reciprocation* or *communion*.

Dramatic dialogue uses distinctive thoughts or words to link the lines together. Ordinarily, the method is one complete idea to a line of speech with the last thought of one line suggesting the first one for the next line. This is not a rigid rule, but whenever something intrudes to break the connection, it will probably have a special purpose. The following excerpt shows effective dialogue linking in *The School for Scandal*. In this scene, Snake has just reported to Lady Sneerwell that he successfully managed to place scandalous reports about Charles Surface in the newspapers. Lady Sneerwell and Charles were once lovers. She wishes to win Charles back, or at least wound him, by discrediting him with the woman he loves now. Charles' brother, Joseph Surface, joins the scene. Careful reading will show how the final words in each line suggest the initial words in the succeeding line.

JOSEPH SURFACE

My dear Lady Sneerwell, how do you do today?
Mr. Snake, your most obedient.

LADY SNEERWELL

Snake has just been teasing me on our mutual
attachment; but I have informed him of our real
views. You know how useful he has been to us;
and believe me, the confidence is not ill
placed.

JOSEPH SURFACE

Madam, it is impossible for me to suspect a man
of Mr. Snake's sensibility and discernment.

LADY SNEERWELL

Well, well, no compliments now; but tell me
when you saw your mistress, Maria—or, what is
more material to me, your brother.

JOSEPH SURFACE

I have not seen either since I left you; but I
can inform you that they never meet. Some of
your stories have taken good effect on Maria.

LADY SNEERWELL

Ah, my dear Snake! the merit of this belongs to
you. But do your brother's distresses increase?

JOSEPH SURFACE

Every hour. I am told he has had another
summons from the court yesterday. In short, his

dissipation and extravagance exceed anything I
have ever heard of.

LADY SNEERWELL

Poor Charles!

JOSEPH SURFACE

True, madam; notwithstanding his vices one
can't help feeling for him. Poor Charles! I'm
sure I wish it were in my power to be of any
essential service to him; for the man who does
not share in the distresses of a brother, even
though merited by his own misconduct, serves—

LADY SNEERWELL

O Lud! you are going to be moral and forget
that you are among friends.

JOSEPH SURFACE

Egad, that's true! I'll keep that sentiment
till I see Sir Peter. However, it is certainly
a charity to rescue Maria from such a
libertine, who, if he is to be reclaimed, can
be so only by a person of your ladyship's
superior accomplishments and understanding.

SNAKE

I believe, Lady Sneerwell, here's company
coming. I'll go and copy the letter I mentioned
to you. Mr. Surface, your most obedient.

JOSEPH SURFACE

Sir, your very devoted.

It will be worth the effort to study this passage closely. Sheridan's dialogue is a model of conventional linking. Each line connects firmly but inconspicuously with the line before and the line following. The conversation progresses smoothly from one topic to the next without any breaks in logic or feeling. The two lines without verbal links are linked by non-verbal means. Lady Sneerwell's expression—"Poor Charles!"—seems to end her line abruptly before furnishing a link with Joseph Surface's next line. The two lines are actually linked by the unspoken thought of Lady Sneerwell's secret love for Charles. The dramatist expects the actors to provide a facial expression, gesture, or stage business to fill the pause. At first glance, Snake's line announcing the arrival of visitors also seems unlinked; however, the off-stage sounds of guests approaching provides the link here.

We have seen that linking isn't always expressed verbally in the dialogue. This is particularly true in modern plays where verbal expression is frequently less important than physical expression of feelings. Much of the dialogue in *A Lie of the Mind*, *Angels in America*, and *Streamers*, for example, seems to skip from one line to another in an unlinked fashion, almost telegraphic in its terseness. In performance, the effect is less formal and more lifelike, as well as edgier.

Internal Arrangement

Just as dramatists orchestrate obstacles leading to a climax so also do they arrange the internal dynamics of speeches to achieve the strongest effects. Most speeches build toward a climax; they may do so, however, in different ways. The start may be bold, as in the previous example from *A Raisin in the Sun*, or the beginning may be a low-conflict point of departure. A resting point often occurs somewhere in the middle of a long speech, followed by the final progression to the climax at the end. Another example of the principle of *beginning, middle, and end*. Sometimes the climax may be followed by a simple, quiet close. Of course, the actor's interpretation can never be overlooked, but in any event, the internal arrangement of a speech is chiefly governed by writing considerations.

Arthur Miller arranged Linda's final speech by Willy's grave site at the close of *Death of a Salesman* in skillful climactic fashion. The speech intensifies as it builds toward the end.

LINDA

Forgive me, dear, I can't cry. I don't know
what it is, but I can't cry. I don't understand

```
it. Why did you ever do that? Help me, Willy, I
can't cry. It seems to me that you're just on
another trip. I keep expecting you. Willy,
dear, I can't cry. Why did you do it? I search
and search and I search, and I can't understand
it, Willy. I made the last payment on the house
today. Today, dear. And there'll be nobody
home. (A sob rises in her throat.) We're free
and clear. (sobbing more fully, released) We're
free. (Biff comes slowly toward her.) We're
free . . . We're free . . .
```

Linda's speech begins quietly, then builds to a small crest ("Willy, dear, I can't cry"). After a brief emotional rest, the intensity builds once again to a final peak of emotion ("We're free and clear"), then it ends with a simple, quiet close ("We're free . . ."). Such musically orchestrated speeches also distinguish the dialogue in *The Piano Lesson* and *Three Sisters*.

External Arrangement

Chapter 5 explained how scenes are dramatic progressions structured like miniature plays. Now let's analyze the inner workings of a scene to learn how the speeches themselves also build to peaks of emotional intensity. The climax of *Death of a Salesman* is the quarrel between Willy and Biff near the end of the play. In this scene, Biff finally summons the courage to challenge his father's opinion of him. This is the scene that the entire play has prepared us to expect. Prior to this moment, the dramatist stockpiled a large inventory of dramatic tension in the earlier scenes. He created the necessary suspense by revealing in small increments information about Willy and Biff's relationship and by inserting complementary scenes with the other characters.

The scene begins when Biff comes into the backyard and tells Willy that he is leaving home for good. Biff is trying to appear calm, but he is withholding his real feelings because he doesn't want another argument with his father. Willy is preoccupied at this point and doesn't fully understand what Biff is saying anyway. The tension accumulates in the next unit. They go into the house together, and Biff tells his mother of his plans in the same restrained manner. Then Biff extends his hand to Willy to say good-bye, and the first emotional eruption occurs as Willy refuses Biff's gesture. When Linda intervenes, Willy curses Biff and refuses to accept any blame for Biff's failures. At this point, Biff can't hold back his feelings any longer, and he challenges Willy openly: "All right, phony! Then let's lay it on the line." Then Biff shows the rubber hose that Willy planned to use to commit suicide by connecting it to the gas line from the water heater in the basement. This is the second emotional flare-up in the scene. When Happy tries to stop him, Biff turns on his brother, mocking his dream of becoming a businessman. Willy grows more distressed and Happy and Linda begin to panic.

Suddenly Biff turns on Willy and denounces him: "I never got anywhere because you blew me so full of hot air I could never stand taking orders from anybody!" When Willy still doesn't understand what is happening, Biff explodes into self-reproach. It almost seems as though Biff is going to strike Willy: "Pop, I'm nothing! I'm nothing, Pop!" but then he collapses against his father and breaks down. This is the major climax of the play. Finally, Willy begins to understand: "What're you doing? Why is he crying?" Biff struggles to contain himself, pulls away, and moves to the stairs, "I'll go in the morning," he says to Linda, "Put him—put him to bed," and he goes to his room. After a long pause, Willy says quietly, "Isn't that—isn't that remarkable? Biff likes me!"

Of course this is only one example of how a very good playwright orchestrates the emotional peaks and valleys in one scene. Others arrange their plays in different ways to suit their own characters and situations. Moreover, readers should never overlook the important interpretive contributions to a scene that the actors, director, and designers provide. Studying the orchestration of speeches in climactic scenes can provide practical artistic information about playable values.

SPECIAL QUALITIES

From the preceding discussion it should be apparent that understanding theatrical dialogue involves meticulous attention to words, sentences, and speeches. Appreciation is increased further if we can also recognize when dialogue has special literary beauties of its own. Dialogue that merely asserts the facts of the plot, characters, and idea may be no more than workmanlike and satisfying. Playwrights who feel strongly about this issue have always tried to make the dialogue entertaining in itself. Some have tried to overlay appealing qualities onto their dialogue like frosting on a cake. Occasionally they have succeeded, at least for their immediate audiences. Mostly they have not because the added qualities did not arise logically from the characters and situations. Yet many dramatists are artists in words as well as actions and characters. As writers, naturally they love the subtleties of language.

To understand how dialogue can be inherently entertaining, consider the following questions. Is the dialogue poetic? Does it simply reveal the basic facts in a practical way, or does it also display a distinctive literary style? Does the dialogue contain colorful idiomatic speech? Not every analysis needs to deal extensively with these topics, but most plays require at least some understanding of the potential literary appeal of the dialogue.

Poetry

Anyone who is serious about the theatre can't help being interested in the dramatic possibilities of poetry. Since most of us are not used to reading poetic dialogue, however, many of its dramatic possibilities tend to be overlooked. Prose dialogue, for all its potential complexity, primarily runs straight ahead. Poetry, on the other hand, is always calling up associations from within itself, a practice that complicates and enriches its pattern of sound and meaning. Moreover, prose dialogue chiefly reveals plot, character, and idea, while in poetic plays, there is additional pleasure in the dialogue as literature. It basically sounds pleasant. There is no need to spend time here discussing the long catalogue of literary devices that can be found in poetry. Play readers should at least be aware that poetic dialogue has many more expressive resources at its command than does unadorned prose.

Theoretically, poetic plays should be more exciting than are their prose counterparts. Their emotional peaks and valleys are more vivid, and they contain more obvious rhythmic feelings. This is true for poetic dialogue as well as for poetic plays in general. Short selections from two plays will illustrate this. One play is formally poetic, the other written in poetic prose. The first selection is from 4,7 of *Hamlet*. Claudius and Laertes have been plotting to murder Hamlet when Queen Gertrude enters unexpectedly with news of Ophelia's suicide. We'll explain in a moment why the plot lines are in bold print.

QUEEN

One woe doth tread upon another's heel.
So fast they follow.
Your sister's drown'd, Laertes.

LAERTES

Drown'd?
O, where?

QUEEN

There is **a willow grows ascant the brook**
That shows his hoar leaves in the glassy
  stream;
There with fantastic **garlands did she make**
Of cornflowers, nettles, daisies, and long
  purples
That liberal shepherds give a grosser name,
But our cold maids do dead men's fingers call
  them.
There, on the pendant boughs her cornet weeds
Clamb'ring to hang, an envious **sliver broke;**
When down her weedy trophies and **herself**
Fell in the weeping **brook.**
Her clothes spread wide,
And, mermaid-like, awhile they **bore her up;**
Which time **she chanted** snatches of old **lauds,**
As one incapable of her own distress,
Or like a creature native and imbued
Unto that element;
but long it could not be
Till that **her garments,** heavy with their drink,
Pull'd the poor wretch from **her** melodious lay
To muddy **death.**

```
                          LAERTES
       Alas, then she is drown'd!


                          QUEEN
       Drown'd, drown'd.
```

The passage develops in seven stages: (1) the Queen's distress, (2) the news of Ophelia's death, (3) where it happened and what she was doing there, (4) her collapse into the water, (5) how she sang as her clothes held her up, (6) how she finally drowned, and (7) Laertes' grief. As the bold print shows, the bare plot information could have been conveyed using only forty words, yet Shakespeare has provided over one hundred additional words to convey the feelings and thoughts that Ophelia's suicide calls up in the characters. We could further analyze the literary features of this passage, but no written description would do justice to its lyrical beauty. For complete expression, it must be performed by an actress who has a sense of its music as well as its drama. Incidentally, although this passage contains highly polished and refined poetry, the same literary principles pertain to poetry that is intentionally poor. Doggerel or negligent grammar or syntax can be as dramatically revealing in poetry as is the good-bad prose speech we discussed earlier.

The tradition of poetry has not completely disappeared from the modern theatre. In the last one hundred years, individual playwrights have repeatedly made attempts to achieve in the theatre the expressive feelings of which poetry is capable. Some authors, like William Butler Yeats, T.S. Eliot, and Maxwell Anderson, returned to writing explicitly poetic dialogue. Others, like August Strindberg, Eugene O'Neill, Tennessee Williams, Samuel Beckett, August Wilson, David Mamet, and Sam Shepard have written prose that can be as expressive as poetry. Modern poetic prose dialogue doesn't conform to historical rules; its poetic flavor is exclusively its own. It is poetic in the sense of how it is used in the play and from its context, not necessarily from its content or form.

A few lines from *Happy Days* will illustrate. Throughout the play, Winnie is physically entrapped in a wasteland, isolated from human contact. She passes the time with trivial activities in the vain hope that her life will improve. Among the objects in her handbag is a revolver. This is how an excerpt early in the play is printed in the script:

```
But something tells me, do not overdo the bag,
Winnie, make use of it of course, let it help
you . . . along when stuck, by all means, but
cast your mind forward, something tells me,
cast your mind forward, Winnie, to the time
when words must fail—(Pause. She turns to look
at the bag.)—and do not overdo the bag.
```

Winnie, of course, is elliptically debating her own suicide. In view of the dramatic context, her everyday words, her pantomime, even her imperfect grammar and syntax, reveal important meanings in this passage. In fact, it would be instructive to recast it as a free verse poem about the futility of hope.

```
But something tells me,
Do not overdo the bag, Winnie,
Make use of it, of course,
Let it help you . . . along,
When stuck,
By all means,
But cast your mind forward,
Something tells me,
Cast your mind forward, Winnie,
To the time when words must fail—
And do not overdo the bag.
```

One of the distinctive rhythmical features of this passage is Beckett's way of repeating a simple phrase, bouncing it in the air like a ball. Besides repetition, the speech also employs a large number of other formal literary devices. This points up once again the difficulty of dealing with poetic speech of any kind in the modern theatre. We understand that dialogue should not be considered exclusively as literature, yet in many cases it is written as much for sound as it is for sense.

Charm

Still another value of dialogue is its inherent capacity to please through wit, irony, gracefulness, or surprise. For lack of a better term, we might call these qualities collectively *charm*. The prose dialogue of many dramatists appeals to the imagination, the appreciation of beauty, and the sense of humor in this way. Some of the most attractive qualities of *The School for Scandal* and *Angels in America*, for example, are the clever remarks and graceful turns of phrase spoken by the characters. The large measure of ironic humor in *The Wild Duck* and *Three Sisters* is one reason these early realistic plays sustain their appeal for contemporary audiences. Brecht may be a social dramatist, but the surprising literary inversions ("How can you have morality without a war?") and musical interludes found in *Mother Courage* are very important parts of its continued appeal.

The poetic quality of Sam Shepard's prose has been well documented. Here is a short passage from *A Lie of the Mind* in which Sally interrupts her brother Jake, who is secretly preparing to run away to find Beth. Jake is shaving in front of a mirror.

JAKE

(*Whisper*) Don't think about her feet or her calves or her knees or her thighs or her waist or her hips or her ribs or her tits or her armpits or her shoulders or her neck or her face or her eyes or her hair or her lips. Especially not her lips. Don't think about any of these things. You'll be much better off.
(*He turns upstage just as Sally enters through the up left door, wearing a jacket, jeans, and western boots and carrying a suitcase. Pause. Sally closes the door, then turns back to Jake. She keeps hold of the suitcase.*)

SALLY

How're you feelin', Jake?

JAKE

Me?
(*Pause. He moves fast to the bed, pulls the flag off his neck as he crosses, kneels down beside the bed, stuffs the flag under the bed, pulls*

out a small black toilet case, unzips it, puts
the shaver inside, zips it back up, and shoves
it back under the bed. He rises to his feet,
then sits on the edge of the bed, facing Sally,
and rubs his knee as he stares at her. Pause)

SALLY

(*Sets her suitcase on floor*) Where's Mom?

JAKE

(*Rapid speech*) I don't worry anymore about
where anybody is. I don't think about that.
Anybody can move wherever they want. I just try
to keep track of my own movements these days.
That's enough. Have you ever tried that? To
follow yourself around? Like a spy? You can
wind up anywhere. It's amazing. Like, just now
I caught myself shaving. I was right over
there. Shaving my face. I didn't know I was
doing that until just now. It's kinda scary, ya
know.

SALLY

Scary?

JAKE

Yeah. I mean there's a possibility that you
could do something that you didn't even know
about. You could be somewhere that you couldn't
even remember being. Has that ever happened to
you?

SALLY

No. No, it's the opposite with me. Everything
just keeps repeating itself.

JAKE

Oh. Well, then you don't know what I'm talkin'
about.

A poetic mood is established with Jake's opening remarks. Sally's abrupt questions continue the mood. Jake follows with curt rapid speech in which he makes up a lame excuse for shaving. Throughout, Jake is nervously suspicious of Sally, whom he believes will prevent him from escaping. The plot here is not complicated, but the poetic mood created by the dialogue lends the moment a haunting quality. The charm of Shepard's dialogue here and all through his work is part of what elevates his plays to the level of a parable. We remember the words as well as the characters and situations in his plays partly because of the charming qualities of the dialogue.

Dialects and Accents

Dialects have similar charming appeal. The regional and folk dialects of Brooklyn, the rural South, New England, and Appalachia, as well as those of various ethnic cultures, have all decorated our American language. The accents of native Germans, Swedes, Italians, Russians, Latin Americans, French, Japanese, Chinese, and recently various Asians and Africans are also attractive and entertaining to the ear. The appeal of these dialects and accents comes from our appreciation of their musical intonations, imaginative word choices, and stirring speech rhythms. Playwrights Eugene O'Neill, Bertolt Brecht, Arthur Miller, Tennessee Williams, Lorraine Hansberry, David Rabe, August Wilson, and Sam Shepard, to name only a few, have shown skill in using these speech qualities. Dialects and accents enhance plausibility, aid in rapid recognition of given circumstances, and provide additional opportunities for emotional expression.

THEATRICALITY

Besides strictly literary features, dialogue also possesses theatrical qualities. This doesn't imply the sensational, the melodramatic, or the artificial; it refers to those effects that are achieved only through the actors and the production values on stage. Any lay reader can find literary meanings on a printed page, but it takes professional skill to perceive the latent action, emotion, and subtext that is present in dramatic dialogue when it is spoken. This kind of perception depends on dramatic as well as literary imagination.

Action

It's hard to think of dialogue without also considering physical action as an expressive outcome. As was explained earlier, an important quality of dialogue is its ability to convey stage or indigenous business. Lorraine Hansberry has provided a great deal of such business directly in the dialogue of *A Raisin in the Sun*. Mama's first appearance in Act 1 offers a good illustration. It is morning; everyone is getting ready for the day's activities.

> MAMA
> Who that 'round here slamming doors at this
> hour.

> RUTH
> That was Walter Lee. He and Bennie was at it
> again.

> MAMA
> My children and they tempers. Lord, if this
> little old plant don't get some more sun than
> it's been getting it ain't never going to see
> spring again. What's the matter with you this
> morning, Ruth? You looks right peaked. You
> aiming to iron all them things? Leave some for
> me. I'll get to 'em this afternoon. Bennie,
> honey, it's too drafty for you to be sitting
> around half dressed. Where's your robe?

> BENEATHA
> In the cleaners.

> MAMA
> Well, go and get mine and put it on.

BENEATHA

I'm not cold, Mama, honest.

MAMA

I know—but you so thin . . .

BENEATHA

Mama, I'm not cold.

MAMA

(*Seeing the make-down sofa-bed as young Travis
has left it.*) Lord have mercy, look at that
poor bed. Bless his heart—he tries, don't he.

RUTH

No—he don't half try at all 'cause he knows
you going to come along behind him and fix
everything.

The author has provided a busy round of activities for Mama in this short selection of dialogue. During these ten lines, Mama briskly enters the room to begin her daily chores: she waters the plant in the kitchen, she moves to help Ruth with her ironing, she crosses to Bennie at the table and fusses over her clothing. Then she closes the window, moves to the sofa bed, and begins straightening the covers. These activities quickly characterize Mama as an energetic, hard-working caregiver who always thinks of others first. Some of the actions are directly stated, others implied. Alert readers can probably recognize additional illustrative actions in her lines.

Pantomime like we have just seen has become increasingly important in modern drama. Much of Winnie's role in *Happy Days* consists of pantomime that Beckett orchestrated with considerable care. Since Winnie hardly moves in the entire play, her pantomime with the small objects becomes a necessary expressive accompaniment to her dialogue. Some professional actors, directors, and designers possess astonishing skill in discovering appropriate interpretive action to accompany the dialogue. Readers should be alert for any opportunities to reinforce the dialogue by use of direct or latent illustrative action.

We already know that action in dramatic dialogue also means something more than physical activity. In the following selection from *Tartuffe* there is no obvious physical action stated or implied, but the moment is comical in performance because of the contrasting patterns of qualities, or behaviors. Orgon has just returned from a visit to the country. He interrogates the servant Dorine about Tartuffe's welfare while he was away.

> ORGON
>
> Has everything gone well the few days I've been away? What have you been doing? How is everyone?
>
> DORINE
>
> The day before yesterday the mistress was feverish all day. She had a dreadful headache.
>
> ORGON
>
> And Tartuffe?
>
> DORINE
>
> Tartuffe? He's very well: hale and hearty; in the pink.
>
> ORGON
>
> Poor fellow!
>
> DORINE
>
> In the evening she felt faint and couldn't touch anything, her headache was so bad.
>
> ORGON
>
> And Tartuffe?
>
> DORINE
>
> He supped with her. She ate nothing but he very devoutly devoured a couple of partridges and half a hashed leg of mutton.

                    ORGON

Poor fellow!

                    DORINE

She never closed her eyes all through the
night. She was too feverish to sleep and we had
to sit up with her until morning.

                    ORGON

And Tartuffe?

                    DORINE

Feeling pleasantly drowsy, he went straight to
his room, jumped into a nice warm bed, and
slept like a top until morning.

                    ORGON

Poor fellow!

                    DORINE

Eventually she yielded to our persuasions,
allowed herself to be bled, and soon felt much
relieved.

                    ORGON

And Tartuffe?

                    DORINE

He dutifully kept up his spirits, and took
three or four good swigs of wine at breakfast
to fortify himself against the worst that might
happen and to make up for the blood the
mistress had lost.

                    ORGON

Poor fellow!

This event requires a small amount of simple staging as Orgon takes off his coat and hat, sets down his traveling bag, and pursues Dorine around the stage with his questions. The physical action would probably not generate much interest, however, without Orgon's continuous questions about the welfare of Tartuffe and Dorine's increasingly provocative insistence on refusing to tell him. Orgon's remarks are as comically unexpected as they are persistent.

Emotion

Another important function of dialogue—some would say its most important function—is the expression of emotion. Characters don't just state facts, they also express their feelings toward conditions they feel strongly about. The most highly emotional dialogue is often a free release of feelings stemming from an open clash of wills. Molière has provided a tense emotional encounter like this between Orgon and his son Damis in *Tartuffe*. Damis has discovered Tartuffe seducing Elmire. He thinks his father will condemn Tartuffe when he finds out, but Tartuffe outwits him. By candidly admitting the accusation, Tartuffe seems to Orgon to be selflessly taking the blame for Damis' slander. Thus Orgon misinterprets Damis' accusation and turns his anger on his son instead.

ORGON

(*to Damis*) Doesn't your heart relent, you dog!

DAMIS

What! Can what he says so far prevail with you
that . . .

ORGON

Silence, you scoundrel! (*raising up Tartuffe*)
Rise, brother—I beg you. (*to his son*) You
scoundrel!

DAMIS

He may—

ORGON

Silence!

DAMIS

This is beyond bearing! What! I'm to . . .

ORGON

Say another word and I'll break every bone in
your body!

TARTUFFE

In God's name, brother, calm yourself. I would
rather suffer any punishment than he should
receive the slightest scratch on my account.

ORGON

(*to his son*) Ungrateful wretch!

TARTUFFE

Leave him in peace! If need be, I'll ask your
pardon for him on my knees . . .

ORGON

(*to Tartuffe*) Alas! What are you thinking of?
(*to his son*) See how good he is to you, you
dog!

DAMIS

Then I . . .

ORGON

Enough!

DAMIS

What! Can't I . . .

ORGON

Enough, I say!

Tartuffe, Orgon, and Damis come into open conflict at this moment. They almost get into a brawl, yet their apparent loss of self-control is very deliberately orchestrated for them in the dialogue. Molière has skillfully written accusations and counter-accusations, epithets, connotative words, and broken sentences to go with their strong feelings.

We explained before how dialogue can narrate and explain ideas. Characters under stress, however, rarely stop to describe and analyze their thoughts and feelings. Such dialogue is seldom a cool scholarly debate. Instead it must reveal the strong emotions that the characters feel for the practical outcome of their ideas. In *The Wild Duck* when Dr. Relling scoffs at Gregers Werle's idealistic image of Hjalmar Ekdal, he does so with feeling. He believes Gregers is ruining other people's lives with his meddlesome brand of idealism. Relling is not just debating abstract ideas here, he's talking about the welfare of his friends.

GREGERS

(*indignantly*) Is it Hjalmar Ekdal you are
talking about in this strain?

RELLING

Yes, with your permission; I am simply giving
you an inside view of the idol you are
groveling before.

GREGERS

I should hardly have thought I was quite stone-
blind.

RELLING

Yes, you are—or not far from it. You are a sick
man, too, you see.

GREGERS

You are right there.

RELLING

Yes. Yours is a complicated case. First of all,
there is that plague of integrity fever, and

> then—what's worse—you are always in a delirium
> of hero worship; you must always have something
> to adore, outside yourself.
>
> GREGERS
> Yes, I must certainly seek it outside myself.
>
> RELLING
> But you make such a shocking mistake about
> every new phoenix you think you have
> discovered.
>
> GREGERS
> If you don't think better than that of Hjalmar
> Ekdal, what pleasure can you find in being
> everlastingly with him?
>
> RELLING
> Well, you see, I'm supposed to be a sort of a
> doctor—God help me! I have to give a hand to
> the poor sick people who live under the same
> roof with me.

Relling may be cerebral, but he is not the coldhearted cynic Gregers thinks he is. He originally chose to be a doctor because he wanted to help people in a practical way. Unfortunately, his own idealism was crushed in the process, and he became an alcoholic as a result. His lingering sympathy for the suffering of others still shows in the strong emotions of this passage. For Dr. Relling, as for other characters who speak about their most cherished beliefs, ideas have practical consequences.

Similar examples of egoistic emotion masking as social ideals appear in *Angels in America*. Louis Ironson seldom misses an opportunity to challenge his friends to a political debate. Act 2,2, Part I starts with Louis provoking Belize, "Why has democracy succeeded in America?" Belize, who sees that Louis' political rant is really a cover for his guilt about abandoning Prior, brings their debate to an end with an account of a love story that pointedly declares, ". . . real love isn't ever ambivalent." The politics in the dialogue masks the latent action, which is necessary to make the scene work on a theatrical level. Without the underlying action, the political debate would be simply abstract and not very entertaining.

Subtext

Some plays reveal plot, character, and idea mainly through their words. A great deal of their beauty can be found in their texts and in the actual structure of words in the dialogue. The words provide most of the thoughts the author considers necessary for the characters. The acting, directing, and design are straightforward illustrations of the text, and the basis of their entertainment value is largely contained in it. Many of these are excellent plays, yet in the theatre, the spoken word is not always as valuable in itself. Sometimes it is the unspoken subtext that is, or should be, the most important source of entertainment.

Subtext consists of the unspoken words that run directly beneath the dialogue. It is one of Stanislavski's most widely honored contributions to the study of plays, and it stems from two basic premises. First, characters actually speak only a small percentage of what they are thinking. Second, a point-to-point correspondence exists between what the characters are saying and what they are thinking. Subtext is much more than simply reading between the lines; it is a carefully crafted technical feature of the dialogue. In many plays, studying the dialogue alone is not enough; knowledge of the specific subtext is necessary to energize the dialogue and make it theatrical, entertaining. Success depends on the vocal intonations, facial expressions, gestures, and other illustrative actions that can be provided only by performing the subtext along with the text. One of the professional reader's serious tasks is to define the subtext so that it may take explicit form in production.

Certain writers extend the definition of subtext to include all the thoughts and feelings not expressed in the dialogue as well as the shape of the plot and the patterns of the imagery—in other words, the entire internal life of the play. There is no need to enforce a standard vocabulary, but knowing the distinction can be useful sometimes in the rehearsal hall.

Subtext plays an important role in *The Wild Duck*. Not much of an external nature happens in the play. There are none of the big scenes we traditionally associate with the stage. The major confrontations between

Gregers and his father, Hjalmar and Gina, and Gregers and Relling are brief and relatively subdued, not climactic in the usual sense. Even Hedvig's death occurs off stage; we only see its effects on the characters afterward. The real drama is expressed chiefly through the subtext. Uncovering the subtext means close reading for all evidence of conflicts, in this case those conflicts involving Gregers and Hjalmar. It's particularly important to understand Gregers' relationship with his father, whom he believes was responsible for his mother's death. A large part of Gregers' so-called mission in life is to punish his father for this. Most of the information comes out frankly in the background story, which Ibsen scholar P.D.F. Tennant has shown to be among the most intricate in all of the dramatist's plays. *The Wild Duck* becomes truly dramatic, however, only when its subtext is fully expressed by the actors.

One contemporary playwright whose plays often languish from the absence of subtext in performance is Sam Shepard. The subtextual core of *A Lie of the Mind*, for example, is too commonly neglected or overlooked in production, leaving audiences and actors in a muddle. A clear and steady look at what actually happens in the play can quickly solve the puzzle. It's a modest love story about a sensitive but abusive husband who finds out what love really means only after he almost destroys his wife. The subtext throughout the play is plugged into the transforming power of love. Without this, the play's dramatic potential is dissipated and falls off to little more than a bewildering narrative.

Subtext is not restricted to modern plays. An enlightening example is provided by Stanislavski from his production of *Tartuffe* described in Vasily Toporkov's book, *Stanislavski in Rehearsal*. The passage happens to be the same one between Orgon and Dorine used earlier in this chapter in the discussion of action. It won't be reproduced here, but readers can consult Toporkov's book if they wish. In the context of a rehearsal, Stanislavski furnishes fresh and imaginative subtext for each line to help the actors find and express the latent humor. Actors and directors will find his comments about subtext worth their attention.

SUMMARY

Dramatic dialogue is a very austere form of writing. Normally, it is denied any expressiveness that is not exclusively devoted to the practical workings of the play. Even when dialogue employs special literary qualities of its own, they cannot be artificially applied. From beginning to end, good dialogue is crafted so that each line advances the action, adding to the harmony and strength of the whole play.

Readers can be successful at analysis of dialogue because prior to production there is usually enough time to do so at the table. Closely studying the literary features of dramatic dialogue, however, should not be cause to overlook its dramatic role in performance. Drama is in danger when too much theoretical interest is taken in language or when language becomes the continuous subject of study. If theatre is really to happen, language must be an integral part of it, not independent from it. It is important to understand the dialogue, but it is necessary to guard against thinking too much about it. Dramatists are generally more concerned with what they have to say than with the way they say it.

QUESTIONS

Words   Does the dialogue employ abstract words? Concrete words? Formal words? Informal words? Do any of the characters specifically do so? Are there any examples of professional jargon or slang? Are there any words that convey more than their dictionary meanings (connotations)? If so, who speaks them? What associations do the words suggest?

Sentences   How long is the average sentence in the play? Does anyone speak sentences that are obviously longer or shorter than the average? What types of sentences are represented? Are the types of sentences generally similar, or is there a variety of sentence types? Do any characters speak in distinctive types of sentences? What do the sentences in the play sound like? Is their rhythm special or unusual in any way?

Speeches   Is punctuation strictly grammatical, or is it also used for dramatic purposes? Can examples of dramatic punctuation be cited? How are the speeches linked to one another? By words? By thoughts? Is verbal linking present in the lines? Are there any examples of dialogue linking by means of action? How are the sentences dramatically arranged within the longer speeches? How are the speeches dramatically orchestrated within units and scenes?

Special Qualities   Is the dialogue written in verse? If so, what types of verse are represented? Is the dialogue written in carefully composed prose? If so, what makes it special or unusual? Is the dialogue appealing in any other way? If so, how? Are there any examples of dialects or accents? If so, what kinds?

Theatricality   Does the dialogue express physical or psychological action? Is the dialogue highly emotional? If so, how is emotion expressed? Does the dialogue contain a great deal of unspoken inner tension (subtext)? If so, how is it meant to be expressed?

CHAPTER 9

Tempo, Rhythm, and Mood

The words *tempo, rhythm*, and *mood* are used here to describe a feature Aristotle called *music* or *song*. Greek tragedies were written in verse that was sung accompanied by music, and critics believe that Aristotle's term referred to the music and/or the musical rhythms of the poetry. He observed that such rhythms were capable of inciting emotions directly, and he concluded that these emotions enhanced the dramatic impact of plays. From this idea, he deduced that "the music of the language" should be considered one of the six basic elements of drama.

Although not many plays use verse today, they do employ tempos, rhythms, and moods to express feelings just as verse and music do. Rhythmical cadences can stimulate overt emotional responses such as laughter, tears, and applause. They can also stimulate more subtle physical adjustments in breathing, heartbeat, blood pressure, and muscular tension, which we associate with the emotions. Whether they acquire their powers from poetry, music, or nature, the features of tempo, rhythm, and mood can convey authentic feelings.

Some might argue that these features cannot be empirically observed in a play script. They would say that these are metaphysical dimensions that do not represent actual material reality. Others disagree. Psychologist William James maintained that there is no reason to call emotional sensations unreal just because they may be unseen. If something produces real effects (and most people would argue that emotions are real), it must be a form of reality itself. Stanislavski was familiar with James's

Principles of Psychology and seems to have agreed with him, if by coincidence. In his book, *Building a Character*, Stanislavski devoted two chapters to defining these features and explaining their importance for actors. His principle of *tempo-rhythm* stems from the struggle between internal and external tempos, rhythms, and moods in a character. Richard Boleslavsky, Georgi Tovstonogov, Alexander Dean, Lawrence Carra, F. Cowles Strickland, Curtis Canfield, Francis Hodge, and Tyrone Guthrie have also written about the empirical aspects of tempo, rhythm, and mood. Apparently there are some objective, teachable elements involved. They are subtle and complex but need to be understood because they help to shape the emotional experience of a play.

Understanding latent tempo, rhythm, and mood in a script requires wide experience in play reading and production. That's why analyzing them is one of the last stages of table work. Even then a reader will not be able to perceive them with much clarity before rehearsals begin. During the preliminary reading phase, tempo, rhythm, and mood may only be minimally there and sometimes as educated guesswork. It is almost impossible to plan them in advance authoritatively. A production will convey these features, but they may emerge very differently in practice than they did at the table. Nevertheless, analysis is needed to remove as many confusions as possible and to clarify thinking before rehearsals begin.

TEMPO

First some definitions and distinctions are needed. Timing, speed, pace, tempo, and rhythm are five different but related concepts. They have no precise definitions in the theatre; however, the definitions stated here are for use in this book. *Timing* means the temporal relationship between one spoken word and another or between a spoken word and a physical action. *Speed* is the measurable rate of movement or speech in real time, and *pace* means the spectator or director's subjective perception of speed. These three terms deal with aspects of time in a live performance. The following chapter relates to tempo, rhythm, and mood stemming from the script itself.

As has been discussed in earlier chapters, every moment in a good play is aimed at expressing the plot, the character, and the idea. How these features emerge from within the script has also been examined. *Tempo* at this point refers to how often information about plot, character, and idea occurs in the dialogue, the frequency of information. In this special context, tempo is not related to the usual meanings of velocity or measurable speed but is closer to the concept of texture or density. When a sequence of dialogue is crowded with information about plot, character, or idea, the inner tempo is slow because there is a large quantity of information to express. When such information is scarce, the content is thinner (less dense) and the inner tempo is swift because there is less for the mind to dwell on. The questions to ask are, "Where and when does the author present important dramatic information?" "What kind of information is it? Plot? Character? Idea?" "How much information is there?" The answers to these questions, according to the definition, describe tempo. Rhythm and its features will be defined later. Now the sources of tempo and tempo patterns are most relevant.

In the Plot

Chapter 3 explained how the background story is the secret part of the plot. In Chapter 4 we learned that plot in the dialogue consists of entrances and exits, blocking, use of properties, special physical activities, and particularly assertions, plans, and commands. Chapter 5 taught further that plot develops in progressions arranged in an escalating pattern of major and minor climaxes. These issues are the focus when trying to determine the tempo of the plot. Ibsen was an excellent craftsman when it came to conveying plot information in the dialogue and arranging it in clear, logical progressions. In the scene between Gregers and his father near the end of the first act of *The Wild Duck*, the chief dramatic interest is plot. Although some information about the characters is revealed through what they talk about and how they treat each other, very few lines express character as such. One line in the scene relates to the idea of the play. None contain any special literary qualities (in the English translation at least), and there is very little physical action to speak of.

The scene occurs on stage while the dinner party is going on in an adjoining room. The assertions, plans and commands in the dialogue advance the plot in four stages: (1) Gregers reproaches his father for the social and economic decline of the Ekdal family, (2) Gregers threatens to disclose his father's sexual relationship with their former housemaid who is now Hjalmar Ekdal's wife, (3) Werle informs Gregers of his engagement to Mrs. Sorby, and (4) Gregers condemns his father and announces his intention to leave home and embark on his life's mission.

The first beat (six lines) establishes Gregers' urgent wish to speak to his father privately.

GREGERS

Father, won't you stay a moment?

WERLE

(*stops*) What is it?

GREGERS

I must have a word with you.

WERLE

Can't it wait until we are alone?

GREGERS

No, it can't, for perhaps we shall never be alone together.

WERLE

(*drawing nearer*) What do you mean by that?

Notice the suspenseful link to the following beat in the last line: "What do you mean by that?" Next is a beat of twelve lines, composed of six rhetorical questions (i.e., assertions about the background story) by Gregers and six angry replies (i.e., counter-assertions about the same facts) by Mr. Werle. The entire beat deals with the illegal timber harvesting incident, but seven related topics are also treated, each expressed in two or three lines of dialogue. Each brief topic forms its own *sub-beat*, so to speak, because each adds its own fragment of new information about forward motion of the plot: (1) the decline in the fortunes of the Ekdals, (2) the former friendship between Lieutenant Ekdal and Mr. Werle, (3) their mutual participation in the timber affair, (4) Ekdal's responsibility in drawing up the fraudulent boundary map, (5) Ekdal's illegal cutting of the timber, (6) Werle's alleged ignorance of Ekdal's actions, and (7) the guilty verdict handed down against Ekdal together with the acquittal of Mr. Werle for lack of evidence. Sub-beats are delineated here by a double bar for clarity.

GREGERS

How has that family been allowed to go so
miserably to the wall?

WERLE

You mean the Ekdals, I suppose?

GREGERS

Yes, I mean the Ekdals. // Lieutenant Ekdal was
once so closely associated with you.

WERLE

Much too closely; I have felt that to my cost
for many years. It is thanks to him that I—
yes I—have had a kind of slur cast upon my
reputation. //

GREGERS

(*softly*) Are you sure that he alone was to
blame?

WERLE

Who else do you suppose?

GREGERS

You and he acted together in that affair of the
forests— //

WERLE

But was it not Ekdal that drew the map of the
tracts we had bought—that fraudulent map! // It

was he who felled all the timber illegally on
government property. In fact the whole
management was in his hands. // I was quite
in the dark as to what Lieutenant Ekdal was
doing.

                    GREGERS
Lieutenant Ekdal himself seems to have been
very much in the dark as to what he was
doing.

                    WERLE
That may be. // But the fact remains that he
was found guilty and I was acquitted.

                    GREGERS
Yes, I know that nothing was proved against
you.

                    WERLE
Acquittal is acquittal.

Mr. Werle takes the offensive in the next beat. It consists of four new
topics expressed in two or three lines each, totaling nine lines: (1) Werle's
wish to put the timber affair behind him once and for all, (2) Ekdal's emotional collapse after his release from prison, (3) Werle's attempt to assist
Ekdal with money and a job, and (4) Werle's decision not to record this
generosity in his financial accounts.

                  WERLE (*continued*)
Why do you rake up these old miseries that
turned my hair gray before its time? Is that
the sort of thing you have been brooding over
up there all these years? I can assure you,
Gregers, here in the town the whole story has
been forgotten long ago—as far as I am
concerned. //

GREGERS

But that unhappy Ekdal family—

WERLE

What would you have me do for those people?
When Ekdal came out of prison he was a broken
man, past all help. There are people in the
world who dive to the bottom the moment they
get a couple of slugs in their body and never
come to the surface again. // You may take my
word for it, Gregers, I have done all I could
without positively laying myself open to all
sorts of suspicion and gossip.

GREGERS

Suspicion? Oh, I see.

WERLE

I have given Ekdal copying work to do for the
office, and I pay him far, far more than his
work is worth.

GREGERS

(*without looking at him*) H'm; that I don't
doubt.

WERLE

You laugh? Do you think I'm not telling you the
truth? // Well, I certainly can't refer you to
my books, for I never enter payments of that
sort.

GREGERS

(*smiles coldly*) No, there are certain payments
it is best to keep no account of.

The first unit ends here. The remainder of the scene comprises seven
more units: Gregers presses Werle to admit he paid for Hjalmar Ekdal's

photography lessons and helped to set him up in business; Gregers accuses Werle of having an affair with their former housemaid and then arranging her marriage to Hjalmar Ekdal; Werle accuses Gregers and his neurotic mother of conspiring against him; Werle informs Gregers of his illness and his forthcoming marriage to Mrs. Sorby; Werle offers Gregers a partnership in his firm (a payoff?); Gregers criticizes his father's immoral behavior; Gregers announces he has found his mission in life and departs. Because Ibsen's dialogue in this scene is packed with detailed plot information, the internal tempo of the plot is slow. It unfolds gradually, fact by fact, in very small increments, and each fact adds a little more information to the plot of the play.

The tempo of the information in the plot influences the speed with which a scene is performed. According to this way of thinking, this scene would be performed slowly and deliberately with the actors accentuating everything they say. It is also quite possible, however, that the plot may not need as much emphasis in a modern performance as this early realistic play seems to indicate. After many years of experience with realism, audiences have been conditioned to deal with the complicated background material that is a hallmark of realistic playwriting. This being the case, in the contemporary theatre the scene might be performed faster than it was in the past. Perhaps there would be more emphasis on the tense emotional relationship between Gregers and Werle, building to a climax at the end of the act. Of course, this is a matter of interpretation. Beats that are too long can oversell a topic and weaken the tension. They may have to be performed rapidly to sustain the level of conflict. Beats that are too short may have to be expanded in performance with illustrative action. In either case, the tempo of the plot as such in the script would remain unchanged.

Compare this scene with the climax of *Death of a Salesman*, which was treated in Chapter 8. In that scene, except for Biff's announcement of his intention to leave home, neither Biff nor Willy furnish any new information about the plot. Essentially, they reiterate in more forceful terms facts that each of them expressed earlier in the play under different circumstances. The inner tempo of the plot is fast because most of the facts are already known. Once again, however, the speed of the actual performance will depend on the interpretive considerations of the actors and directors involved.

In the Characters

As seen in Chapter 6, many scenes contain material the dramatist has introduced essentially to express character. When examining character tempo, find out what kind of character information is being introduced and how much. Look closely for information about objectives, qualities, conflicts, values, personality traits, and relationships. The largest amount of such information tends to occur near the beginning of the play or when an important character appears for the first time.

The dialogue in Sophocles' *Oedipus Rex* offers an instructive example of character tempo in a period play. Creon's first appearance occurs in Episode 2. In that scene, Oedipus demands to know if Teiresias accused him of being Laius' murderer many years ago when it was discovered that Laius had been murdered. This is background story and assertions. Most of the scene, however, is devoted to illustrating the characters of Creon and Oedipus—their behavior qualities, role conflicts, values, personality traits, and relationship. In the first beat, Creon reacts angrily to Oedipus' accusations of treason. He asserts that he values citizenship, honor, and loyalty above everything else. Character information is in bold type.

CREON

Men of Thebes:
I am told that heavy accusations
Have been brought against me by King Oedipus.
I am not the kind of man to bear this tamely.
If in these present difficulties
He holds me accountable for any harm to him
Through anything I have said or done—why, then,
I do not value life in this dishonor.
It is not as though this rumor touched upon
Some private indiscretion. The matter is grave.
The fact is that I am being called disloyal
To the State, to my fellow citizens, to my
    friends.

In the next beat the Choragos attempts to persuade Creon that Oedipus didn't mean what he said (personality trait). He is implying (quality) that

Oedipus is impulsive and hot-tempered (personality trait). He is reluctant (quality) to say so, however, and this makes Creon impatient (personality trait). The excuses (quality) the Choragos offers to explain Oedipus' behavior reveal as much about his own character (role conflict) as they do about Oedipus.

CHORAGOS

He may have spoken in anger, not from his mind.

CREON

But did you not hear him say that I was the one
Who seduced the old prophet into lying?

CHORAGOS

The thing was said; **I do not know how**
  seriously.

CREON

But you were watching him! **Were his eyes**
  steady?
Did he look like a man in his right mind?

CHORAGOS

I do not know.
I cannot judge the behavior of great men.

Oedipus enters in the next unit, whose first beat contains eight balanced lines of dialogue. Oedipus' first five poetic lines reiterate what is already known about the plot. The remainder of the beat is devoted to the expression of character. We see Oedipus' stubborn pride (personality trait) contrasted with Creon's stubborn reasonableness (personality trait). In the final four lines of dialogue, Oedipus ridicules (quality) Creon's educated (quality) style of speech.

OEDIPUS

So you dared come back.
Why? How brazen of you to come to my house,
You murderer!

Do you think I do not know
That you plotted to kill me, plotted to steal
  my throne?
Tell me, in God's name, am I a coward, a fool,
That you should dream you could accomplish
  this?
A fool who could not see your slippery game?
A coward, not to fight back when I saw it?
You are the fool, Creon, are you not? hoping
Without support or friends to get a throne?
Thrones may be won or bought: you could do
  neither.

CREON

Now listen to me. **You have talked; let me talk,**
  too.
You can not judge unless you know the facts.

OEDIPUS

You speak well: there is one fact; but I find it
  hard
To learn from the deadliest enemy I have.

CREON

That above all I must dispute with you.

OEDIPUS

That above all I will not hear you deny.

CREON

If you think there is anything good in being
  stubborn
Against all reason, then I say you are wrong.

OEDIPUS

If you think a man can sin against his own kind
And not be punished for it, I say you are mad.

CREON

I agree.

The beat that follows reinforces plot information already known from the previous scene with Teiresias. The next beat returns to expression of character. It contains a speech in which Creon stands up for himself (personality trait) by defending his values. Readers should note how he uses rhetorical speech (personality trait) and supports his arguments with aphorisms (personality trait). The final beat is devoted to an exchange of short lines (contrasting qualities) that emphasize the difference between them (contrasting values, role conflict, and the significance of their relationship).

CREON

But now it is my turn to question you.

OEDIPUS

Put your questions. I am no murderer.

CREON

First, then: you married my sister?

OEDIPUS

I married your sister.

CREON

And you rule the kingdom equally with her?

OEDIPUS

Everything that she wants she has from me.

CREON

And am I the third, equal to both of you?

OEDIPUS

That is why I call you a bad friend.

CREON

No. Reason it out, as I have done.
Think of this first: Would any sane man prefer
Power, with all a king's anxieties,
To that same power and the grace of sleep?
Certainly not I.
I have never longed for the king's power—only
  his rights.
Would any wise man differ from me in this?
As matters stand, I have my way in everything
With your consent, and no responsibilities.
If I were king, I should be a slave to policy.
How could I desire a scepter more
Than what is now mine—untroubled influence?
No, I have not gone mad; I need no honors,
Except those with the perquisites I have now.
I am welcome everywhere; every man salutes me.
And those who want your favor seek my ear,
Since I know how to manage what they ask.
Should I exchange this ease for that anxiety?
Besides, no sober mind is treasonable.
I hate anarchy
And never would deal with any man who likes it.
Test what I have said. Go to the priestess
At Delphi, ask if I quoted her correctly.
And as for this other thing: if I am found
Guilty of treason with Teiresias,
Then sentence me to death! **You have my word**
It is a sentence I should cast my vote for—
But not without evidence!
You do wrong
When you take good men for bad, bad men for
  good.
A true friend thrown aside—why, life itself
Is not more precious!
In time, you will know this well:
For time, and time alone, will show the just man,
Though scoundrels are discovered in a day.

CHORAGOS

This is well said, and a prudent man would
ponder it.

OEDIPUS

But is he not quick in his duplicity?
And shall I not be quick to parry him?
Would you have me stand still, hold my peace,
  and let
This man win everything, through my inaction?

CREON

And you want—what is it, then? To banish me?

OEDIPUS

No, not exile. It is your death I want.
So that all the world may see what treason
  means.

CREON

You will persist, then? You will not believe
me?

OEDIPUS

How can I believe you?

CREON

Then you are a fool.

OEDIPUS

To save myself?

CREON

In justice, think of me.

OEDIPUS

You are evil incarnate.

CREON

But suppose that you are wrong?

OEDIPUS

Still I must rule.

CREON

But not if you rule badly.

OEDIPUS

O city, city!

CREON

It is my city, too!

The plot tempo in this unit is moderately fast because little is revealed about the plot that is not already known. The tempo of character disclosure is slow, however, because so much of the dialogue is devoted to its expression. The stately character tempo and reliance on words instead of illustrative actions are standard playwriting techniques in period plays. When speaking in public or in a court of law, classical conventions often required speakers to establish their credibility by declaring their family lineage and personal values. If the beats revealing character seem too long for modern tastes, they might be speeded up with illustrative character business to supplement the dialogue.

When modern dramatists write dialogue devoted to character expression, they usually do so in shorter passages. They are also inclined to supplement the dialogue with more opportunities for illustrative business. The first entrance of Anna Fierling in *Mother Courage* is a representative case. The plot at this point in the play involves the Recruiting Sergeant's demand (command) for Anna's identity papers (conflict of objectives), but he must wait (role conflict) while she chatters (personality trait) about herself (values) throughout the entire unit. In the first beat, she makes wisecracks (quality) about how she got her nickname (personality trait). In the second beat, she jokes (quality) about the useless collection of official papers (values) she has accumulated (personality trait) over the years. She also "asserts" her reputation for honest dealing (values). All this talk is a pure expression of her character. In fact, she reveals almost everything about her character in these thirteen lines. Brecht has created a slow character tempo at this point to introduce this character. He has also provided plenty of opportunities in the dialogue for illustrative business with props to illustrate her personality traits.

In the Idea

When dramatists choose to express idea directly in words, the tempo slows to conform to the quality and amount of intellectual information being presented. The slowest tempos arising from idea are found in period plays, where the practice was to present ideas in speeches composed according to classical rhetorical principles. Cleante's initial scene with Orgon in the first act of *Tartuffe*, for example, includes two very long idea speeches (set speeches). Together they contain a total of twenty-five sentences averaging over twenty-five words each. Close analysis reveals them to be skillfully arranged expressions of the central intellectual issues at stake. Whatever the tempos may be elsewhere in the play, the tempo of the idea is slow and deliberate throughout these speeches.

Modern dramatists are inclined to incorporate talk about ideas more realistically within the character and situation. In *Death of a Salesman*, Arthur Miller demonstrates considerable skill at expressing intellectual issues in the dialogue without appearing to do so. His characters present ideas in the form of aphorisms that sound like expressions of simple personal values. Willy offers instructions to his sons: "The man who makes an appearance in the business world, the man who creates personal interest, is the man who gets ahead. Be liked and you will never want." "Start big, and you'll end big." Ben advises Willy: "Never fight fair with a stranger . . . You'll never get out of the jungle that way." Linda admonishes Biff: "A small man can be just as exhausted as a great man." Charley warns Willy: "When a deposit bottle is broken, you don't get your nickel back." These simple expressions are not meant to slow the tempo as much as Cleante's speeches do. Instead they should slow the tempo for a moment, like a brief retard in music, while they harmonize or counterpoint the main idea of the play.

Chapter 7 explained that epilogues provide opportunities for the characters to speak about the ideas in the play. Arthur Miller uses an epilogue in *Death of a Salesman* although he calls it a "Requiem." He also provides a funeral to give the scene the plausibility that modern conventions require. Biff reflects about his father, "He had all the wrong dreams. All, all, wrong." Then Charley admonishes him for dishonoring Willy's memory.

CHARLEY

Nobody dast blame this man. You don't
understand. Willy was a salesman. And for a
salesman, there is no rock bottom to life. He
don't put a bolt to a nut, he don't tell you
the law or give you medicine. He's a man way
out there in the blue, riding on a smile and a
shoeshine. And when they start not smiling
back—that's an earthquake. And then you get
yourself a couple of spots on your hat, and
you're finished. Nobody dast blame this man. A
salesman got to dream, boy. It comes with the
territory.

The way the dramatist expresses idea in this passage is characteristic of modern playwrights. Biff's line is a statement about idea, but within the context of the situation, it sounds like a spontaneous emotional outburst. Charley's speech is also an extended expression of idea, similar to Cleante's in *Tartuffe*. The tempo of his dialogue is slow because the speech is long, also like Cleante's. Charley's speech, however, sounds realistic because Miller has placed it in a solemn situation and divided it into eleven short sentences averaging nine words each. The dramatic situation plus the halting emotional progress of the words conceal the intellectual content of the speech and make it sound like an expression of character and feeling.

RHYTHM

Rhythm is the pattern of changing tensions in the beats, units, scenes, and acts—a pulsing sensation that occurs when the dramatic intensity rises and falls within each progression. Rhythm operates the same way in drama as it does in metrical poetry. It uses recurring stresses and variations in the placement of accents to stimulate feelings and associations that enhance the meaning. Rhythm assists progressions in establishing interest, maintaining suspense, developing the main idea, and concluding interest in the work. Dramatic rhythm does not depend on regular metrical pulses, however, like those found in poetry or music. As already seen, there is a large variety in the speed with which tensions are built up and released within progressions. Along with tempo, rhythm is the second element of drama capable of expressing and inciting feelings directly. Because it is based in natural human instincts, rhythm induces feelings effortlessly. Most of us are inclined to accept its emotional effects without even thinking about them.

In the Plot

Almost any good play will employ strategies to create plot rhythm. The trouble is that dramatists use rhythm so skillfully that its features are hidden from untrained observers. This is where close analysis becomes helpful once again. To some extent, rhythm was already dealt with while considering Freytag's principles of dramatic technique. Recall in Chapter 5 his point that a plot is not a flat, featureless composition. It consists of obstacles and climaxes arranged by the dramatist to convey the meaning desired. Freytag's pyramid was an attempt to describe an idealized arrangement of these features. But in doing so, he also provided a picture of how dramatic rhythm operates. By visualizing the maximum and minimum tensions (climaxes) and the intervals between them, a pyramid like Freytag's can furnish a rhythmic picture of the total play. Of course, Freytag's approach is not the only way to study rhythm. Readers could also use the simple method of noting the stresses, or emotional pulses, within a series of dramatic actions, something like scanning verse. Director Louis Jouvet described these impressions poetically as masculine, neutral, and feminine. Collecting the stressed and unstressed impressions into coherent groups can furnish a narrative description of the rhythm. In any case, what we are attempting to find at this time is how the dramatic tensions collect and develop to form the pulses of emotional tension, or plot rhythm in a play.

Studying how an individual dramatist uses rhythm will help to account for how it produces its effects. Referring to *The Wild Duck*, remember that Act 1 occurs in Werle's study. As the play opens, the servants are putting things in order (first rhythmic pulse) while a dinner party is under way in the adjoining room (ongoing rhythmic counter-pulse). Petersen lights a lamp and says resentfully, "Listen to them, Jensen!" Then he starts a whispered conversation about Mr. Werle and his son, Gregers (second rhythmic pulse). During the conversation, the other hired waiters can be seen at work through the doorway up center, and banter and laughter comes from the other room. As the two servants speak, the side door opens and Old Ekdal bursts in, drunk. Petersen says, "Good Lord!—what do you want here?" and Ekdal asks to be allowed into the office to get his salary (third rhythmic pulse). After Ekdal goes into the office, Jensen asks skeptically, "Is he one of the office people?" Then there is a restrained conversation about Old Ekdal (fourth rhythmic pulse). Soon Petersen hears the dinner party breaking up and warns Jensen, "Sh! They're leaving the table" (fifth rhythmic pulse). The double doors are thrown open, and Mrs. Sorby enters (sixth rhythmic pulse). The two servants stop their conversation and hurry on to perform their duties.

The rhythm in this scene is controlled by the tension of the first whispered conversation about Werle and Gregers, the increase in suspense accompanying Ekdal's surprise appearance, the tension of the second whispered conversation about Ekdal, and the interruption of the conversation when Mrs. Sorby appears. The accumulated tension is held in check during the next unit. It is a transitional moment consisting of nine lines in which Mrs. Sorby and several guests engage in small talk as they pass through the study on their way to another room. Gregers and Hjalmar are then left alone on stage.

The scene between Gregers and Hjalmar contains seven units, seven rhythmic pulses, crowded with fragments of background story. There is immediate suspense when Hjalmar begins by responding to a caustic remark made by one of the guests about his appearance at the dinner party, "You ought not to have invited me, Gregers." After Gregers restores his confidence, they begin to talk about their school days together, their subsequent separation for seventeen years, Old Ekdal's imprisonment, Hjalmar's photography career, the Ekdal family's separation from their original circle of friends, Hjalmar's marriage to Gina, and Werle's financial backing of Hjalmar's photography business. As Gregers is about to ask more about his father, Mrs. Sorby again enters and again brings the conversation on stage to an abrupt halt. Each of these topic-rhythms is introduced, then interrupted by the introduction of the next topic-rhythm. Although each topic is crucial to both characters, the rhythmic pulses continue to swell because no topic is completely explained.

Director Tyrone Guthrie believed that anyone who wishes to know a play well ought to be able to observe the rhythm of a play like a graph similar to a patient's hospital chart or a company's sales statistics. In other words, the reader should see the emotional peaks and valleys and be able to picture the shape of the scene in a graphic form that helps to make the rhythm clear. Graphing can also help in understanding the relation to adjoining scenes better. Ideally, each scene should have its own small graph and eventually a graph of each act should emerge. It is possible to understand the rhythmic peaks and valleys of the entire play like this.

Rhythm arises from the words and actions of the play. However, the acting, speech, and blocking, as well as the scenery, lighting, and costumes also contribute to the rhythm of the performance. In *The Wild Duck* these elements are composed of, but not limited to, the sounds of the dinner party off stage and the piano music, the entrances and exits of the characters and the sounds of their footsteps, the movements of Petersen and Jensen and the other servants, and even the pauses in the dialogue. In production, everything is part of the rhythm, including the speed and intensity of the light changes and the fast or slow curtains or blackouts between acts. Although awareness of rhythm begins with understanding what's going on in the script, it also demands sensitivity to the contributions made by all the elements involved with the performance.

In the Characters

The rate and sum of change shown by the characters marks their rhythm. How much change occurs in the characters from beginning to end? How much from one entrance to the next? In his useful handbook, *Acting: The First Six Lessons*, Richard Boleslavsky offered the following explanation of character rhythm. He and his student took an elevator ride to the top floor of New York's Empire State Building. Boleslavsky maintained that the reason they were exhilarated by the view from the 102nd floor is because it is so different from the view at street level. He said that if, instead of taking the elevator, they had ascended one floor at a time, they would still know where they were and how high. They would continue to recognize the change, but there would be none of the earlier feeling of exhilaration because the view from one floor to the next did not change very much. The final view would be the same, but the gradual, step-by-step manner of getting there would make it feel different, less exhilarating.

The thrill they experienced after taking the elevator to the top floor resulted from several features: (1) the sudden shutting-out of the complex sights and sounds at street level when they stepped into the quiet elevator, (2) the silent, accelerated ascent through space, and (3) the infinite expanse of open space that greeted them when they emerged onto the viewing deck. They were transported from a noisy, restrictive world of chaotic impressions, placed in an isolation chamber, and then thrust into a new world of openness, freedom, and silence.

Boleslavsky's lesson illustrates how rhythm operates in the illustration of character. Hamlet's character is different at the end of the play, for example, than it was at the beginning. We won't argue whether he has been transformed or has revealed traits that initially were hidden. The point is that however the changes occur, the alterations in Hamlet have occurred in small increments one scene at a time. The rhythm of Hamlet's character development is slow and steady, and the final effect is cumulative rather than surprising. Character development is patterned like this also in *Death of a Salesman*, *Streamers*, *The Piano Lesson*, and *Angels in America*. On the other hand, Oedipus changes from an arrogant dictator to a blind outcast in five enormous leaps. His personality is different in each episode, and the emotional impact of his final appearance is that much greater because of the rhythmic leaps. A similar rhythmical development is employed in *Tartuffe*, *A Raisin in the Sun*, and *A Lie of the Mind*.

The rhythm of character development in *Three Sisters* is similar, if not as apparent. There are three plots, three love triangles, in the play: Masha-Kulygin-Vershinin, Andrey-Natasha-Protopopov, and Irina-Tuzenbach-Solyony. At most, each affair has one or two scenes in each of the four acts. Our composite picture of their relationships is based on a total of four or five brief encounters, each separated by a period of several months or sometimes up to a year or more. Their separate love affairs are woven together in such a seamless fashion that we don't realize how little we really know of them or how far each affair has progressed since its previous appearance. Each affair progresses over great leaps of time, of which we see only selected events. Chekhov directs us to fill in the gaps for ourselves. Readers should understand that the method dramatists choose for developing character rhythmically is an important feature in conveying the meaning of a play to the audience.

MOOD

Everyone agrees that successful plays evoke strong moods in performers and audiences. Mood doesn't mean moodiness, the condition of being gloomy or sullen. In drama, *mood* is a particular state of persistent emotion that includes the whole range of possible human feelings. Mikhail Chekhov and his followers refer to this feature as *atmosphere*. Some of these emotional states lie within the play; others refer to a world outside the play. Chekhov made the distinction by using the terms *atmosphere* and *individual feelings*. Although both work together, the main concern here is the moods that arise from within the closed context of the play itself.

The given circumstances of time, locale, season, and social conditions can be effective sources of mood. Plot can elicit mood through tension, suspense, climax, and release. Moods can be activated by the mental states and emotions of the characters and the things they do, and in certain plays, connotations associated with the main idea can induce moods as well as intellectual awareness. Dialogue can also evoke moods by means of word choices, rhythms, imagery, and sound. In short, every play has the potential for creating moods using a variety of means. As a rule, in a play there will be one dominant mood that works like a dominant chord in music, while additional emotional shadings emerge from this controlling mood.

In the Given Circumstances

Although the specific function of the given circumstances is to provide the temporal, spatial, and social context of the play, mood can be a by-product of those elements. Seventeenth-century, war-torn Europe creates a mood of bleakness and despair in *Mother Courage*. The late seasons (fall and winter) and the desolate locales (a highway, outside a half-demolished church, an army camp, and so on) contribute to the mood. The barren coldness of the military cadre room in *Streamers* enhances the dominant mood in that play.

A dinner party at the home of a successful businessman (the bustle of servants, sparkling candles, a comfortable fire in the fireplace, cheerful piano music, luxurious furnishings, and expensive decorations) produces an incongruously pleasant background mood for the first act of *The Wild Duck*, with its tense family conflict. Compare this to the mood created by the given circumstances of the rest of the play, which takes place in Hjalmar Ekdal's flat. Instead of luxury, cheer, and warmth there is a cramped tenement with snow blowing through broken windows.

Chekhov is considered a playwright of moods. In his influential book, *The Joy of Rehearsal*, Russian director Anatoly Efros explained his understanding of the moods in *Three Sisters*. Notice that the moods are not laid on by Efros, but generated from the actions in the play, notably the time of day.

> The first act of *Three Sisters* takes place in the morning. The second in the evening. The third at night. And the fourth again in the morning.
>
> Morning: hopes, sunshine, Sunday breakfast, name days. But in the morning there is also melancholy. Because of yesterday's unfortunate events, yesterday's suffering.
>
> Evening: company, the table full of food, chit-chat, disputes, quarrels, cheerfulness, and nervous uneasiness.
>
> Night: sleep, nightmares, hysterics, overwrought impressions.
>
> Morning again: departures, hangovers, denouement. The pallor of the faces and ennui in the postures. The need for work. And again hope.

These are a few examples of how playwrights use moods in the given circumstances to strengthen the emotional impact of the other dramatic elements in a play.

In the Plot

Among the most noticeable moods are those created by the emotional dynamics of the plot. Murder mysteries offer some of the best examples of this principle. The moods created by the tensions, suspense, and surprises in mystery plots are a major part of their entertainment appeal. Though character is the dominant element in *Hamlet*, the broad scope of the plot has an emotional influence as well. It contains scenes of mystery, intrigue, lyricism, humor, horror, pomp and circumstance, irony, and conspiracy and concludes with savage killings and a military funeral procession. Eugene O'Neill's drama *The Hairy Ape* and Tony Kushner's *Angels in America* provide other examples of powerful plot dynamics. Some playwrights take the opposite approach. The mordant mood created by the flat plot dynamics of Beckett's *Happy Days* is a key to that drama's unusual brand of theatricality. In these plays and many others, the forces released and withheld in the plot contribute to the creation of mood.

In the Characters

Characters themselves create mood through their actions, desires, and behavioral mannerisms. Molière's characters are excellent examples. Tartuffe's audacious and clever hypocrisy, Dorine's merry rebelliousness, Mariane's romantic affection, and Orgon's impulsive temperament contribute mood values to *Tartuffe*. The characters in *A Raisin in the Sun* create moods both individually and as a group. Each brings a special feeling to the total mood of the play: Mama's moral strength, Walter's longing, Ruth's forbearance, Asagai's optimism, and Beneatha's exuberance. Character moods also add to the total mood appeal of *A Lie of the Mind, The Piano Lesson, Mother Courage, Streamers,* and *Death of a Salesman*.

Some characters are so compelling that their individual moods determine the controlling mood for the entire play. The characters of Oedipus and Hamlet, for example, tower over everyone else. They define the dominant moods of their respective plays regardless of whether they are on stage. In a like manner, the quirky moods of Jake and Beth control the overall mood of *A Lie of the Mind* and the rambunctious mood of Boy Willie governs that of *The Piano Lesson*. In monodramas, the leading character must be so interesting that the character's moods replace those provided by plot, characters, and idea in multicharacter plays. Winnie in *Happy Days* is an example. Similarly, Yank's moods both dominate and characterize *The Hairy Ape*, which is almost a monodrama in production.

In the Idea

Idea can incite strong moods dependent on what's going on in the mind of the observer and in the everyday world outside the play. Spirited feelings arise when ideas in the play make direct contact with real world ideas about politics, economics, science, religion, and art. The politics in *Mother Courage*, for example, were so provocative that its productions in this country enraged some audiences in the 1950s. When *Death of a Salesman* was produced in 1949, it was not unusual for fathers in the audience to weep openly. Its intellectual issues were relevant and affecting during the post-World War II economic boom. The anticapitalist implications of *Death of a Salesman* were also a subject of spirited debate in the press. David Rabe's 1976 play *Streamers* is another instance. Today the play seems to be a compassionate plea for human sympathy. In 1976, however, the Vietnam War and social unrest were the immediate background. The motifs of homosexuality and the brutality of war incited audiences and at the same time made them think. Some readers may still have vivid memories of the commotion raised by the ideas presented in *Angels in America* when it premiered in 1992 and even thereafter. As was discussed in Chapter 7, dramatists employ ideas in their plays in the belief that they will not merely interest us intellectually, but will mainly excite our feelings. Readers could provide many other examples of plays in which ideas incite emotions.

SUMMARY

Tempo, rhythm, and mood are empirical human experiences, just as thinking, feeling, and behavior are. This chapter showed that plays depend for much of their appeal on these emotional experiences that lie hidden in plot, character, idea, and dialogue. The patterns formed of these experiences are not formal; they tend to be irregular and free. In a production, it is the director who deals with issues of tempo, rhythm, and mood. It helps, however, if the entire artistic team at least understands these features and knows how they influence a performance. In this way, everyone will be capable of comprehending what the dramatic effects should be and how they should come about. Of course, there is always the possibility of confusing internal tempo, rhythm, and mood with their external realization in performance, which is Michael Chekhov's distinction between *atmosphere* and *individual feelings*. It is important to remember that analysis is just part of what needs to be done to understand moods. It is a way of helping to define mood goals and making the most of creative ideas.

QUESTIONS

Tempo   Studying the beats and units, how often is information presented about plot? About character? About idea? Is the play crowded with such information? What kind of information appears most often? Or is there comparatively little information? Where in the play is most of this information presented? Which characters express these elements most?

Rhythm   How do the emotional tensions collect and develop in each scene? Each act? The entire play? Can the rhythmical pattern of tensions be described? Graphically represented? How much, if at all, do the leading characters change or develop from one scene to the next? From the beginning of the play to the end?

Mood   Are there any feelings associated with the period in which the play is set? The season? The time of day? The locale? Any feelings associated with the social groups? Are the characters distinguished by their own unique moods? Any strong feelings associated with the specific characters selected? Any feelings associated with the major or minor ideas? What has stimulated the ideas in the play to create strong moods?

CHAPTER 10

The Style of the Play

The previous chapters explained the basic elements of a play and how they work their effects. How the dramatist selects and arranges these elements to fashion a unique, imaginative creation comprises the final stage of formalist analysis. This is what is meant here by the term style. Every dramatist has a special individual style and he or she can also be influenced by existing writing practices, but it is still worthwhile to analyze the style of each play. This is particularly true if the dramatist is known to make use of different styles, as is the case with Ibsen, O'Neill, and Miller. Analyzing the technical particulars of a play and their relationship to each other reveals important stylistic impressions.

Style may come from the dominance of certain elements in a play. In *A Raisin in the Sun*, for example, it is the element of character that makes the strongest impression. The play expresses itself through the attitudes, ideas, and actions of the characters, and the dramatist has fashioned the play for them. The main idea is also important because it is an important issue in contemporary American culture. But even though idea helps to give the play significance and scope, it is not as important as are the characters themselves. The most vivid impressions are of Mama, Walter, Beneatha, and Ruth, as well as the other memorable characters in the play.

In *Mother Courage*, on the other hand, the dominant element is idea. Brecht attempts to present the life of Anna Fierling and her children as evidence of the immoral effects of a certain brand of capitalism. Anna and the other characters are entertaining, but their significance stems from their relation to the idea expressed by the play. The elements of plot and dialogue plus a whole range of other theatrical and journalistic devices serve to keep attention focused on the socio-intellectual issues at stake.

Style may also be recognized by the degree to which a play adheres to or departs from everyday reality. At one end of this scale are plays that attempt to reflect reality as closely as possible. *The Wild Duck*, *Three Sisters*, *A Raisin in the Sun*, *Streamers*, and *The Piano Lesson* are in this group as is any other play that presents a plausible picture of everyday life. At the other end of the scale are plays that don't involve real-life situations, such as *Happy Days* and August Strindberg's *The Ghost Sonata*. Between these poles are plays that sometimes reflect everyday reality and sometimes don't. *Hamlet*, *Tartuffe*, *The School for Scandal*, *Death of a Salesman*, *A Lie of the Mind*, and *Angels in America* belong to this group. In the choice and arrangement of given circumstances, background story, plot, and character, stylistic principles are at work. As the level of reality changes, so also the technical features will change.

This chapter will return to the basic building blocks of plays and reconsider them individually. This time, however, attention will not be on what they are as such, but on how they are fashioned and how they relate to each other and to the entire play. The division of analysis into factual and stylistic phases involves some repetition, but it is a good way to learn. In addition to learning about the play's style, this method evaluates how suitable are the stylistic features to the play's meaning. It's important to determine whether style is achieved merely through technical means, or through the meaning, or through both working in harmony.

GIVEN CIRCUMSTANCES

Time

Any features that differ from conventional expectations have the potential of becoming stylistic signs. The treatment of time is no exception. For example, dramatic time in *Death of a Salesman* is unconventional because it exists in several dimensions at once. In addition to the customary forward progress of time in the main plot, there are also flashbacks. In Willy's imagined or recollected reveries, time seems to go backward. Furthermore, there are no realistic transition scenes to clarify the switching between present and past. The time changes occur almost imperceptibly, creating the impression of seamless continuity.

Time is treated in a like manner in *Angels in America*. The dramatic time covered by the play is about six months between 1986 and 1987. Within that framework time moves forward realistically, but there are also split scenes that take place in two places at the same time, flashbacks, and hallucinatory scenes that occur in imaginary time. Since little direct information about time is provided in the script, time seems to jump at odd intervals from scene to scene. Readers and audiences are expected to fill in the gaps themselves. Comparably irregular treatment of time is found in *A Lie of the Mind*.

The dramatists wrote in this manner so they wouldn't have to devote valuable stage time (i.e., dialogue) to formal connecting scenes and scenes that allowed enough time for events to happen realistically. The authors chose instead to write scenes that revealed the central events of the play without delay. They wanted to emphasize that essential point and restrict themselves to it. Shepard and Kushner take this goal even further than Miller did by eliminating almost any references to the time of day in their plays. Taken away are most conventional entrances and exits, the lighting or dimming of lamps, the putting on or taking off of coats and hats, the "Good mornings" and "Good nights," and all the other bits and pieces needed to denote time realistically. As a result, we are dropped immediately into the stream of the action in the manner of contemporary films. This is a departure from the detailed realistic treatment of time in, for instance, *The Wild Duck*, but it is not new. It is a return to the unrestrained way in which time is handled in historical plays such as *Hamlet*. What is new is the application of Shakespeare's emancipated treatment of time to contemporary drama.

Dramatic time in Beckett's *Happy Days* stands still throughout the entire play. The harsh bright stage light never changes, as there is no passage of time. A loud bell off stage is the signal for Winnie to wake and sleep. Winnie often speaks about time, but when she does, it emphasizes the fact that time in the traditional sense no longer exists.

In these several plays, the treatment of dramatic time is meant to be distinctive stylistically because it departs from conventional, meaning realistic, expectations.

Place

To answer the question "Can place be stylistically important in the play?" it is helpful to learn if one of the chief interests in the play is its general or its specific locale. The attic in *The Wild Duck* is a useful example. Ibsen describes it in detail. The room contains "odd nooks and corners, stovepipes running through it from the rooms below, . . . [and] a skylight through which clear moonbeams shine in." Inside are doves flying, hens cackling, rabbits and other small animals, assorted small trees, and the wild duck. Access is through a sliding door in the back wall of the studio and through a specially constructed curtain—"the lower part consisting of a piece of old sailcloth, the upper part of a stretched fishing net." Throughout the play, the dialogue, action, visual interest, and sound effects are associated with this specific locale. Old Ekdal treats the attic as if it were a shrine, Hjalmar uses it as a hideaway, and Hedvig kills herself there. In *The Wild Duck*, the attic assumes almost symbolic importance, and its design and use should be a stylistic feature in production.

Beyond special locales, style can also be found in the use of multiple locales or complex changes of locale. The Loman house in *Death of a Salesman* should evoke a realistic sense of place, but it should also provide enough scenic flexibility to permit the fluid expression of time in the play. This calls for the complex and distinctive scenery and costuming that has become one of the hallmarks of the play in production. How, for example, do the characters manage to change their costumes when they appear in adjacent scenes but in different time frames? How are the lighting changes handled? These will be important stylistic features in any production.

The multiple locales in *The Hairy Ape* are as unusual as they are diverse. They consist of the fireman's forecastle, promenade deck, and stokehole of an ocean liner, a corner on Fifth Avenue in New York City, a prison on Blackwell's Island, a union hall, and the monkey house at a zoo. The succession of curious locales, each quite different from the other, contributes to the feeling of disorientation in the play and highlights Yank's dilemma. The multiple locales in *Mother Courage* also contribute to the style of that play. The action travels all over central Europe, yet the constant presence of the canteen wagon adds a note of timelessness to the scenic transitions. Multiple locales are also characteristic of *Hamlet* and *Angels in America*. *Hamlet* ranges throughout the castle of

Elsinore and its surrounding grounds. The locales in *Angels in America* include various places in and around New York City, the Kremlin, heaven and hell, and Antarctica. The emotional impact of multiple locales—individually, sequentially, and collectively—add stylistic expressiveness to a play.

Society

Interesting observations about a play's style and a playwright's creative thinking can be uncovered by studying the social features of the given circumstances. In his influential book *Mimesis*, for example, Erich Auerbach has discussed the meaning of Shakespeare's fixation with the aristocratic classes of society. Auerbach points out that when members of the middle or lower classes appear in Shakespeare's plays, they almost always speak and behave in comic, or at least unserious, ways. Shakespeare's aristocratic characters may lapse into unserious ways of expression or behavior, but the reverse rarely happens. Auerbach contends that this is evidence of the aristocratic values implicit in Shakespeare's plays. The plays of Sophocles and Molière show similar stylistic tendencies. On the other hand, the plays of Sheridan, Miller, Brecht, Hansberry, Wilson, Shepard, and Kushner suggest a deep-seated mistrust of accepted social values; the middle- and lower-class characters that comprise the dominant social groups in plays by these playwrights speak and behave in serious, meaningful ways. It is the wealthy, upper-class, or bourgeois characters that talk and act in comic, satiric, or unserious ways. This stylistic feature can be interpreted as an implicit critique of wealthy, or at least of conformist bourgeois, society.

In contrast to the drama of earlier centuries, modern drama is characterized by its concern with middle- and lower-class working society, but there are still variations in the social groups, even in modern plays. Eugene O'Neill's plays are among the most produced American plays worldwide. We can arrive at some useful observations about the universal appeal of his style by examining the social groupings in *The Hairy Ape*. The main social group consists of working-class seamen, but within this category are found stokers, engineers, and mates, and Irishmen, Germans, Cockneys, Frenchmen, Scandinavians, Chinese, Dutch, and Italians. Also present are Marxists, capitalists, policemen, criminals, prison guards, trade unionists, and anarchists. There is variety even among the wealthy classes represented, including industrialists, robber barons, high society, religious leaders, and politicians. Apes and monkeys have their day too. The number and variety of social groups lead to the feeling of seeing the whole world spread out and contribute to a sense of universality to Yank's plight.

The choice of fashionable social groups or fashionable values may also lead to some helpful stylistic insights that may have been overlooked or at least underexpressed in earlier interpretations. *The School for Scandal* is a satire about a small circle of characters that entertain themselves by passing comic judgment on the reputations of others. One of these characters is Joseph Surface, whom Sheridan has singled out for special comic disapproval. Joseph admits to being a "sentimentalist." The sentimentalists were a fashionable social group current in eighteenth-century London. They were distinguished by their obvious aristocratic class-consciousness, their flamboyant moral self-righteousness, and their habit of sprinkling conversations with clever aphorisms drawn from popular sentimentalist literature. Joseph displays all these traits. In opposition to Joseph and his sentimentalists, Sheridan places Charles Surface and his egalitarian circle of friends, who disdain class distinctions and sentimental cant and champion democratic ideals. Sheridan's style in this play is marked by the contrast between these two social groups.

Three Sisters deals with Russian educated society, the so-called *intelligentsia*. In *A Lie of the Mind* are found the blue-collar classes of society, a few of them first-generation college educated. While the leading characters in *Angels in America* are of course gay, the social groups also include lawyers, doctors, religious figures (including angels), and politicians and their families and associates—in other words, members of America's ruling classes. *The Piano Lesson* is similar to *A Raisin in the Sun* in that both plays deal with African Americans from the lower economic and educational levels of society. Why do these plays deal with these social groups and no others?

Other Stylistic Considerations

A close study of other given circumstances can uncover further theatrical values that contribute to a play's style. Under the category of intellect (science and technology), for example, there are details about a late nineteenth-century photography studio described in *The Wild Duck*. Hjalmar's studio contains "photographic instruments and apparatus of different kinds, boxes and bottles of chemicals, instruments, tools, photographs and small articles, such as camel's-hair pencils, paper, and so forth." Act 3 opens with Hjalmar colorizing and retouching photographs. At the beginning of Act 4, Gina has finished a photographic sitting. She's shown "with a little box and a wet glass plate in her hand," and later she "slips the plate into the box and puts it into the covered camera." Hjalmar's photography business is a plot motif that runs throughout the play.

A little supplementary study reveals that Ibsen has described the practice of wet-plate photography that was used during the period. Historians of photography also suggest that, in its infant stages at least, photography was considered as a shortcut for artists so that they could avoid the necessity of having to learn basic drawing and painting. With a little imagination, readers should be able to recognize the potential stylistic appeal of these technological and historical details. Photography was still novel in 1884, and Hjalmar's studio may have been one of the first in his city. He would be proud of that. The fact that photography was considered by some to be a shortcut to art calls to mind Hjalmar's desire to be treated as an artist without having to do the actual hard work of making art. He maintained this illusion about himself by leaving to Gina the messy work of taking pictures and developing them while reserving for himself the artistic work of touching up and adding color to the final results. The scientific dimension of photography also provided him with public proof of his desire to be thought of as an inventor, another illusion of his. The fact that in this play about sexual infidelity Hjalmar specializes in wedding pictures is a little example of Ibsen's wry sense of humor. That's how the given circumstances connected with photography reveal some interesting features of Hjalmar's personality.

BACKGROUND STORY

Dramatists treat background story with special care because they know that it will provide at least as much dramatic potential as the on-stage action. They break lengthy narration into parts and interrupt it with other speeches, permit other characters to underscore the speaker's feelings by intruding with their own comments, and arrange all the pieces in a climactic pattern. Because background story is often more complicated than the on-stage plot, its treatment can be an important feature of a play's style.

Content

Apart from having occurred in the past, what type of information is expressed in the background story? Ordinarily, it consists of events. Early in *Streamers*, for instance, Roger informs Billy about Sergeant Rooney's military specialty when he was fighting in Vietnam, "You know what's the ole boy's MOS? His Military Occupation Specialty? Demolitions, baby. Expert is his name." He also reveals Rooney's experience in World War II, "Ole Sarge was over in Europe in the big one, Billy. Did all kinds a bad things."

Background story, however, can also contain other information besides events. Again in *Streamers*, Billy asks what Rooney's feelings were when he learned he had been reassigned to Vietnam, "Was he drinkin' since he got the word?" Roger uses a sensory response about the past to imply that Rooney was frightened, "Was he breathin', Billy, was he breathin'?" As their conversation continues, they discuss events, feelings, and sensory responses from their own pasts.

In Roger's portrayal of the NCO, there are also examples of background story containing character descriptions. Past events in themselves play a minor role in *Streamers*; past feelings, character descriptions, and sensory responses, however, are important features of style in the background story.

Quality

How the background story is disclosed is another stylistic feature. As already discussed, playwrights use various methods also used by other kinds of writers. In period plays, the practice was to tell the background story in sustained direct narration somewhere near the beginning of the play. The use of direct narrative persisted through the eighteenth century and in some cases still continues. David Rabe's *Streamers* is admired for its realism, but in the handling of background story, Rabe relies on the tested method of prolonged direct narration. Billy's speech at the end of Act 1 is a good demonstration. Its function is character description enhanced with other types of events and feelings. Even though Billy's story is 457 words long, Rabe has ensured that the uninterrupted presentation remains realistically plausible. The situation establishes that the characters are in their bunks about to go to sleep for the night. It is dark and quiet. The striking events of the previous scene have stirred the characters' feelings. Billy reflects on the experiences of a boyhood friend or maybe of Billy himself. His sentences are short, and the grammar and syntax are irregular. In this context, the length and placement of Billy's background story does not sound artificially laid on or improbable.

August Wilson and Sam Shepard are two other dramatists who use historical technique to disclose background story. In *The Piano Lesson*, the characters of Doaker, Boy Willie, and Wining Boy reveal the past in speeches composed almost as sermons or arias. Sally tells her mother, Lorraine, about Jake's murder of their father in several speeches of direct narrative without any obvious attempt at literary disguise.

Modern background story technique, influenced by realism, develops retrospectively in fragments. The chapter devoted to background story discussed the enterprising ways in which Ibsen and others treated background story. It also discussed the contemporary practice of withholding, concealing, or even ignoring background information to achieve dramatic interest.

Samuel Beckett has done this so well that it has become one of the chief stylistic features of his plays. A great deal of the background story in *Happy Days*, for instance, is either hidden within elliptical suggestions and accidental remarks or else it has been eliminated altogether. Beckett's treatment of background story has entertainment value. It's part of the play's overall style. It evokes ambiguity, ominous forebodings, and, most importantly, the quality of mythic universality. Sam Shepard in *A Lie of the Mind* uses a similar technique with similar results.

It's curious, too, that *Three Sisters* and *Angels in America* do not seem to depend on background story the same way as some other modern plays do. There are no hidden crimes or clandestine love affairs, for example, which might generate tensions for on-stage action. What dramatic reasons could there be for this stylistic feature?

Premises for Disclosure

One difficulty in writing realistically is the time and effort needed to establish realistic believability. Apart from the visual considerations, characters must be occupied doing plausible actions and speaking in believable ways. They must observe all the details of ordinary life that have little purpose on stage other than to make what is going on seem real. This is particularly true for background story. It takes a great deal of time and extraordinary skill to incorporate technical devices into a plot to justify the disclosure of the past by the characters. This means that, besides the nature and quality of background story, there is also the possibility of style in the premises used for its disclosure. Tennant's study, *Ibsen's Dramatic Technique*, provides useful insights into the development of Ibsen's background story technique. He explains how Ibsen sustains realistic believability when disclosing the background story by using the conventions of confidants, the meetings of old friends, inquiring strangers, *raissoneurs*, and written correspondence. Ibsen's methods worked so well that they have become the model for later realistic dramatists.

In *Death of a Salesman*, Arthur Miller shows how he is a beneficiary of Ibsen's craftsmanship. Miller uses the conventional devices of returning characters and confidants to justify the disclosure of the past realistically. In the opening scene of the play, Willy's surprise return from a sales trip provides a plausible reason for him to explain why he came back. Willy also talks about Biff's recent return home after a long absence. In the next scene, Biff's return furnishes the chance for him to talk about his childhood with Happy and also about what has happened during the intervening years. Later in the act, a confidant appears in the form of Charley, the Loman's' next door neighbor. Charley's questions permit Willy to unburden himself about Biff's return and other related information. Ben's appearance in a flashback supplies the justification for him and Willy to discuss their pasts. The use of returning characters and confidants to justify disclosure of the background story realistically is a feature of this play's style.

In *Three Sisters*, the arrival of Colonel Vershinin offers an opportunity to talk about the past. The arrival of Lorraine, Baylor, and Meg provides a premise for talking about the past in *A Lie of the Mind*. Later in the play, Sally functions as a confidante when she discloses Jake's murder of their father. August Wilson uses the visits of Boy Willie and Wining Boy as opportunities to talk about the past in *The Piano Lesson*. Much of the background story in *Angels in America* is revealed through Belize, a confidant, and Hannah Pitt, an arriving visitor. The visits of the Angel and Prior's ancestors also serve the same purpose.

Historical authors and some modern authors as well do not bother so much about surface realism. They dispense background story as swiftly as possible, often in long passages. This does not mean the background story is handled clumsily, just that it is disclosed speedily in order to devote more attention to plot, character, and idea. The conventional, nonrealistic devices for narrating the background story in nonrealistic plays are asides, prologues, choruses, messengers, soliloquies, and dumb shows (plays-within-plays). Many of these devices are used in *Mother Courage*.

PLOT

Type

That there is a need for understanding the genre, or collective emotional spirit, of a play is clear. This book, however, is not concerned with the theoretical definitions of tragedy, comedy, melodrama, and farce (see Appendix B for more information about these topics). The purpose behind studying the spirit of a play's actions is not to comply with theoretical categories; rather it is to understand the emotional feel of a play as the basis for an approach to acting, directing, or designing. For the time being, it is enough to recognize that in comedies unhappy situations are prevented from becoming too unhappy so that they will not break the comic mood, and in tragedies, serious situations develop to the fullest possible extent. The difference is more of degree than it is of kind. In the technical treatment of plot, character, idea, dialogue, and other features, dramatic genres are essentially alike.

The type of actions depicted in a play reveal a great deal about its emotional spirit, which is a significant part of its style. In the past, the actions depicted in plays were consistent with classical conventions. Comedies like *The School for Scandal* contained cheerful incidents and happy endings. Tragedies like *Oedipus Rex* contained serious incidents and unhappy endings. Enforced uniformity, however, was never completely accepted. In even the earliest plays, comic or at least unserious moments were found within the most serious of plays and vice versa. One of the characteristics of Shakespeare's style and his point of departure from other writers was his mixture of comic and serious actions. For example, although most of the incidents in *Hamlet* are serious, unserious or ironic moments continually intrude. This is true in speeches, in individual characters, in scenes, and throughout the entire play. Molière's plays show similar tendencies. *Tartuffe* is cheerful in spirit although some scenes, notably those between Elmire and Tartuffe, contain serious moments. To maintain dramatic focus, some plays try to sustain a consistent overall mood even though they may depict contrasting types of actions. *Death of a Salesman*, *Three Sisters*, and *A Lie of the Mind*, for example, contain unserious and ironic moments, but their dominant mood is serious.

There are modern plays that combine serious and unserious actions to a much greater extent. In the final scene of *The Wild Duck*, Hedvig's suicide shares the stage with the drunkenness of Ekdal and Reverend Molvik and the bombast of Hjalmar's self-admiration and self-pity. The combination of contrasting actions is as incongruous as it is unique.

At the end of *The Hairy Ape*, Yank encounters an ape at the zoo. In another context, the combination of characters would not be serious, but O'Neill has chosen to draw a parallel between Yank's alienation from society and the ape's isolation from his natural environment. The result is a distinctively serious conclusion. The ending of *Streamers* also depicts contrasting types of actions. After a violent scene in which two characters are graphically murdered, Sergeant Cokes indifferently sits down on a footlocker and sings a ballad to the tune of "Beautiful Dreamer." *Angels in America* combines unserious and serious scenes too, but the overall mood remains unserious, or at least positive, not darkly serious. After all, how else should we take its extravagant departures from realism? Mixing otherwise incongruous actions is discomforting, but makes an important stylistic statement. Few plays today maintain the kind of consistent emotional tone once found in historical plays. Instead, like *The Hairy Ape*, *Angels in America*, and *Streamers*, they tend to employ unusual combinations of actions, and the uncomfortable feelings that arise from them as part of their style.

Organization

Most plays are organized by cause and effect. They lead through a series of consecutive, apparently inevitable events without anything missing or out of place, from an initial situation to its logical conclusion. The chain of events and consequences is the essence of causally organized dramas such as *Tartuffe*, *The School for Scandal*, *The Wild Duck*, *Death of a Salesman*, *A Raisin in the Sun*, *The Piano Lesson*, and *Three Sisters*. Starting with the opening lines, questions, forebodings, and possibilities are raised that carry our interest from unit to unit and act to act to a logical conclusion.

Cause and effect is among the most common organizing principles of plays, but to be effective, this principle needs to be seen at work in the performance as well as at the table. Think of *The School for Scandal*. Although plot summaries tend to overlook the influence of Lady Sneerwell in the play, the origin of the entire tangled story is her wish to undermine the love between Charles Surface and Maria. Unless Lady Sneerwell's super-objective has a probable and satisfactory cause, however, she is not a credible character, and the play becomes little more than a collection of high jinks. Several things could account for her super-objective: malice, hatred, spite, envy, revenge, and even entertainment. The task is to determine which cause motivates her, and then to illustrate it in performance through her super-objective.

The answer is in the opening scene. Lady Sneerwell was the victim of scandal once herself, stemming from a love affair she had with none other than Charles Surface. What made the scandal cruel was the class distinction between her and Charles and rumors of an illegitimate child. To recover from her misfortune and win back or at least injure Charles, she says she would "sacrifice everything." This important information is disclosed in a short casual conversation with Mr. Snake, but it is the root cause of her super-objective. It is logical and it certainly is strong enough to explain the extreme nature of its consequences. For the cause-and-effect sequence to work right, Lady Sneerwell must disclose her motive in a way that clearly emphasizes its relationship to her super-objective. This sets off the chain of events and consequences that ultimately leads to the comic conclusion.

Cause-and-effect principles are taught in logic classes. Nonetheless, actors, directors, and designers need to be aware of them too and should recognize how they should work in a play. The questions to ask are: (1) Which cause, out of all the possible and probable causes, is the one that activates the effect? (2) Can that cause plausibly produce that particular effect? (3) How are cause and effect disclosed? As the example from *The School for Scandal* shows, readers should be careful dealing with cause and effect in plays having complicated plots.

Not all plays are organized by cause and effect. Although this has been the dominant manner, many plays use other methods. *Oedipus Rex* is interrupted by improbable choral interludes. The stream of action in *Hamlet* often comes to a complete standstill while the leading character reveals his most intimate thoughts. Signs, songs, and other journalistic and cabaret devices punctuate the scenic development in Mother Courage. *The Hairy Ape* and *Happy Days* do not depict causally related chains of events; they move ahead not by dramatized actions but rather by varieties of set speeches. Harper and Prior's hallucinations seem to defy ordinary cause and effect in *Angels in America*, as do many of Jake's actions in *A Lie of the Mind*.

Some plays work by abstract logic, not causation. Take *Happy Days*. The play is presented in two sections. In the first, Winnie is sunk in the ground up to her waist. In the second, she's in it up to her neck. The second section develops causally from the first, but only by accident. The real organizing principle is abstract, not dramatic in the ordinary sense. Winnie exists as the ironic symbol of humanity entrapped in a universe that has no answers, only dilemmas. She's a pathetic victim, and the earth in which she's embedded is a symbol of the fickle, malfunctioning universe.

This play is not organized by cause and effect. It's a demonstration of the relationship between human nature and the universe, which attempts to show Winnie as humanity in a comic-pathetic light. Of course the play does more than this, but it is organized as a demonstration, not a conventional cause-and-effect chain of events. Its parts exist for the sake of demonstrating an abstract idea that in turn must be reasoned out from the situation being demonstrated. *The Hairy Ape* and *Mother Courage* are organized along similarly unconventional lines. Some readers find this kind of arrangement unsettling, and they should; but there have been an increasing number of examples recently, so it would be worthwhile to understand how a demonstration works to achieve its effects.

Simple and Complex Plots

Whether the plot is technically simple or complex is another important stylistic consideration. Chapter 4 explained that a complex plot contains a reversal in the fortunes of the leading character and a change in that character's self-knowledge. Think for a moment of *Tartuffe* and note that the plot is technically complex. At the moment when Orgon understands how misplaced his devotion to Tartuffe has been, he simultaneously suffers the loss of his personal fortune and reputation, not to mention the respect of his family. The plot of *Death of a Salesman* also presents interesting considerations. The playwright has stated that Willy Loman comes to a profound understanding of his situation. This means the plot is technically complex and Willy is elevated to the stature of a tragic hero. Critic Francis Fergusson contends in *The Idea of a Theatre*, however, that the plot is technically simple. It is not clear to Fergusson that Willy passes from ignorance to self-knowledge. The answer to the question lies in the scenes where Willy is planting in his garden. Does Willy attach any special significance to his actions in these scenes? Does he associate the garden symbolically with his role as a father? Is the garden emblematic of the future or of posterity? If the answer to these questions is yes, the play might be a tragedy; if it is no, then it probably is not tragic. As this example shows, the issue of complex or simple plots is more than theoretical. It has practical implications because it involves specific actions in the play and how actors and directors interpret and portray them. Stylistically, the play may depend for its effects on the emotional dynamics inherent in simple or complex plotting.

In a simple plot, there is no significant reversal either in the nature of the situation or in the self-knowledge of the leading character. *The Wild Duck* is an example of a play with a simple plot. Hedvig's death is a major change of fortune for Hjalmar and Gregers. Ibsen points out the error of this impression, however. When Gregers insists that Hedvig's suicide has changed Hjalmar's character, Dr. Relling corrects his sentimental interpretation, "Before a year is over, little Hedvig will be nothing to him but a pretty theme for declamation," nor does Gregers give any indication that Hedvig's death has had any serious effect on his arrogant idealism. Censured by Relling for interfering in other people's lives, Gregers replies: "I am glad that my destiny is what it is. . . . To be thirteenth at table." The stylistic feature that lies behind the use of a simple plot in this play is Ibsen's own skepticism and his avoidance of traditional climactic endings. By declining to provide a conventional resolution for the situation, the action of the play underscores a belief that people don't change, unfortunately, no matter how much others may want them to.

Other plays that use simple plots are *Mother Courage* and *Happy Days*. Chekhov, too, employed a simple plot in *Three Sisters*. For despite all their intelligence and self-analysis, in the end the three sisters and their brother understand no more about themselves than before. Things may grow from bad to worse in simple plots, but no one is any the wiser for it. That's what is so compelling about them, and so frustrating. To express the meanings of these plays, it is important to portray the simple or complex nature of their plots as clearly as possible. It could be a stylistic disaster to interpret simple plots as complex or vice versa.

Scenic Linking

Chapter 8 treated linking as one of the basic features of dialogue. As parts of a whole, scenic actions are also linked. Actions are linked in practical terms by the repetition of selected features from one scene to the next throughout the play. Their connections prepare for the sequence of events and help to form a coherent world within the play. The ways in which plot, character, dialogue, and idea achieve linking determine the stylistic feature to be emphasized. In period plays, direct statements placed at the ends and beginnings of scenes link them together. The last topic in one scene forms the first topic in the next. Key issues are also repeated inside each scene. Scenic linking operates this way in *Oedipus Rex*. Moreover, important facts like the murder of Laius, Oedipus' past, and the prophecies of the oracles are also repeated inside scenes as further linking devices.

Understandably, the practice of linking actions is subtler in realistic plays. Tennant has shown that the linking in *The Wild Duck* consists of repeated hints about certain fatal objects, words, and actions. Close reading reveals frequent accenting of selected plot incidents—Hjalmar's youth, Ekdal and Werle's pasts, Gina's past, Hjalmar's marriage, Hedvig's birthday, Werle and Hedvig's weak eyesight, the wild duck, and the fatal pistol. The links converge in the final misfortune of Hedvig's suicide.

Ibsen's style of linking employs allusions, direct and indirect statements, and inadvertent remarks.

Linking in drama is more than literary foreshadowing to arrange things so that later events are prepared for audiences beforehand. By intentional repetition, linking underscores the main idea and provides artistic coherence and completeness to the play.

Scenic Openings and Closings

In older plays, a scene was identified by the introduction and development of a single complete topic. A new scene opened either with the entrance of a new character or with the reappearance of an earlier character conveying fresh information. It closed after the information was developed and concluded. A quick review of *Hamlet*, *Tartuffe*, or *The School for Scandal* will show this pattern. The scenic openings and closings are influenced by plot considerations, but they are plausible in performance because other features distract attention from whatever realistic improbabilities they might possess. Similarly utilitarian openings and closings are also used in modern plays. The openings and closings in *A Lie of the Mind* and *Angels in America* are governed by the mechanics of the plot. Yet the emotional impact of the performance permits any improbabilities in the openings and closings to go unnoticed. The same holds true for the openings and closings in almost every drama on television and in films. Theatre directors and actors can learn useful lessons from observing how scenic openings and closings are handled in these other mediums.

The appearance of the modern realistic style of playwriting altered this practice markedly. In modern realism, characters are often introduced not to present new information but rather to interrupt conversations before they are developed. This practice creates suspense by delaying the full disclosure of information until later. This can be seen at work in *Streamers*. In Act 1 Carlyle's arrival interrupts the conversation just when Richie is trying to find a way to conceal Martin's attempted suicide from the military authorities. Then Billy comes in and interrupts Carlyle just as he is about to release his aggression on Martin and Richie. Not until much later in the act does Carlyle reappear and furnish complete information about himself. In *Death of a Salesman*, the action is interrupted by the flashbacks and the appearances of Uncle Ben. The flashbacks in turn are interrupted by a return to the main action. In this way, the real reason why Biff didn't graduate from high school is not disclosed until late in Act 2, just before the final build toward the climax. *The Piano Lesson*, *Three Sisters*, and *A Raisin in the Sun* operate in a similar manner. These openings and closings are written according to realistic conventions. Characters do not turn up or depart on demand as they do in older plays. The realistic style of interruption requires that the utmost tension and suspense should be expressed in these openings and closings.

CHARACTER

Objectives

Theatrical appeal is often produced by what characters want and by the nature of the forces that oppose them. Oedipus strives for information in direct opposition to the will of the gods. Although he loses on the physical level, he nonetheless achieves tragic stature by a heroic exertion of his will. By contrast, both Willy Loman and Walter Younger seek to maintain their goals in a world controlled by other values. Willy becomes a victim (perhaps), but Walter overcomes and leads his family to a new beginning. Jake wakes up to the social values that control him in *A Lie of the Mind*, and then rejects them. Berniece in *The Piano Lesson* is in the unique position of being an outsider in two cultures. She can't do much about the dominant culture, but she does learn a lesson about her own culture. Anna Fierling and Yank also try to survive in a hostile world, but in their cases, they are merely pawns in a larger struggle beyond their understanding or control. Stylistic appeal in all these plays results from the nature of the characters' goals, from what opposes them—fate, personal ideals, or socioeconomic forces—and from their final victory or defeat.

Values

In the past, established standards of right and wrong were more widely accepted, or at least tolerated. There was little obvious effort on the part of dramatists to use their plays to challenge the dominant values of their times. On the contrary, dramatists endorsed the established conventions of good and bad. They had to or else they risked losing their aristocratic financial backing. Hamlet and Orgon exist within societies where established standards of virtue and vice were generally acknowledged as true. Their personal challenges consisted of striving to understand and conform to normal values.

Modern dramatists, on the other hand, tend to challenge accepted ideas of right and wrong. This is not the place to consider the historical circumstances that led to such a shift in the general view of the world. Whatever the reasons, the results are there for everyone to see. The aim of many modern dramatists is to replace old values with new values based on the conditions of life here and now. Plays such as *The Wild Duck*, *Death of a Salesman*, *Mother Courage*, *Streamers*, *A Lie of the Mind*, and *Angels in America* attempt to reveal the motives hidden behind accepted standards of good and bad. In doing so, accepted values are turned upside down. What was considered good becomes bad, and what was bad becomes good. The clash of old versus new values forms a major part of the stylistic appeal of these plays.

Depiction

Characters may be revealed through either narration or action. The relative balance between the two methods is part of a play's style. That two of the major restrictions of playwriting are time and proportion has already been shown. Since most plays are written to conform to a two-and-a-half-hour time limit, attention must be focused on the most important elements of a character. Moreover, the play must be devoted largely to showing the actions of a single character. Supporting characters need to be presented as economically as possible, often through narration. This fact is apparent every time the secondary characters in a play are studied.

When narration furnishes the majority of the information about major characters, however, the reasons may be other than practical. George Pierce Baker pointed out that the essential distinction between character drawing in drama and fiction is the difference between action and narration. A corollary to this is that narrated characters are by definition more literary than they are dramatic. Certain major characters in *Mother Courage*, *A Raisin in the Sun*, *Streamers*, and *The Piano Lesson* fall into this category. Whether these are dramatic necessity or lapses in technique is a matter for the reader to determine after studying the other features in the plays.

One major character that is almost completely narrated for sound reasons is Haakon Werle, Gregers' father and the alleged father of Hedvig in *The Wild Duck*. The paradoxes of his personality are disclosed through the judgments of Gregers, Hjalmar, Gina, and Mrs. Sorby, all of whom seem to have conflicting opinions of him. The only substantial actions he performs on stage are the announcement to Gregers of his engagement to Mrs. Sorby in Act 1 and his visit to the Ekdals' flat to offer Gregers a position in the firm in Act 3. Everything else known about him comes through others. Of course, Ibsen's use of narration in this case should not be attributed to faulty writing. He avoided showing too much of Werle's real character in order to create an ambiguous impression of him. Werle's character is a diversionary tactic. What he did in the past matters little to the outcome of the play. The key issue is what others think of him, particularly what Gregers and Hjalmar think of him. Ibsen's choice of a narrative style of disclosure for Werle is in harmony with the main idea of the entire play.

In older plays, it was often the stylistic practice to present major characters through a balanced combination of narration and action. Notable among them is *Tartuffe*. The title character forms the chief topic of conversation in Acts 1 and 2 of Molière's play. By the time of his first appearance in Act 3, a very considerable amount is known through other people's opinions of him. Unlike Haakon Werle, however, throughout the remainder of the play, Tartuffe's personality is revealed through his own words and actions. The audience has ample opportunity to test the impressions of the other characters by witnessing Tartuffe play at piety, seduce Elmire, and swindle Orgon out of his assets.

Narration defines Werle, and a balance of narration and action defines Tartuffe, but action is the chief method of presenting most major characters. It is by their actions that it is possible to understand major characters in dramatic literature such as Oedipus, Hamlet, Orgon in *Tartuffe*, Gregers Werle and Hjalmar Ekdal in *The Wild Duck*, Willy Loman in *Death of a Salesman*, Winnie in *Happy Days*, Walter in *A Raisin in the Sun*, the Prozorov siblings in *Three Sisters*, Prior in *Angels in America*, and Jake in *A Lie of the Mind*. The way that narration or action is used for presenting character is an important element of a play's style. Of course, regardless of the final balance in the script, the performer's responsibility remains unchanged. Both narrated and illustrated characters must always be acted to the fullest extent possible. The difference is that for narrated characters the actors need to discover illustrative actions on their own without the direct aid of the playwright.

IDEA

The dramatist settles on the meaning to convey and selects and arranges everything in the play to express it with maximum effectiveness. It follows that the ideas that playwrights choose to deal with are important features of a play's style. In scrutinizing ideas in a play, the principles of logic usually help. Plays are emotional experiences, however, and the value of logical truth is always less important than is emotional truth. In art, the word *truth* has a broader meaning. It means not that the play is logically accurate but rather that we agree with it or that the feelings it evokes will lead to better human understanding.

Persuasiveness

The ideas in a play arise from the actions and characters created by the playwright. The credibility of the playwright's ideas stems from their suitability to the actions and characters and from how they stand up to scrutiny. But psychological reliability is not the sole reason an idea can be persuasive. Sometimes ideas may be compelling for conventional theatrical reasons. The extravagant ideas presented in broad comedies, for instance, work satisfactorily even though they will seldom withstand close examination. Comic ideas have momentary appeal as entertaining premises for the plot, though they must be at least consistent.

The religious hypocrisy in *Tartuffe* is believable, as is the economic pragmatism in *Death of a Salesman*. They persuade because they arise from their dramatic contexts. Likewise, the racial discrimination that forms the world of *A Raisin in the Sun* and *The Piano Lesson* is indisputable. On the other hand, certain readers may be doubtful about the economic determinism depicted in *Mother Courage*, or the scientific materialism in *Happy Days*, or the all-inclusive tolerance advocated in *Angels in America*. They may feel that the actions and characters have not justified these ideas satisfactorily. Some plays strain credibility despite the best efforts of dramatists. In any case, the persuasive power or lack of it in the main idea is an important stylistic consideration.

Scope

The extent of the idea's actual relevance to life is another part of its style. Many dramas attempt to deal with universal artistic truths. These are feelings or understandings that are valuable to society under all circumstances. Solving sharp political, social, or moral questions is not part of their style. Although social and political ideas are present in *Oedipus Rex*, Sophocles does not try to judge his characters on this basis exclusively. Most readers would also agree that even though Shakespeare deals with ideas about society and politics in *Hamlet*, he is more concerned with the characters trying to solve their own problems than with solving them himself. Some critics have attempted to label Anton Chekhov as a social dramatist, but most readers should see beyond this conclusion. These dramatists observe, select, and combine ideas for the sake of art. Their styles are based on the assumption that theatre is an entertaining and illuminating artistic experience. Interpreting their plays otherwise is a risky exercise, although there are many exceptions.

Socially responsive playwrights question whether universal ideas stand the test of time. The world has changed, they argue. The stylistic theory of *art for art's sake* may be a noble ideal, but it leaves much to be desired in the real world. Consequently, some writers feel they should make a stand in their plays on the vital social and political questions of the day. Dramatists from Ibsen to Kushner have come out on one side or another of important moral and political issues. The ideas in *The Wild Duck*, *Mother Courage*, *Streamers*, *The Piano Lesson*, and *Angels in America*, for example, attempt to contribute toward the creation of a potentially new social order. The style of these ideas suggests dislike for, or at least dissatisfaction with, outmoded values that perceived as unhealthy for society. Ideas are decisive in these plays, and audiences look forward to being challenged intellectually by such productions.

But there are questions with this stylistic approach too. George Bernard Shaw was one of the most articulate representatives among the socially responsible playwrights. Yet even Shaw (in an essay entitled "The Problem Play") expressed concern about the authority of the playwright to pronounce judgment on social or political issues, his own work notwithstanding. He pointed out that dramatists tend to lead literary lives. They dwell for the most part in the world of the imagination (like Hamlet?) instead of the world of politics, business, and law and statecraft. Shaw argued that although such authors may seek to raise social issues in their plays, some of them remain surprisingly unaware of real life as it is lived by ordinary people. Many modern playwrights present moral and political ideas with high degrees of conviction, imagination, and sharp senses of observation, but the key issue for readers here is more than one of technical skill. It is necessary to judge whether authors have the wisdom to make the ideas in their plays both desirable and practical.

DIALOGUE

Since dialogue is the most noticeable part of a play, it certainly is an important component of a play's style. The large assortment of its interesting features can appeal to audiences as strongly as does any other element in the play. Apart from its literary aspects, however, dialogue also functions as the container for the plot, character, and idea. These theatrical functions may be less obvious to an untrained observer, but they are no less important in determining style.

Literary Features

Literary style in the dialogue includes all of those features studied in Chapter 8, including verse forms, rhetorical or telegraphic or emotional speech, imagery and formal symbolism, songs, jokes, colorful and unusual words, idiomatic phrases, dialects, and anything that calls attention to the dialogue as dialogue. There are many examples of plays that employ these features. *Oedipus Rex*, *Hamlet*, and *Tartuffe* contain a lot of different verse forms as well as rhetorical speech, aphorisms, and historical charm. These literary devices indicate that, even though the chief features in these plays are character and idea, dialogue is still important in achieving the overall style.

The expectation of everyday talk in modern plays may lead some readers to find little literary appeal in realistic speech. Many modern realistic dramatists, however, also use literary features, though less noticeably than their nonrealistic counterparts. Arthur Miller's language in *Death of a Salesman*, as was mentioned earlier, contains pronounced rhythms, colorful words and phrases, and emotional speeches that contribute to its style. Dialogue is one of the main stylistic attractions of Brecht's plays—almost as much as it is in older or so-called *stylized* dramas—although with Brecht the language has a more surprising effect because of its contrast with the homespun nature of the characters. O'Neill's use of dialects, imagery, and rhythms is not as important as is character revelation and idea in *The Hairy Ape*, yet the dialogue appeals to the ear as José Quintero's radio production confirmed. Intelligence and wit are very much part of the appeal of the dialogue in *Angels in America*. Poetic language plays a large role in the success of *The Piano Lesson*. Both historical and modern playwrights have used a rich variety of literary stylistic devices to focus attention on their language.

Text and Subtext

The question of speech rhythm brings up consideration of another element of style found in dialogue. One of the chief differences between older and modern dialogue is compression. Modern plays tend to use language economically. They dispense with highly structured modes of expression and cut out everything that is not essential. This radical reduction of the number of words in modern plays has had important stylistic results. It has caused a corresponding enlargement of unspoken inner tensions. Stanislavski called these inner tensions the *subtext*, the unspoken words behind the text.

An important question for Stanislavski was how to determine the relative balance between words on the one hand and subtext on the other. Literary dialogue places more emphasis on spoken words, less on subtext. By contrast, economical modern dialogue capitalizes on subtext to express character, feelings, and ideas. Thus, some realistic dialogue may sound conversational, but in reality, it may be far different from relaxed, everyday speech. Forceful subtext revealed through vocal rhythms and word choices energizes the dialogue and makes it dramatic in a modern way. In the plays of Beckett and Shepard, for instance, characters say what they mean using the fewest possible words, yet they seem to understand subtle hints and veiled allusions almost at first hearing. When this occurs, it is for a stylistic purpose, and it is a sure sign that subtext is a prominent element of the play's style.

MOOD

Once again, mood does not mean moodiness. Mood in drama is a particular state of sustained emotion that includes the whole range of human feelings. Production values contribute to mood, but mood values develop best in harmony with other values already present in the script. Mood is an important stylistic factor in the play when the persistent feelings generated by the plot, the characters, or the idea are potent enough to be memorable in themselves. As the chief element of dramatic interest, however, a unified persistent mood is important only in a few plays and in the works of the symbolists. Although the ideas in symbolist plays are important as well, the semiconscious dreamlike atmosphere that suffuses the action is the outstanding stylistic feature. It should be conspicuous in production, or the play will surely suffer.

There are a number of modern plays in which mood plays at least a minor role. The plays of Anton Chekhov, William Saroyan, and Tennessee Williams are valued for their sustained feelings of nostalgic charm. The moods in these plays are unique, but they seldom overpower the principal interest in character. Fantasy plays like James Barrie's *Peter Pan* or Jean Giraudoux's *The Madwoman of Chaillot* also emphasize mood. Even though mood is not their dominant appeal, their atmosphere of make-believe must be understood if they are to be successfully produced. Not least important among the list of plays in which mood is stylistically important are comedies, above all romantic comedies, and satires. In such plays, the influence of sustained moods of cheerfulness, romance, or irony are, or should be, fundamental parts of their appeal. A word should also be said about the mysterious moods in the plays Sam

Shepard and like-minded writers, which arise from the withholding of background story and use of laconic dialogue.

SUMMARY

The assumption underlying this chapter is that playwrights are self-conscious artists. They know what they want to do and have the skills to achieve their goals using the most effective means possible. Playwrights fashion plot, character, idea, and dialogue as well as tempo, rhythm, and mood to concentrate attention on the important features in their plays. In many plays, the dominant stylistic attraction might be character with supporting interests in idea, plot, or dialogue. In others, the main appeal might be idea with characters, dialogue, and plot in supporting positions. In still other plays, the plot might be the center of attention, and "What's going to happen next?" becomes more important than who the characters are, what they're saying, or even what it all means. In a few plays, the primary technical features appeal so much that the subordinate elements may have almost no intrinsic interest.

Playwrights make the stylistic values of their plays apparent in various ways. The length and number of scenes devoted to a particular feature, the qualities of thoroughness and detail, and the spirit of the main idea all contribute to stylistic focus. Studying the artistic reasons behind these choices may seem abstract and theoretical compared to the crisp kind of analysis presented in the earlier chapters, but it is necessary for the discovery of still more playable values. Each reader will form personal impressions, of course, but they can never be separated from the elements of style within the play itself.

QUESTIONS

Given Circumstances   How is time handled? Is it continuous or interrupted? Does it flow logically from beginning to end, or is there another pattern? How is continuity of time maintained? Is there anything special about the geographical locale? The specific locale? How many specific locales are presented? How is continuity of place maintained? What social groups are presented? What is the point of view expressed toward them by the play as a whole? Are any unusual or outsider groups presented? Anything special about the economic circumstances? Political and legal circumstances? Intellectual and cultural circumstances? Religious circumstances? Any special scientific or technological details in the plot? Any unusual social or professional practices?

Background Story   What does the background story consist of? Events? Character descriptions? Feelings? Sense impressions? Is the background story disclosed in large pieces? Retrospectively? Is it stated, or does it consist of subtle hints and veiled allusions? What situations in the play are used to justify disclosure of the past? Who discloses most of the background story?

Plot   What types of actions are depicted? Are the actions serious? Comic? Ironic? Why? Are different types of actions presented simultaneously? How is the introductory portion of the play managed? How is the main subject introduced at the beginning of the play? What is the play's point of view toward its subject? Serious? Comic? Ironic? Critical? How is the point of view introduced? How are the incidents arranged? Through cause and effect? Chronologically? In progressively more intensive scenes? From familiar to unfamiliar? How is the conclusion managed? Restatement? Amplification? Emotional call-to-arms? Upbeat? Does the plot contain a reversal of fortune for the leading character? Does the leading character come to a new understanding of himself or herself? How are the scenes linked? How are the scenic openings and closings managed? Is the story completed in each scene? Interrupted? How are the curtain scenes managed? How are the act endings handled?

Character   What do the characters want out of life? Power? Knowledge? Love? Wealth? Fame? Personal fulfillment? What do the characters consider to be good or evil in the world of the play? How completely are the characters depicted in the script? Are the characters revealed through action? Narration? Both?

Idea   What ideas are dealt with in the play? Why? How are they related to one another? Is the main idea persuasive? How credible is the author's authority to speak about the idea? Is the central idea artistic? Practical? Moralistic?

Dialogue   Is the dialogue literary? If so, what are its literary features? Is the dialogue conversational? If so, what are its conversational features? How important is the text as compared to the subtext? Why? What should be their relative balance in performance?

Mood   Is a single predominant mood sustained throughout the play? If so, what is it? What features in the play create mood? Any sequences of unusual, interesting, or effective moods? If so, what are they? Any contrasting moods within the same or adjacent scenes? Are the moods independent of one another? Are they mixed?

Statement of Play Script Style   What is the single most important dramatic element in the play? Plot? Character? Idea? Dialogue? Mood? Why? What are the secondary dramatic elements? Why?

A Final Word about
Dramatic Form

This is the end of a long, close look at the wide-ranging subject of play script analysis. Yet one of the difficulties with analytical principles when they are defined and explained in a textbook is that they can remain inactive on the printed page. Or worse, the intellectual frame of mind required for analytical study interposes itself between the actors, director, and designer on one hand and the concrete human behavior that is the lifeblood of drama in performance on the other. When this happens readers will remain just as mystified about how plays work as they may have been before they read the book, despite the best efforts of author and teachers. One remedy is to consider that the principles might work better as questions that encourage a search for answers. The questions at the end of each chapter offer a guide to what should be included in script analysis. They are meant to encourage as much familiarity as possible with all the dramatic potentials of a play and all of the possible relationships among them. Equally important, the questions encourage examination of the facts behind the automatic assumptions the reader faces in any encounter with a play. Questions also reinforce the practice of systematic study, which after all will ordinarily be conducted without the benefit of an expert guide.

Even though not all of the topics will be equally helpful all the time, readers should determine for themselves which ones are more valuable and which ones less so for each play. This means answering completely, or attempting to answer, all the questions. It means thinking out the subtlest implications of what the characters say and do and what the play means. By the same token, script analysis should never be allowed to become fussy or overwrought. The ultimate goal is to stir up the imagination and to provide suggestions for acting, directing, and design. As much as possible, this objective should be kept foremost in mind, and other considerations should be kept in the background.

I hope to have shown that there is a wonderful artistic self-sufficiency to a play latent with meaning. Economy, control of shape and details, the search for a structure with independent beauty are all worked into excellence by the playwright. It is not always clear what is meant by form in a play. It has something to do with a beginning, middle, and end; with harmony and sharp thematics; with the relationship of different features to the events of the plot; and with the determinations of theatre itself. Formalist Analysis heightens awareness of these features. It invites us to admire the inseparable coexistence of form and content. As professionals, we can develop a sense of form as an integral part of the total experience of play production, the summation of what is meant by the art of theatre.

Supplementary Topics for Script Analysis

Throughout this book a play is treated as an independent object with its own self-contained context. A good play becomes even better, however, when its external connections as well as its internal features are understood. After studying the life of the author, his or her other works, and the author's world, a play becomes more fascinating, the characters grow, the plot thickens, and the whole work seems to mushroom. It becomes part of something on a scale greater than itself. In other words, while Formalist Analysis and Action Analysis can reveal the internal qualities of a play, outside information is necessary for a completely professional understanding.

Topics to guide the initial steps of this process are provided below, at least insofar as I have been able to comprehend them. Some of the more radical critical approaches are omitted because they are notoriously hard to pin down. In any case, my own prejudices as a director and a critic should be clear from this book. Consequently, readers should be sure to consult other books for more authoritative information about the individual approaches discussed here.

A word of caution should be added before concluding this preamble. Theoretical statements, the biography of the author, the historical or social context, the history of the play, variations of the text, and so forth—evidence that goes beyond the play—can offer only hints about the main idea. Actors, directors, and designers should always consider external information secondary and confirm its results by close study of the play itself. External information should be tested against internal analysis in order to be employed properly in the rehearsal hall.

BIOGRAPHY AND HISTORY

A play is certain to be more meaningful when its environment and that of its author are understood. Since plays express a wide range of human experience, they can often benefit from knowledge of these considerations. How are the playwright's life and times reflected in the play? Consider personal, social, political, economic, religious, and artistic circumstances of the author and the period when the play was written. Note that point-to-point correlations between the author's life and his works seldom exist, at least not as often as some critics believe they do. Authors are both too skillful and too subtle to employ such simple methods. The search for influences will be more rewarding if this tip is kept in mind.

THE TEXT

Try to establish an authoritative version of the play. Are there any other editions or translations? If so, compare and contrast the differences, including spelling, punctuation, capitalization, and italicization as well as any kind of more substantial variances that might appear in the dialogue, characters, scenic arrangements, and endings. Examine any commentary by editors or translators for additional insights.

PHILOSOPHY AND MORALITY

Some writers believe that the major function of literature, including dramatic literature, is to teach morality and inquire into philosophical issues. How does the play relate to the philosophical and moral ideas of the period? Of a particular school or coterie? Of the author? What philosophical and moral issues does the play seem to embrace or advocate?

PSYCHOLOGY

The psychoanalytical theories of Sigmund Freud and his followers emphasize the unconscious aspects of the mind, the sexual motives of behavior (libido), and the involuntary repression of undesirable memories. Furthermore, mental processes may be assigned to three different regions, called the *id* (the source of dangerous aggressions and desires), the *ego* (the conscious controlling agent of the id), and the *superego* (conscience and pride). Other features include the reality principle, the pleasure principle, the morality principle, and the Oedipus complex, to name only the most well known. What insights can be gained from applying Freud's theories to the characters in the play?

MYTHOLOGY AND ARCHETYPES

Myths are stories of allegedly historical events. They unite social groups together through common activities and beliefs and are found everywhere in human society. Certain mysterious elements related to myths in plays can excite universal human reactions. Furthermore, certain myths tend to summon common meanings or responses or serve similar functions throughout many different societies. These common images or themes are called *archetypes*, or universal symbols.

Does the play promise to become a classic? Does it express the kind of reality that generates a universal response? What archetypal patterns does the play emphasize that might summon a deeply subliminal response in audiences? What symbolic expressions of hope, fear, moral values, and desires are expressed in the play? Does the play correlate with any prehistorical spiritual forces or rituals? What is the abstract core of action that gives the play its form or meaning?

FEMINISM

Did a man or a woman write the play? What male-female issues may have conditioned the play? What are the concealed male-female power imbalances, patriarchal premises, gender prejudices, and other signs of misogyny in the play? How are they reflected, endorsed, or questioned by the play? Are the women in the play constrained in their environment? Are the women in the play exploited in ways related to their economic circumstances? Do the women in the play experience any additional oppression as members of a minority group?

STRUCTURALISM AND POSTSTRUCTURALISM

What deep structures, or systems of relationships, are found in the play? What words or physical items in the play gain special meaning from these relationships? Can the play be equated with language forms, architecture, landscaping, kinship, marriage customs, fashion, menus, furniture, popular culture, politics or any other knowable social or cultural phenomenon? If so, what additional meanings are obtained? On the other hand, what internal contradictions or self-contradictions may be found in the play? Is there any kind of concealed power in the author that may unintentionally undermine the immediate meaning of the play?

MARXISM

Place the play within the context of larger social, political, economic, and historical forces. Does the play reflect, endorse, or question any of these great forces operating in opposition to each other? In particular, can any negative social effects of the capitalist system be found in the play? How does the play (or the characters in the play) come to terms with issues of class, race, sex, oppression, and liberation? Does the play provide a workable solution to well-known socio-economic problems?

COMMUNICATION AND RHETORIC

Consider the possible interactions between the play, the author, and the audience. How does the process of communication in the play operate among these three groups? What does the play communicate to the audience and how does it do so? What can the play reveal about the author? Whom is the playwright addressing with the play? How is the audience expected to respond? Is there a distinction between the beliefs of the author and those expressed by the characters in the play?

Introduction to Genres and Styles of Drama

The topics of genre and style have traditionally provided the basis for courses in dramatic literature and criticism. They have also been the subjects of countless books and articles. A direct outcome of all this attention is that many terms and definitions are available for inspection. In the interests of brevity, however, this appendix treats only major genres and styles and mainstream viewpoints. The purpose is to review the range of genres and styles that actors, directors, and designers must convert into theatrical form and to understand some of their major features. Genre and style are complicated but important subjects. Readers are encouraged to consult some of the specialized writing listed in the Bibliography before attempting to arrive at anything like a complete artistic understanding. Georgi Tovstonogov's essay, "Genre," in *The Profession of the Stage Director* is a lucid and practical introduction for theatre students.

GENRES

The word *genre* was adopted from the Latin words for *genus* and *gender*. Broadly speaking, it refers to a kind or type of object, usually concerning works of literature. Dramatic genres are distinguished by the nature of a play's content, that is, by the ideas, feelings, events, and characters of which the play is composed. In classical drama, the genres were tragedy, comedy, and farce, to which melodrama, or (serious) drama, was added later. From the time of the Italian Renaissance through the eighteenth century in Europe dramatic genres were meticulously defined, and authors were obliged to adhere to the rules prescribed for them. Later the notion of *purity of genre* grew less important as authors began to mix contrasting actions within their plays and create works containing multiple points of view.

Genre is a theoretical and historical concept, but the need for actors, directors, and designers to understand it is just as important as it is for critics and historians to do so. Classification by genre is an attempt to define the play's point of view toward the world. In a play, life may be viewed as tragic, comic, or farcical; it may change from one attitude to another during the course of the action; or it may even mix viewpoints to produce a feeling of absurdity or insanity. Consequently, in practical artistic terms, genre sets the tone for the production approach. It controls the general mood or spirit as well as the emotional rhythm of the play. By guiding the play in this way, genre helps to unify all of the elements of production into a harmonious totality.

Tragedy

Tragedy means literally the song of the goat, referring to a sacrificial animal (scapegoat) used in certain religious rituals of preclassical Greece. Classical Greek tragedy emerged from such a form of ritualistic sacrifice accompanied by choral songs performed in honor of Dionysus, the Greek god of fields and vineyards. Today, a tragedy may be any serious play with an unhappy or disastrous ending brought about by the leading character who is compelled by fate, moral weakness, or by psychological maladjustment or social pressures. It is impossible to arrive at a more precise definition because the term has different meanings in various theoretical schemes. Broken down to its simplest terms, however, tragedy contains a powerful force, a victim aware of his condition, and the strong will of the victim to struggle against the force and overcome it.

In tragedies, serious events are carried to their extreme psychological and physical limits. The plots are complex in the technical sense, containing a psychological realization on the part of the leading character (*anagnorisis*), together with a major reversal of fortune from good to bad (*peripeteia*). It is crucial that the reversal is accompanied by physical and emotional violence, which often, though not always, leads to death. Tragedies are dominated by a central character that possesses psychological stature either of a historically majestic kind or that of a modern ordinary person. In either case, the character possesses a will at least strong enough to confront the major opposing force on equal terms. The value system espoused by the leading character is said to contain a serious personal misjudgment or *tragic flaw (hamartia)* that forms the basis of his or her realization at the climax of the play. In a successful tragedy, the universal importance of the subject can lead to both sympathy for the tragic hero and apprehension for his or her plight—so-called *pity* and *fear*. This combination of feelings is said to create a social bond between the play and its audience that is unique to tragedy. According to Aristotle, pity and fear combine to produce a therapeutic release of tensions in the audience that is known as *catharsis.* Minor genres of tragedy include domestic, heroic, modern, neoclassical, and revenge tragedies and tragicomedy.

Melodrama

Although melodramatic plays have existed throughout history, melodrama as a distinct genre is believed to have originated toward the end of the eighteenth century in France. The main features included a thrilling plot with songs and musical accompaniment. Hence the French source for the composite term, *melo* (music) plus *drame* (drama). Its leading characters were either markedly virtuous or markedly evil, and its endings were life affirming. This was the original form, but melodrama did not remain fixed in this state for long. Dramatists soon began to combine melodramatic techniques with the those of the more subtle and dignified genre of tragedy.

Today the term *melodrama* may refer to any serious play with thrilling, often violent, actions and strong emotions. Sometimes modern melodrama can be as serious as tragedy, but still retaining the life-affirming ending of its eighteenth-century ancestor. Historical and modern melodramas continue to share a major emphasis on plot, on "What's going to happen next?" They also share the same intention of attracting wide audiences by means of exciting scenes, tense suspense, and strong conflicts. In France, the term *drame* was given by Diderot to a type of eighteenth-century play that was neither tragedy nor comedy but rather a serious play that fell somewhere in between the two. Diderot's term is now formally applied to *sentimental comedy*, a minor historical genre. Today, the Anglicized term *drama* is used by critics to refer to modern serious melodrama to distinguish it from historical melodrama.

The basic plot premise of melodrama tends to be larger-than-life, but not enough to make it too hard for the audience to accept as plausible. Individual scenes are often dramatic in themselves, and the social circumstances play an important role. Scenes are marked by sudden changes in incident and mood and linked by taut suspense with contrast provided by comic scenes or characters. In modern melodramas, there is a clear hierarchy of character depiction with the major characters much more fully written (sometimes with the most up-to-date neuroses) than are the supporting characters. Melodramatic dialogue tends to swing from exaggerated to understated emotion with sharply defined spoken rhythms to strengthen mood. Socially relevant main ideas that point to a clear moral are another major characteristic of modern melodramas. Today this genre dominates the Hollywood film industry, which has the technical resources to make the most of melodrama's exaggerated given circumstances, characters, and events.

Comedy

Comedy can be traced to classical Greek source words for *banquet* and *song*. Much like tragedy, the earliest examples of comedy were related to fertility rituals and the worship of the god Dionysus. Gradually the early folk practices became formalized, and since the fifth century BC in Athens comedy has been associated with drama. Aristotle distinguished comedy from tragedy by pointing out that it deals in an unserious way with ordinary characters in everyday situations, and although comedy has passed through many different historical stages, the basic intention has always remained the same—to portray human behavior in an amusing and playful way. Historically, any play that was not tragic was considered a comedy, and for many centuries, critics expected authors to maintain the distinction between them. Although some of the thinking behind this contrast may still be valid, it was much too narrow for practical creative purposes, and it eventually yielded to a broader understanding. Currently, almost any play that deals with ordinary life in an amusing way and ends happily is called a comedy. Contemporary writers have discovered that in some situations comedy may be as serious as tragedy, and the ideas found in some contemporary comedies can be as profound as those in tragedies.

Unlike tragedy, the comic point of view is intellectual rather than emotional. Comedy is a way of looking at life coolly with the mind, and its success depends on keeping things at a distance so as not to stir up deep feelings that might obscure the entertainment values. Of course, some emotional involvement is always necessary in live theatre, but in general, real comedy appears when deep feelings are held in check. Comic plots may arise from a variety of ordinary situations. Sometimes the release of restrained behavior results in comedy. Incongruous contrasts, repetitions, inverted situations, mistaken identities, misunderstandings, and character automatism are other common plot premises.

Farce

Farce comes from the French term *to stuff*, as in cooking. Some say this is because early examples were used to fill in the intervals between the parts; others say that it refers to vernacular passages inserted into Latin liturgical texts. Farce is a broader and simpler form of comedy in which everything is aimed at creating the most outright laughter. Its *slapstick* (visual and physical humor), *horseplay* (rough, noisy fun), *gags* (practical jokes with unexpected turns), *high jinks* (noisy pranks), and *jokes* (amusing tales), regardless of how artificial, are meant only for the sake of laughter. Since its earliest sources stemmed from an improvised folk tradition, farce hasn't left much in the way of written records. The chief historical examples were written at the beginning of the classical periods of Greece and Rome, during the Middle Ages, during the seventeenth century in Italy and France, and in the eighteenth and nineteenth centuries for English and American stages in one-act form as parts of bills with longer plays.

Except when it contains aphorisms, epigrams, or wisecracks, as in Oscar Wilde's play *The Importance of Being Earnest*, farce has little literary merit as such. It depends on physical humor, surprising entrances and exits, and its chief interest is to entertain through inventive plots and characters designed to produce laughs. Even when the goal is social satire or commentary, as in Alan Ayckbourn's *Bedroom Farce* or Michael Frayn's *Noises Off*, farce is still markedly contrived. But despite its exaggerated and excessive humor, farce is nonetheless fun to believe. Its strong popular entertainment value stems from its consistent internal logic and from the fact that its conflicts are resolved amicably, often with the use of unexpected endings.

Farce also employs appealing leading characters written in large, bold strokes. Originally they were stock characters drawn from stereotypes, but nowadays farces like those of Alan Ayckbourn can display more detailed character depiction. Still, farcical characters are more impulsive than they are rational. They are gripped by a fixed idea and fail to respond to obvious clues. Reacting mechanically to everything around them, they seldom learn anything and seldom even think about what is happening to them. Through their wit and cleverness, however, they compensate for their lack of psychological plausibility. At any rate, farce is not about character but rather about characters that are caught in funny predicaments.

STYLES

Genres are distinguished by their content. In contrast, style is distinguished by the form of a play, that is, by the shape and organization of the technical components out of which the dramatist has fashioned the work. The major historical, or period, styles are classicism (including neoclassicism), Greek and Roman comedy, morality drama, and romanticism. Modern styles are classified according to self-conscious schools and movements, or according to manners and modes of artistic expression. The most widespread modern styles are realism (including naturalism), symbolism, and expressionism (including epic theatre and theatre of the absurd).

Dramatic styles originally appeared as historical expressions of dominant points of view about the world whereas today all styles are mixed and modified liberally—for example, *Romeo and Juliet* produced as modern psychological realism or *Tartuffe* done in terms of twentieth-century religious skepticism. Sometimes it seems as though style may become little more than a game of dress-up or hide-and-seek. Even though the idea of dramatic style is sometimes misunderstood, the basic issues remain important. For audiences, the play is always a single, continuous experience, but for theatre artists, style is the distinct imaginative reality in which the story of the play takes place. Style is a particular way of playwriting that creates its own distinctive artistic world.

Theatricalism and Illusionism

Dramatic styles may be broadly divided into two categories: *theatrical* (non-realistic or presentational) and *illusionistic* (realistic or representational). In theatrical styles, creating an impression of everyday life on stage is of little importance. The main purpose is to express the content with as little as possible coming between the play and the audience. Direct expression may mean the use of a chorus, verse forms, candid narration, slides and film, television, or anything else it may take to communicate effectively. A character's inner life may be expressed openly, sung, or even displayed on photographic slides or television screens. Scenic locales may be conveyed by narrative descriptions or perhaps not at all. In short, there will be no conscious attempt on the part of the playwright to create the illusion of everyday life. By far, most plays have been in this general style from classical Greek tragedies through modern musicals. In contrast, illusionistic plays aim at being non-theatrical. Plot, characters, and dialogue are selected and arranged to give the closest approximation to actual life.

Although the two approaches are opposed by intent, it is a misunderstanding to think of these functional definitions as hard-and-fast rules. As pointed out repeatedly, even in the most realistic plays plot, character, dialogue, idea, and tempo-rhythm-mood have been selected and arranged. In other words, realism is also a style, although one whose conventions require the illusion of daily life. Conversely, theatricalism does not exist in a pure state. Many scenes from classical Greek tragedies, the plays of Shakespeare, or theatre of the absurd are as honest and real as anything written by Arthur Miller or David Rabe. The use of one style does not hinder the use of the other by the same playwright or even within the same play. Identification of style is a question of determining the relative importance or unimportance of selected features within the play.

Classicism

A *classic* is an outstanding or superior achievement, which has endured in time or is the peak expression of a culture or epoch. In drama, the classical period is considered to be the fifth and fourth centuries BC in Greece and first centuries BC and AD in Rome. Examples include the plays of Aeschylus, Sophocles, and Euripides as well as those of Seneca (read though not performed). Classical tragedies are characterized by compactness and single-minded, economic concentration on artistic unity. Scenic episodes separated by choral odes comprise the main structural pattern of the plays, which also contain verse recitatives, songs, and prose narration. Although they include violent physical action of the most extreme kind, such actions occur offstage, leaving them to be depicted more dramatically through long emotional narratives. Specific production features like masks, limitations on the number of actors, and the use of a singing and dancing chorus are unusual today but do not present too much difficulty in modern productions. In modern times, the term *classical* can refer to any play that emulates Greek and Roman models by the use of restricted plots, refined language and characters, a carefully crafted structure, emotional restraint, and economy of dramatic means.

Today classicism is sometimes called *neoclassicism*; strictly speaking, however, neoclassicism means a conscious imitation of classicism. Scholars say that in Europe the period 1650–1750 was characterized by respect for classical literary tradition plus attentive study and application of its predetermined artistic principles. Neoclassical drama is associated with the plays of the seventeenth-century French playwright Jean Racine. Although there is no chorus, music, or dance as was the case in the original Greek models, in other respects his plays are comparable to their historical counterparts. Neoclassical plays, however, observe the concept of artistic unity even more closely than did the Greek plays, expanding it to include strict singleness of plot, character actions and personality traits, scenic locale, and passage of time. Such academic attention to formal rules tends to render neoclassical plays troublesome for modern audiences. As a result, although neoclassical drama is still read in the classroom, its production is virtually extinct today, at least in the United States.

Greek and Roman Comedy

Greek comedy was a form of rowdy, bawdy topical satire about contemporary public issues connected with politics, religion, education, and literary fashion. It employed music, dancing, and songs and was extravagant and fantastic. Its plots were loosely linked by emotional contrasts and surprises rather than by cause and effect, and characters were drawn from exaggerated types. Because the plays of Aristophanes are the only existing examples, this form is also called *Aristophanic comedy*.

Roman-style comedy began with the later Greek playwright Menander and continued with the Roman writers Plautus and Terence. It was not lyrical, fantastic, or satirical like its Greek predecessor. Its subjects were everyday domestic affairs, especially romances and family squabbles. Characters were stock types—braggarts, parasites, young lovers, aging parents, and so on. Roman comedy plots were more conventional and complicated than were their Greek predecessors. Character reactions were more down-to-earth, not as exaggerated or fantastic. The dialogue was meant to sound realistic, containing numerous colloquial expressions.

Aristophanic, or old comedy, is strictly theatrical, whereas Roman, or new comedy, was more illusionistic. Roman comedy is also considered *comedy of character* because it dealt with characters caught in recognizable human conflicts and *comedy of manners* because it reflected the manners and morals of the period in which it was written. It is also *domestic comedy* because the characters and plots stem from everyday family situations. Roman-style comedy has been revived in medieval farces and interludes, Renaissance *commedia dell' arte*, Elizabethan romantic comedies and comedies of humours, Molière's comedies, Restoration comedies, sentimental comedies, comedies of ideas (Shaw), and in the popular comedies of modern theatre, film, and television.

Morality Drama

Mystery (also called *miracle*) plays were medieval dramas stemming from Christian ceremonial sources. Often performed on religious holidays, each work formed part of a cycle of plays based on the Bible (beginning with the creation and continuing through the end of the world) or on the lives of holy people. Mystery plays were simple religious stories written in the uncomplicated manner of folk tales. *Morality plays*, on the other hand, were a later and more sophisticated style. They were allegorical and instructional, and their characters were personifications of abstract vices and virtues, like the characters of Good Deeds and Riches from *Everyman*. The appeal of medieval religious drama lies in its folk charm and, in the case of morality plays, its clever use of allegorical characters. Although the original mystery and morality plays were religious, later plays adapted some of their simplified techniques to suit more modern humanistic attitudes. Allegorical elements traced to medieval moral drama may be found in the plays of Eugene O'Neill *(The Hairy Ape)*, Samuel Beckett *(Waiting for Godot)*, Edward Albee *(Tiny Alice)*, and Harold Pinter *(The Caretaker)*, to name a few.

Romanticism

Romanticism is represented by the dramas of Elizabethan England (1555–1642) and the Spanish Golden Age (1575–1675) as well as by the dramas of Johann Wolfgang von Goethe and Friedrich von Schiller, the plays of Victor Hugo and Edmund Rostand, and Ibsen's early verse dramas. The important stylistic issues are plots with multiple actions, scenes, and locales plus considerable freedom in the treatment of time. Political intrigues often form the background. Romanticism's major feature, though, is its liberal mixing of comedy, farce, tragedy, and melo-drama, and of upper- and lower-class characters within the same plays, according to the authors' individual manners. The plays of Shakespeare, Goethe, and Schiller also contain large amounts of poetry, though not of the formal, classical variety. Romantic drama is idealized, that is, the characters speak the expressive fluent language of poets and strive to achieve highly idealistic goals. It often uses non-illusionistic features like soliloquies, asides, choruses, music, songs, narration, and direct address although some modern examples may still attempt to be illusionistic.

Realism

Realism has already been explained in terms of illusionism, but a few more words should be added. It is a flexible literary term whose many qualifications and equivocations can often be more trouble to understand than they are worth. What is clear, however, is that as the expression of an attitude toward life, realism attempts to be scientifically objective. It assumes that everything and everyone exist as integral parts of nature and uses illusionistic methods to convey the notion that human behavior is explained by natural (that is, material) causes, instead of supernatural or spiritual ones. Along with naturalism, its more extreme cousin, early realism was influenced by Charles Darwin's biological theories and by Auguste Comte's theories about the application of scientific principles to the study of society. To this end, realism's advocates concentrate on the depiction of social environment, for the most part on the deficiencies and shortcomings of characters. This explains realism's reliance on social given circumstances as crucial features of its plots.

It should be noted too that strict adherence to the principles of illusionism existed only in realism's earliest phase. Later realistic works contain many non-illusionistic elements such as multiple locales, tele-scoping dramatic time, allegorical characters, lengthy narratives, and direct address. The illusion of plausibility, however, disguises them from all but the closest detection.

Symbolism

The symbolist viewpoint asserts that truth can be found only in the inner life of the human spirit, not in the realistic appearances of everyday life. The unspoken assumption is that the real world is a failure and that imagination is therefore truer and better than life. As exemplified in the plays of Belgian author Maurice Maeterlinck and Russian author Leonid Andreyev, the main characteristics of symbolism are sustained self-conscious moods of dreamy meditation. A *symbol* is something that stands for something else, and in their extreme forms, symbolist dramas contain abundant examples of formal symbols and allegorical characters. In Andreyev's *King Hunger*, for example, the intellectual idea of hunger is illustrated by the allegorical figure of the King himself. But such plays also invite a large amount of informal symbolism by combining dreamy suggestiveness and calculated physical actions with external reference points supplied by the audience. In Maeterlinck's *The Blind*, for instance, the sightless characters conjure up images of spiritual deprivation, and the Priest becomes a representative of spiritual dogmatism. Legitimate symbolist plays require meticulous analysis to understand and deft interpretation to express their true ideas.

Less radical instances of symbolism occur in plays like *The Wild Duck*, *The Seagull*, *The Hairy Ape*, and *Happy Days*. In these works, the characters are realistic, but certain other features are symbolic. Symbolism is less important as a major point of style in them, but the plays would not make sense without a clear comprehension of their symbolic features and a clear-cut illustration of their meaning.

Expressionism

A response to excessive illusionism, expressionism was an artistic concept that developed during the early years of the twentieth century in Germany. It is the most frankly theatrical of all dramatic styles. Plot, character, dialogue, and tempo-rhythm-mood are employed frankly as artistic devices to achieve the greatest expressiveness possible. Little attention is devoted to creating sustained illusionistic believability, but mixing theatricalism with illusionism is a common stylistic feature. The beginning and end of *The Hairy Ape*, for example, are traditional illusionistic scenes while the scenes between them are theatricalized illustrations of the frightening social world in which Yank finds himself increasingly a stranger. Critics say that the distortion of given circumstances that accompanies expressionism is a reflection of the leading character's state of mind. In other words, Yank's world is portrayed in distorted fashion in an attempt to communicate his personal conflicts more vividly. By the use of telegraphic speech, long narratives, asides, goodbad speech, and frequent repetitions, dialogue becomes another device to accentuate the leading character's conflicts.

One of the more important variations of expressionism is *epic theatre*. Arising in the late 1920s in Germany, it was originally the idea of director Erwin Piscator, but later it was adopted and expanded by playwright Bertolt Brecht, whom critics consider its greatest proponent. The term *epic* stems from Aristotle and refers to a type of plot that presents a series of incidents simply and directly, without traditional cause-and-effect linking. The chief stylistic feature is epic theatre's frank admission of being demonstration drama for teaching purposes. The so-called *living newspapers* of America's Federal Theater Project in the 1930s employed epic theatre techniques as did Julian Beck's and Judith Malina's Living Theatre in the 1960s and 1970s.

Epic theatre is different from true expressionism in one way because it employs journalistic and music hall devices to illustrate its meaning. Its ideas are emphasized through visual projections, film, television, and placards; narrators, music, and songs; and obvious pieces of formal symbolism. Their use is understandable because the main purpose of epic theatre is to instruct as much as to entertain. According to Brecht, the main point is that epic theatre appeals less to the spectator's feelings than it does to his reason. For instance, in Brecht's *Mother Courage*, the issue at stake is economic injustice. To illustrate the theme, assorted characters perform self-contained dramatic lesson-scenes; they address the audience with narratives and songs to explain the meaning; and signs appear containing stage directions, penetrating quotations, and relevant statistics. Clearly, epic theatre has a great deal of dramatic expressiveness at its disposal.

In the 1950s, another variation of expressionism emerged, called *theatre of the absurd* or *absurdism*. Originally named by critic Martin Esslin in his book, *Theatre of the Absurd*, it describes an informal group of like-minded playwrights that included Samuel Beckett and Eugene Ionesco. Absurdism is more of an attitude than it is a coherent aesthetic system. The term refers to intellectual irrationality, not comic ridiculousness. Its point of view is that the universe is perceived as irrational (absurd) because the moral and philosophical beliefs of previous ages are outmoded and we allegedly have nothing with which to replace them. Absurdism dramatizes the philosophical anguish that results when human beings attempt to struggle with this irrational universe.

To express their idiosyncratic view of the world, absurdist playwrights employ theatrical devices in somewhat the same candid way as do the expressionists. Instead of telling a story illusionistically, they tend to demonstrate a static condition from a variety of different perspectives. Traditional illusionistic plots with their logical progressions and cause-and-effect linking are avoided in favor of plots that appear to be static and illogical. Absurdist characters attempt to insulate themselves from the metaphysical mindlessness in which they are trapped.

Beckett's *Happy Days* is a typical and excellent example of absurdist style. It contains little plot in the traditional illusionistic sense. In the first act, Winnie is trapped waist-deep in a mound of scorched earth; in the second act, she is in it up to her neck. She doesn't seem to struggle or attempt to escape from her strange condition. Instead she tries to make sense of her life by examining and reexamining the trivial objects she keeps handy in her shopping bag. The end of the play (since it's technically a simple plot, there is no climax in the orthodox sense) comes when her husband, until now unseen, emerges from his hole behind the mound, crawls up within Winnie's view, and reaches for her gun, possibly to shoot himself or her. The plot (especially the detailed pantomime), dialogue, and tempo-rhythm-mood have been selected and arranged to demonstrate the absurdity of her situation. The exaggerated given circumstances of *Happy Days*, as with other absurdist plays, is an expression of its attitude to the world.

Bibliography

Abel, Lionel. *Metatheatre: A New View of Dramatic Form.* New York: Hill and Wang, 1963.

Albright, H. D. and William P. Halstead. *Principles of Theatre Art.* Boston: Houghton Mifflin Company, 1968.

Appia, Adolphe. *Music and the Art of the Theatre.* Tr. Robert W. Corrigan and Mary Douglas Dirks. Coral Gables, FL: University of Miami Press, 1962 [originally published 1899].

Archer, William. *Playmaking: A Manual of Craftsmanship.* Boston: Small Maynard & Company, 1912.

Aristotle. *Poetics.* Tr. S.H. Butcher. Ed. Francis Fergusson. New York: Hill and Wang, 1961.

—. *Rhetoric.* Tr. Lane Cooper. New York: Appleton-Century-Crofts, 1960.

Auerbach, Erich. *Mimesis: The Representation of Reality in Western Literature.* Tr. Willard Trask. Princeton, NJ: Princeton University Press, 1968.

Baker, George Pierce. *Dramatic Technique.* Boston: Houghton Mifflin Company, 1919.

Balatova, N. and A. Svobodin, Eds. *Systema K. S. Stanislavskogo: Slovar Terminov [The Stanislavski System: A Dictionary of Terms].* Moscow: International Conference of Theatre Unions, 1994.

Ball, David. *Backwards and Forwards: A Technical Manual for Reading Plays.* Carbondale, IL: Southern Illinois University Press, 1983.

Ball, William. *A Sense of Direction.* New York: Drama Book Publishers, 1984.

Barrault, Jean-Louis. *Reflections on the Theatre.* Tr. Barbara Wall. London: Rockliff, 1951.

Barry, Jackson G. *Dramatic Structure: The Shaping of Experience.* Berkeley: University of California Press, 1970.

Barzun, Jacques. *The Culture We Deserve.* Middletown, CT: Wesleyan University Press, 1989.

—. *The Use and Abuse of Art*. Princeton, NJ: Princeton University Press, 1974.

Beckerman, Bernard. *Dynamics of Drama*. New York: Drama Book Publishers, 1979.

Benedetti, Jean, Ed. and Tr. *The Moscow Art Theatre Letters*. New York: Routledge, 1991.

Bentley, Eric. *The Life of the Drama*. New York: Atheneum Press, 1964.

—. *In Search of Theatre*. New York: Vintage Books, 1956.

—. *The Play: A Critical Anthology*. Englewood Cliffs, NJ: Prentice-Hall, 1951.

—. *The Playwright as Thinker*. New York: Harcourt, Brace & World, 1946.

—. "The Psychology of Farce." Forward. *Let's Get a Divorce and Other Plays*. Ed. Eric Bentley. New York: Hill and Wang, 1958.

—. *The Theory of the Modern Stage*. London: Penguin Books, 1968.

Berry, Cicely. *The Actor and the Text*. New York: Applause Books, 1987.

Blok, Vladimir. *Systema Stanislavskogo I Problemi Dramaturgii [The Stanislavski System and Problems of Dramaturgy]*. Moscow: All-Russian Theatrical Union, 1963.

Boal, Augusto. *Theatre of the Oppressed*. New York: Theatre Communications Group, 1985.

Boleslavsky, Richard. *Acting: The First Six Lessons*. New York: Theatre Arts Books, 1933.

Brook, Peter. *The Empty Space*. London: MacGibbon & Kee, 1968.

Brooks, Cleanth. *Modern Rhetoric*. New York: Harcourt, Brace, 1958.

—. *Understanding Poetry*. New York: Holt, 1938.

— and Robert B. Heilman. *Understanding Drama*. New York: Henry Holt and Company, 1948.

— and Robert Penn Warren. *Understanding Fiction*. New York: Appleton-Century-Crofts, 1943.

— and William Wimsatt. *Literary Criticism: A Short History*. New York: Alfred A. Knopf, 1957.

Brownstein, Oscar Lee and Darlene Daubert. *Analytical Sourcebook of Concepts in Dramatic Theory*. Westport, CT: Greenwood Press, 1981.

Bruder, Melissa, et al. *A Practical Handbook for the Actor*. New York: Vintage Books, 1986.

Busfield, Roger M. *The Playwright's Art*. New York: Harper & Row, Publishers, 1958.

Callow, Simon. *Being an Actor*. London: Penguin Books, 1995.

Canfield, F. Curtis. *The Craft of Play Directing*. New York: Holt, Rinehart and Winston, 1963.

Cardullo, Bert, Ed. *What is Dramaturgy?* New York: Peter Lang, 1995.

Carlson, Marvin. *Theories of the Theatre: A Historical and Critical Survey from the Greeks to the Present*. Ithaca, NY: Cornell University Press, 1984.

Carnicke, Sharon M. *Stanislavsky in Focus*. London: Routledge, 1998.

Carra, Lawrence. *Controls in Play Directing*. New York: Vantage Press, 1985.

Chekhov, Michael. *Lessons for the Professional Actor*. New York: Performing Arts Journal, 1985.

—. *On the Technique of Acting*. New York: Harper Collins, 1991.

—. *To the Director and the Playwright*. New York: Harper & Row, 1963.

—. *To the Actor*. New York: Harper & Row, 1953.

Clark, Barrett H. *European Theories of the Drama*. New York: Crown Publishers, 1965.

Clay, James H. and Daniel Krempel. *The Theatrical Image.* New York: McGraw-Hill, 1967.

Clurman, Harold. *On Directing.* New York: Macmillan, 1974.

—. *The Divine Pastime.* New York: Macmillan, 1974.

—. *The Naked Image.* New York: Macmillan, 1966.

—. *Lies Like Truth.* New York: Macmillan, 1958.

—. "The Principles of Interpretation," *Producing the Play.* Ed. John Gassner. New York: Dryden Press, 1941.

—. *The Collected Works of Harold Clurman.* Eds. Glen Young and Marjorie Loggias. New York: Applause Books, 1994.

Cole, Toby, Ed. *Acting: A Handbook of the Stanislavski Method.* New York: Bonanza Books, 1973.

Conrad, Joseph. *Joseph Conrad on Fiction.* Ed. Walter F. Wright. Lincoln: University of Nebraska Press, 1964.

Corbett, Edward P.J. *Classical Rhetoric for the Modern Student.* New York: Oxford University Press, 1971.

Corcoran, Anatoly. *Vam Privyet ot Stanislavskogo [Greetings from Stanislavski].* Moscow: Soviet Writer, 1996.

Craig, Edward Gordon. *On the Art of the Theatre.* New York: Theatre Arts Books, 1956.

Daiches, David. *Critical Approaches to Literature.* Englewood Cliffs, NJ: Prentice-Hall, 1956.

Danziger, Marlies K. and W. Stacy Johnson. *The Study of Literature.* Boston: D.C. Heath, 1965.

Dean, Alexander, and Lawrence Carra. *Fundamentals of Play Directing.* New York: Holt, Rinehart and Winston, 1974.

Dietrich, John E. *Play Direction.* Englewood Cliffs, NJ: Prentice-Hall, 1953.

Dukore, Bernard F. *Dramatic Theory and Criticism.* New York: Holt, Rinehart and Winston, 1974.

Eagelton, Terry. *After Theory.* New York: Basic Books, 2003.

—. *Literary Theory: An Introduction.* Minneapolis: University of Minnesota Press, 1996.

Efros, Anatoly. *Rabota Rejhissera nad Spektaklem [The Director's Work on the Production].* Moscow: Central House of People's Culture, 1960.

—. *Repititsia Lyubov Moya [The Joy of Rehearsal].* Moscow: Iskusstvo, 1975.

Egri, Lajos. *The Art of Dramatic Writing.* New York: Simon and Schuster, 1946.

Eliot, T.S. "The Function of Criticism," *Selected Essays: 1917–1932.* New York: Harcourt, Brace and Company, 1932.

Falls, Gregory A. "Intellect and the Theatre," *Educational Theatre Journal.* Vol. 18, No. 1 [March 1966]: 1–6.

Fergusson, Francis. *The Human Image in Dramatic Literature.* Garden City, NY: Doubleday, 1957.

—. *The Idea of a Theatre.* Garden City, NY: Doubleday Anchor Books, 1949.

Fogerty, Elsie. *Rhythm.* London: George Allen & Unwin, 1937.

—. *The Speaking of English Verse.* New York: E.P. Dutton & Co., 1929.

Forster, E.M. *Aspects of the Novel.* New York: Harcourt, Brace & World, 1956.

Freed, Donald. *Freud and Stanislavsky.* New York: Vantage Press, 1964.

Frenz, Horst, Ed. *American Playwrights on Drama.* New York: Hill and Wang, 1965.

Frye, Northrop. *Anatomy of Criticism.* Princeton, NJ: Princeton University Press, 1957.

Gallway, Marian. *Constructing a Play.* Englewood Cliffs, NJ: Prentice-Hall, 1950.

Gardner, John. *The Art of Fiction.* New York: Alfred A. Knopf, 1984.

Gass, William H. "The Nature of Narrative and Its Philosophical Implications." *Tests of Time.* New York: Alfred H. Knopf, 2002.

Gassner, John. *Form and Idea in Modern Theatre.* New York: Dryden Press, 1956.

—. *Producing the Play.* New York: Dryden Press, 1941.

Ginkas, Kama. *Provoking Theatre.* Trans. John Freedman. London: Smith and Kraus, 2003.

Goddard, Harold C. *The Meaning of Shakespeare.* Chicago: University of Chicago Press, 2 v., 1951.

Granville-Barker, Harley. *On Dramatic Method.* New York: Hill and Wang, 1956.

Grebanier, Bernard. *Playwriting.* New York: Thomas Y. Crowell Company, 1961.

Greenberg, Clement. "Modernist Painting," *Clement Greenberg: The Collected Essays and Criticism.* Ed. John O'Brian. Chicago: University of Chicago Press, 1995. V. 4, 85–93.

Gregory, W.A. *The Director: A Guide to Modern Theatre Practice.* New York: Funk & Wagnalls, 1968.

Griffiths, Stuart. *How Plays Are Made: The Fundamental Elements of Play Construction.* Englewood Cliffs, NJ: Prentice-Hall, 1982.

Gross, Roger. *Understanding Playscripts: Theory and Method.* Bowling Green: Bowling Green University Press, 1974.

Grote, David. *Script Analysis: Reading and Understanding the Playscript for Production.* Belmont, CA: Wadsworth Publishing Company, 1985.

Guerin, Wilfred L., et al. *A Handbook of Critical Approaches to Literature.* New York: Harper & Row, 1992.

Hauser, Arnold. "The Origins of Domestic Drama." Tr. Stanley Godman. *The Theory of the Modern Stage: An Introduction to Modern Theatre and Drama.* Ed. Eric Bentley. New York: Penguin Books, 1968.

Hayakawa, S.I. *Language in Action: A Guide to Accurate Thinking.* New York: Harcourt, Brace and Company, 1940.

Hobgood, Burnet M. "Framework for the Study of Directing in the Theatre." *Empirical Research in Theatre.* Vol. 1, No. 1 (August 1984): 1–51.

—. "Central Conceptions in Stanislavski's System." *Educational Theatre Journal.* Vol. 25, No. 2 [May 1973]: 147–159.

Hodge, Francis. *Play Directing: Analysis, Communication, and Style.* Englewood Cliffs, NJ: Prentice-Hall, 1994.

Hopkins, Arthur. *How's Your Second Act?* New York: Samuel French, 1931.

Hornby, Richard. *Script into Performance: A Structuralist View of Play Production.* Austin: University of Texas Press, 1977.

—. *The End of Acting.* New York: Applause Theatre Books, 1992.

—. *Mad About Theatre.* New York: Applause Theatre Books, 1996.

Hyman, Stanley Edgar. *The Armed Vision: A Study in the Methods of Modern Literary Criticism*. New York: Vintage Books, 1955.

James, Henry. *Theory of Fiction: Henry James*. Ed. James E. Miller, Jr. Lincoln: University of Nebraska Press, 1972.

Jones, David Richard. *Great Directors at Work: Stanislavsky, Brecht, Kazan, Brook*. Berkeley, CA: University of California Press, 1986.

Kataev, Vladimir. *If Only We Could Know: An Interpretation of Chekhov*. Ed. and Tr. Harvey Pitcher. Chicago: Ivan R. Dee, 2002.

Katz, Leon. "The Compleat Dramaturg" *What is Dramaturgy?* Ed. Bert Cardullo. New York: Peter Lang, 1995, 13–16.

Kernan, Alvin. *The Death of Literature*. New Haven: Yale University Press, 1990.

Knebel, Maria. *O Deistviye Analizye Pyesi I Roli [Effective Analysis of the Play and the Role]*. Moscow: Iskusstvo, 1982.

—. *O Tom, Shto Mne Kajhetsya Osobenno Vajhnim [What is Particularly Important to Me]*. Moscow: Iskusstvo, 1971.

—. *Poeziya Pedagogikii [The Poetics of Teaching]*. Moscow: Iskusstvo, 1976.

—. *Slovo v Tvorchesve Aktera [The Word in the Actor's Creativity]*. Moscow: Iskusstvo, 1964.

Knight, George Wilson. *The Wheel of Fire*. London: Oxford University Press, 1930.

Kozintsev, Grigori. *Shakespeare: Time and Conscience*. Tr. Joyce Vining. London: Dennis Dobson, 1966.

Lawson, John Howard. *Theory and Technique of Playwriting*. New York: G.P. Putnam's Sons, 1949.

Lemon, Lee T. and Marion J. Reis, Ed. and Tr. *Russian Formalist Criticism: Four Essays*. Lincoln: University of Nebraska Press, 1965.

Levin, Irina, and Levin, Igor. *Methodology of Working on the Play and the Role*. Washington, D.C.: Ladore Press, 1990.

Lewis, Robert. *Advice to the Players*. New York: Harper & Row, Publishers, 1980.

Lukacs, George. "The Sociology of Modern Drama." Tr. Lee Baxandall. *The Theory of the Modern Stage: An Introduction to Modern Theatre and Drama*. Ed. Eric Bentley. New York: Penguin Books, 1968.

Lynch, William F. *Christ and Apollo: The Dimensions of the Literary Imagination*. New York: Sheed and Ward, 1960.

MacGowan, Kenneth. *A Primer of Playwriting*. Garden City, NY: Dolphin Books, 1962.

McMullan, Frank. *Directing Shakespeare in the Contemporary Theatre*. New York: Richards Rosen Press, 1974.

—. *The Director's Handbook*. Hamden, CT: Shoestring Press, 1964.

—. *The Directorial Image*. Hamden, CT: Shoestring Press, 1962.

Meisner, Sanford and Dennis Longwell. *Sanford Meisner on Acting*. New York: Vintage, 1987.

Merlin, Bella. *Konstantin Stanislavsky*. London: Routledge, 2003.

Meyer, Leonard B. *Emotion and Meaning in Music*. Chicago: University of Chicago Press, 1956.

Millett, Fred B. *Reading Drama*. New York: Harper & Brothers, 1950.

Moore, W.G. *Moliere: A New Criticism.* New York: Anchor Books, 1962.

Nicoll, Alardyce. *The Theory of Drama.* New York: Thomas Y. Crowell, 1931.

Nietzsche, Friedrich. "The Birth of Tragedy," *The Birth of Tragedy and The Genealogy of Morals.* Tr. Francis Golffing. New York: Anchor Press, 1956 [orig. pub. 1870].

O'Connor, Flannery. *Mystery and Manners.* New York: Farrar, Straus and Giroux, 1962.

Pfister, Manfred. *Theory and Analysis of Drama.* Tr. John Halliday. Cambridge: Cambridge University Press, 1988.

Pope, Randolph H., Ed. *The Analysis of Literary Texts: Current Trends in Methodology.* Ypsilanti, MI.: Bilingual Press, 1980.

Ransom, John Crowe. *The New Criticism.* Norfolk, CT: New Directions, 1941.

Rowe, Kenneth Thorpe. *A Theatre in Your Head.* New York: Funk and Wagnall's, 1960.

Saint-Denis, Michel. *Theatre: The Rediscovery of Style.* New York: Theatre Arts Books, 1960.

Schechner, Richard, et al. *Stanislavski and America.* Ed. Erika Munk. New York: Hill and Wang, 1966.

Schmid, Herta and Aloysius Van Kesteren, Eds. *Semiotics of Drama and Theatre.* Philadelphia: John Benjamins Publishing Company, 1984.

Selden, Raman. *A Researcher's Guide to Contemporary Literary Theory.* Lexington: University Press of Kentucky, 1989.

Selden, Samuel. *An Introduction to Playwriting.* New York: F.S. Croft & Company, 1946.

Sharp, William L. *Language in Drama: Meanings for the Director and the Actor.* Scranton, PA: Chandler Publishing Co., 1970.

Smiley, Sam. *Playwriting: The Structure of Action.* Englewood Cliffs, NJ: Prentice-Hall, Inc., 1971.

Sontag, Susan. "Against Interpretation" and "On Style." *A Susan Sontag Reader.* New York: Farrar-Straus-Giroux, 1963.

—. "Artaud: An Essay." *Antonin Artaud: Selected Writings.* Ed. Susan Sontag. Berkeley: University of California Press, 1976.

Spurgeon, Caroline. *Shakespeare's Imagery and What It Tells Us.* Cambridge: Cambridge University Press, 1935.

Stanislavski, Constantin. *Selected Works.* Ed. and Tr. Oksana Korneva. Moscow: Raduga Publishers, 1984.

—. *Stanislavski's Legacy.* Ed. and Tr. Elizabeth Reynolds Hapgood. New York: Theatre Arts Books, 1968.

—. *An Actor's Handbook.* Ed. and Tr. Elizabeth Reynolds Hapgood. New York: Theatre Arts Books, 1963.

—. *Stanislavski.* Tr. Sergei Melik-Zakharov and Shoel Bogatyrev. Ed. Vic Schneierson. Moscow: Progress Publishers, 1963.

—. *Creating a Role.* Ed. and Tr. Elizabeth Reynolds Hapgood. New York: Theatre Arts Books, 1961.

—. *Stanislavsky on the Art of the Stage.* Tr. David Magarshack. New York: Hill and Wang, 1961.

—. *Building a Character.* Ed. and Tr. Elizabeth Reynolds Hapgood. New York: Theatre Arts Books, 1949.

—. *An Actor Prepares*. Ed. and Tr. Elizabeth Reynolds Hapgood. New York: Theatre Arts Books 1936.

—. *My Life in Art*. Tr. G. Ivanov-Mumijev. Moscow: Foreign Languages Publishing House, 1925.

—. *Stanislavsky Directs*. Ed. Nikolai Gorchakov. Tr. Miriam Goldina. New York: Minerva Press, 1954.

—. *Stanislavsky in Rehearsal*. Ed. Vasily Osipovich Toporkov. Tr. Christine Edwards. New York: Theatre Arts Books, 1979.

Stevens, Bonnie Klomp and Larry L. Stewart. *A Guide to Literary Criticism and Research*. New York: Holt, Rinehart and Winston, 1987.

Strickland, F. Cowles. *The Technique of Acting*. New York: McGraw-Hill, 1956.

Styan, J.L. *The Elements of Drama*. Cambridge: Cambridge University Press, 1960.

Sutherland, Donald. "Gertrude Stein and the Twentieth Century." *A Primer for the Gradual Understanding of Gertrude Stein*. Ed. Robert Bartlett Haas. Los Angeles: Black Sparrow Press, 1971.

Tarkovsky, Andrey. *Sculpting in Time: Reflections on the Cinema*. Tr. Kitty Hunter Blair. London: Faber and Faber, 1986.

Tennant, P.F.D. *Ibsen's Dramatic Technique*. New York: Humanities Press, 1965.

Thompson, A.R. *The Anatomy of Drama*. Berkeley: University of California Press, 1946.

Thompson, Ewa M. *Russian Formalism and Anglo-American New Criticism*. The Hague: Mouton, 1971.

Tovstonogov, Georgi. *The Profession of the Stage Director*. Moscow: Progress Publishers, 1972.

Van Druten, John. *Playwright at Work*. New York: Harper & Brothers. 1953.

Vaughn, Jack. *Drama A to Z: A Handbook*. New York: Frederick Ungar Publishing Co., 1978.

Waxberg, Charles. *The Actor's Script: Script Analysis for Performers*. Portsmouth, NH: Heinemann, 1998.

Weston, Anthony. *A Rulebook for Arguments*. Indianapolis: Hackett Publishing Company, 1987.

Wiles, Timothy J. *The Theatre Event: Modern Theories of Performance*. Chicago: University of Chicago Press, 1980.

Wimsatt, William K. *The Verbal Icon*. Lexington: University of Kentucky Press, 1954.

—and Cleanth Brooks. *Literary Criticism: A Short History*. New York: Alfred A. Knopf, 1965.

Wolfe, Tom. "Stalking the Billion-Footed Beast." *The Best American Essays: 1990*. Ed. Justin Kaplan and Robert Atwan. New York: Ticknor & Fields, 1990.

Young, Thomas Daniel, Ed. *The New Criticism and After*. Charlottesville: University Press of Virginia, 1976.

Index

Aphorisms, 179–180
Archetypes, 297
Aristophanes, 309
Aristophanic comedy, 309
Aristotelian approach, xxii
Aristotle, xxi–xxiii
  antagonist, 166
  comedy, 304
  complex plots, 141
  music, 239
  plot, 81
  protagonist, 166
  recognition, 140–1
  reversal, 140–1
  simple plots, 141
  song, 239
Art for art's sake, 286
Art of the Theatre, On the (Craig), xli
Assertions, 98–103
At the table, xxxi
Atmosphere, 260
Audiences, xxxv

B
Background story (Ch. 3), 1, 5, 241,
  271–75
  character descriptions, 66–7
  combining events, character
    descriptions, and feelings, 68–79
  content, 272
  deep background story, 63–4
  developing retrospectively in
    fragments, 273
  direct narration, 272–73
  distributed throughout play, 60–1
  early modern technique, 62–3
  events, 65–6
  extended narration, 61–2
  extended passages, 60
  feelings, 67–8
  historical technique, 61–2
  identification, 65–79
  limiting quantity, 64
  modern technique, 63–4

Oedipus Rex, 58
  premises for disclosure, 274–75
  quality, 272–73
  realistic treatment, 77
  retrospective method, 62–3
  shared among characters, 62–3
  speeches, 273
  techniques, 60–4
  Wild Duck, The, 58–60
  withholding, 64
Baker, George Pierce, 283
Barrie, James, 289
Barry, Jackson G., xxiv
Beats, 118–23, 242–53
  acting, 120
  dialogue without, 119
  disclosing new topic, 122–23
  group of related, 123–30
  learning to recognize, 119
  textual, 119–20
Beck, Julian, 313
Beckerman, Bernard, xxiv
Beckett, Samuel, xxxviii, 64, 222, 273,
  289, 313. *See also Waiting for Godot*
  and Happy Days
  allusions, 181
  Anton Chekhov and, 142
  deep background stories, 63
  simple plots, 142
Bedroom Farce (Ayckbourn), 306
Beginning, 13
Below-stairs scene, 62
Benedetti, Jean, xxiv
Bentley, Eric, xxiv
Biography, 296
Becque, Henri, 175
Bits, 123
Black bile, 163
Blackmur, R.P., xxiv
Blind, The (Maeterlinck), 312
Blocking, 86–9
Blood, 163
Boleslavsky, Richard, xxiv, 240
Books, 118

Brecht, Bertolt, xxxv, xxxviii, 226, 288,
    313. *See also Mother Courage*
  mistrust of accepted social values, 269
  simple plots, 142
Brieux, Eugene, 175
Brooks, Cleanth, xxiv
Brunetière, Ferdinand, 153
Building a Character (Stanislavski), 240
Burke, Kenneth, xxiv

C
Cabaret devices, 278
Cambridge Critics, xxiv
Canfield, Curtis, xxiv, 240
Capitalism, 49, 50
Caretaker, The (Pinter), 310
Carra, Lawrence, xxiv, 240
Catastrophe, 140–1
Cause and effect, 277–8
Chapters, 118
Character (Ch. 6), 5, 145
  analysis and sentence length, 206
  balanced combination of narration and
    action, 284–5
  classifying, 163
  complexity, 165–6
  conflicts of objectives, 153–4
  depiction, 283–5
  descriptions, 66–79
  driving, 114
  ideas in, 186–9
  identifying main, 166
  illustration of, 259
  mood, 262–3
  more self-aware, 165–6
  narration, 283–4
  objectives, 146–9, 153, 195
  parallelism, 190–1
  personality traits, 162–5
  position or attitude, 54
  qualities, 149–50
  rate and sum of change, 258–60
  relationships, 166–8
  rhythm, 258–60

role conflicts, 150–3
strong-willed, 154–5
style, 282–5
tempo, 247–54
types, 163, 165
values, 158–62
willpower, 154–8
Charm of dialogue, 223–6
Chekhov, Anton, 63–4, 84–5, 261, 286,
    289. *See also Three Sisters*
Chekhov, Michael, xxiv–xxv, xxvi, 13,
    149–50, 260
Cherry Orchard, The (Chekhov), 49
Chorus, 186–7
Classicism, 308–09
Climaxes, 135, 138–41, 241
  catastrophe, 140–1
  ideas, 192–3
  major climax, 139
  minor climaxes, 140
  recognition, 140–1
  reversal, 140–1
  three major climaxes, 12–18, 139–40
Close reading, xxiv
Clurman, Harold, xxiv, 146, 149
Cohen, Robert, xxiv
Comedies, 176–7, 188–9, 275, 304–305
Comedy of character, 309
Comedy of manners, 309
Commands, 107–114
Commedia dell' arte, 309
Communication, 298–9
Communion, 214
Complex characters, 165–6
Complex plots, 141–2, 279–80
Complications, 137
Complot, 81
Concrete concepts, 21
Concrete words, 202–3
Confidant, 188
Conflict
  of attitude, 151
  behavior and emotions, 151
  ideas, 191–2

Epic theatre, 313
Epilogues, 142, 185–6, 254
Euphemisms, 46–7
Euripides, 308
Events
    background story, 65–6
    characters descriptions, 66
    combining with character descriptions
        and feelings, 68–79
    defining important, 2
    external, 3–5
    internal, 10–12
    sequence of, 2–5, 10–12
Exits, 82–6
Exposition, 57–8
Expressionism, 312–4
External action (Ch. 4)
    blocking, 86–9
    entrances and exits, 82–6
    special activities, 94–8
    use of properties, 89–94
External events, 3–6, 10
Extraversion-introversion, 163

F
Facts, xxxiii, 5–6
Fallacies, xxxv–xxl
Fallacy of faulty generalization
    (overexpansion), xxxvi–xxxvii
Fallacy of half-truth (debunking), xxxviii
Fallacy of illicit process (reductiveness),
    xxxvii
Fallacy of origins, xxxvii–xxxviii
Falling action, 135
Families, 41–3
Farce, 176, 305–306
Faust, 19
Fear of scandal, 46–7
Federal Theater Project, 313
Feelings, 67–79
Feminism, 297–8
Fergusson, Francis, xxiv
Fiction, xxxii
Firm, 154

Foils, 190
Force, 154
Foreshadowing, 90
Form,
    dramatic, 293–4
Formal scenes, 131
Formal words, 203–204
Formalist analysis, xxv
    dissatisfaction with self-imposed limits
        of, xxv
    versus formal analysis or formalistic
        analysis, xxii–xxvi
    inductive reasoning, 1
    New Criticism, xxiii–xxvx
    patterns, 6
    present meaning of, xxi–xxii
    principles of, xxvi
    Russian Formalists, xxiii
Forward motion principle, 13, 19–20
Foundations of the plot. *See Given
    Circumstances and Background
    Story.*
French scenes, 131–2
Freud, Sigmund, 167, 297
Freytag, Gustav, 135, 256
Freytag pyramid, 135
Friendships, 43–4
Frigidity (insensitivity), xxxix
Funding, 90

G
Gags, 305
Gardner, John, xxxix
Genêt, Jean, 63–4
Genetic fallacy, xxxvii–xxxviii
Geniuses, 2
Genres, 301–302
    comedy, 304–305
    farce, 305–306
    melodramas, 303–304
    styles, 306–314
    tragedies, 302–303
Geographical locales, 35–8
Gestalt, 134

climaxes, 192–3
confidant, 188
conflict, 191–2
different concepts of, 176
direct, 176
discussions, 178
epilogue, 185–6
epilogues, 254
imagery, 183–4
indirect, 176–7
main idea, 194–8
moods, 263
narrator or chorus, 186–7
norm character, 188–9
parallelism, 190–1
persuasiveness, 285–6
in plot, 189–93
prologue, 185–86
raisonneur, 187
satires, 176
scope, 286–7
serious plays, 176
set speeches, 182–3
slowest tempos, 254
style, 285–7
symbolism, 184–5
tempo, 254–5
titles, 177
in words, 177–86
Identifications, 102
Illusionism, 307–308
Imagery, 183–184
Imagination, xxv
Implications, xxxiv–xxxv
Importance of Being Earnest, The
    (Wilde), 306
Important issues, 182–3
Impressionism, xxxvi
Incidental symbols, 184–5
Inciting action, 136
Indigenous blocking, 86–9
Indirect ideas, 176–177
Individual feelings, 260
Inductive reasoning, 1

Inferences, xxxiv–xxxv
Inferno (Dante), 181
Informal words, 203–4
Insensitivity, xxxix
Intellect, 51–2, 270–271
Intelligentsia, 270
Intention, 146
Intentional fallacy, xxxviii–xxxix
Intentional symbols, 184–185
Internal action (Ch. 4)
    assertions, 98–103
    commands, 107–114
    plans, 103–107
Internal dynamics, 217–8
Internal events, 10–12
Internal structure, 194
Internal tempo, 246
Ionesco, Eugene, 313
Irony, 180

J
James, Henry, xxxii
James, William, 239
Jargon, 204
Jokes, 305
Jouvet, Louis, 256
Joy of Rehearsal, The (Efros), 261
Judgment-perception, 163
Jung, Carl, 163

K
Kazan, Elia, xxiv, xxxvi, 192
King Hunger (Andreyev), 312
Knebel, Maria, xxvi
Knight, G. Wilson, xxiv
Kouski, 123
Krapp's Last Tape (Beckett), 167
Kushner, Tony, 267, 269 *See also Angels*
    in America

L
Laissez-faire economic system, 49
Late point of attack, 136
Law of conflict, 153